*Children: the Development
of Personality and Behaviour*

Children: the Development of Personality and Behaviour

MARGARET E. WOOD, B. A., Ph. D.

HARRAP   LONDON

First published in Great Britain 1973
by GEORGE G. HARRAP & CO. LTD
182–184 High Holborn, London WC1V 7AX

© *Margaret E. Wood* 1973

ISBN 0 245 51918 1

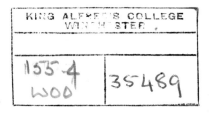
*Composed in Plantin type and Photoset and Printed
by Redwood Press Limited
Trowbridge, Wiltshire*

PREFACE

This is a book about the developing personality of the child. I had three major aims in mind while writing it:

(1) A child's perception of his world, and of the people in it, differs in important respects from an adult's perception and understanding. In addition the child's standpoint, from which he views the behaviour of others and attempts to understand the world around him, is constantly and continually changing from birth until maturity. One of my aims, therefore, has been to attempt to present this changing 'child's eye' view of the world.

(2) The material in the book is both descriptive and interpretative: I cite experimental investigations into the behaviour of children and, where relevant, of animals, and I have attempted to interpret the significance of the findings of such work as far as they concern the handling of children in our Western culture. Because experimental psychology is a relatively new science, and because work which aims at the elucidation of the springs of human behaviour is notoriously difficult to carry out, modern psychologists have been understandably reluctant to offer specific advice which can be applied 'to the concrete problems of the individual person' (Vernon, 1963). Enough knowledge, however, now exists to enable conclusions to be drawn about what is *more*, rather than *less*, advisable in the handling of children. William James, in *Talks to Teachers on Psychology* as long ago as 1899, suggested that psychology should enable us to be 'more clear as to what we are about'; the second aim of this book then is that it should help readers to be more clear 'as to what (they) are about' in regard to their relationship with children.

(3) However, despite certain broad notions which can be deduced from psychological work, and which can be applied to an understanding of *all* children, it is far more important to be able to understand the *individual* child than to have at hand ready-made ideas about child rearing in general; my third aim, therefore, has been to try to present information which will enable the reader to gain an understanding of individual children.

How children are studied

Experimental and observational work in child psychology is basically of two kinds: the 'antecedent-consequential', and the 'developmental-descriptive'. Investigators engaged in the first kind of work are concerned with discovering the possible causes for observed effects; for example, the psychologist may be interested in discovering whether children who are weaned relatively late in infancy differ in some measurable way from children who are weaned early. Workers engaged in the developmental-descriptive kind of investigation are interested in seeking to observe how particular aspects of the personality develop in children as their age increases: for example, the social, intellectual or emotional aspects.

Such studies on children can be carried out either 'cross-sectionally' or 'longitudinally': thus if, for example, it is intended to study children's growing ability with increasing age to make moral judgements, then the investigator may either take samples of different children of varying ages and study the kind of moral judgements children of different ages make, or he may, over a period of several years, study the *same* group of children, observing them as they grow older. The first is a cross-sectional investigation, the second a longitudinal study.

The book itself

(1)   It is hoped that the book will be useful to teachers in training, and particularly to those specializing in primary-school teaching, but that parents and others engaged in the care of children will also find it helpful. (It can also serve as an *introductory* text for students studying Developmental Psychology on undergraduate degree courses.)

(2)   The book is divided into three sections: Section I deals with the history of child rearing and with the theoretical aspects of child development. Section II describes the development of behaviour and the factors which influence this development. Section III is concerned with the role of the adult who comes into influential contact with children. The 'Introduction and Summary' presents a synopsis of the book; and is not easily comprehensible by itself; a list of further readings is appended to each chapter.

(3)   As the development of the child is very rapid in infancy and childhood, I have concentrated on these early periods, though later periods of development are not neglected. Because the book is primarily concerned with suggesting guide-lines for the understanding of individual children, special emphasis is given, particularly in Section III, to those aspects of development which affect the adult's contact with the child.

(4)   There is a certain artificiality in separating discussions of different aspects of development into sections and chapters, as if these aspects of development proceeded independently of each other. However, experimental and observational work has of necessity to limit itself to certain specific aspects of child growth and behaviour, and such work is best described in the terms in which it was carried out. There will also be the inevitable duplication of material: for example, the effects of social-class membership on

psychological development cannot be separated from a study of the influence of language on development, and when the growth of language use is studied the effects of social class must be considered. To reduce unnecessary duplication a system of cross-referencing has been adopted so that only the briefest mention of a particular subject need be made if this subject is reviewed more fully elsewhere in the book.

(5)   I have throughout used the personal pronoun 'he' to refer to the child, and 'she' to refer to the teacher. This has avoided the constant and irritating use of 'he or she'.

(6)   Whenever reference is made to certain specific developmental periods in the child's life it must be borne in mind that this indicates a *predominance* of a particular function, behaviour or ability during that period. It must not be assumed that such function, behaviour or ability either cannot occur earlier, or ceases completely at the end of the period described.

(7)   Asterisked words are defined in the glossary.

(8)   Books suggested for further reading at the end of every chapter are not necessarily the most authoritative, but those which the author considers to be generally helpful and interesting, as well as being usually easily accessible. Thus no reference is made in the Further Reading lists to articles published in learned journals, nor to certain books: for example, to Piaget's own writings (with one exception).

Acknowledgements

I would like to express my grateful thanks to Dr C. M. Loewenthal, Professor P. E. Vernon and Mrs D. Taylor for reading sections of the book and making valuable suggestions. Any errors or misinterpretations, however, remain entirely my own responsibility. Finally, I wish to thank my husband, who has commented on style and accuracy of writing, and whose innumerable suggestions have very greatly improved the readability of the book. He has been responsible for producing the original diagrams and also assisted me in preparing the book for the press.

CONTENTS

LIST OF ILLUSTRATIONS

INTRODUCTION AND SUMMARY

Cross-cultural and historical review of attitudes to child development and rearing

The present-day manner of treating children in our 'Western society' is unique, both culturally and historically. The attitudes adopted by adults towards children vary from one culture to another, and have indeed varied at different periods in history within our own, Western culture.

All children require that their basic needs be met: how these needs are met; what values adults place on children; the amount of discipline administered; the timing and manner of weaning and toilet training; how responsibilities are given; and how and when the transition from childhood to adulthood is accomplished—all these aspects of rearing children are managed differently in different communities.

For a considerable period in the 'West' children were considered to be miniature adults, and only in relatively recent times has the child been seen *as a child*, having his own particular needs and desires. To keep children alive at all was in itself a great problem until the middle of the last century; about this time a large literature on child-rearing problems appeared in the USA. Calvinistic ideas were deeply influential, and the notion was prevalent that a child was naturally depraved and had, through wise rearing and the breaking of his will, to be brought to 'grace'. These views often produced very strict methods of child rearing.

Friendship between parents and children did not seem possible under such a régime, but it is suggested that such friendship did often exist in working-class families. Available information about parent-child relationships and child-rearing habits in the past is largely restricted to what was customary at the time in the middle and upper classes, and does not inform us about working-class families.

Between the middle and end of the nineteenth century paternal oversight of children, founded often on harsh physical disciplining, gave way to gentler maternal rearing based more on the giving or withholding (as a corrective) of 'conditional love'. Nineteenth-century middle-class parents were concerned with character training, and this concern was also dominant in the baby-books of the 1920s and 1930s. Since physical hygiene had been effective in keeping children alive, 'mental' hygiene should produce mentally healthy children; and 'mentally healthy' was probably thought to be synonymous with 'good character'. J. B. Watson effectively stressed the need for the instilling of good habits in order to discipline the mind as well as the body. A sentimental approach was also to be avoided, even to the extent of avoiding close physical proximity between baby and adult.

Children, however, still behaved spontaneously in ways which caused parents concern, particularly in regard to auto-erotic manifestations, and also in regard to the child's apparent wish to dominate!

Although Watson, Freud and the Jesuits all stressed the importance of early experience, Watson alone emphasized the overriding importance of early learning processes as such, while Freud's greatest contribution was to focus attention on the *baby's* needs rather than on the needs of *religion* or *society*. His followers interpreted his teachings into child-rearing advice; for example, Susan Isaacs' recommendation of the need for understanding the child was radically different from those of Watson and Truby King. However, it is questionable whether the influence of psychoanalysis was entirely beneficial; the so-called 'permissive' rearing cult, probably stemming from a misinterpretation of Freudian theory, in its more extreme form has been helpful neither to the children subjected to this freedom, nor to the parents. In addition, even otherwise enlightened psychoanalytic writers made dogmatic pronouncements about rearing which were unsubstantiated by adequate evidence.

The plethora of baby-books written both by behaviourists and psychoanalysts often giving contradictory advice made parents feel deeply responsible for the forming of their children's personalities without giving them unequivocal guidance. In recent years relief from this unhappy state has come from two sources: the one from the experts who now say that dogmatic advice which purports to be applicable to all children is of little value; they no longer give such advice; and the other from the new 'fun morality', which suggests that as long as parents enjoy looking after their baby they are probably treating it properly! This 'morality' in itself presents problems, for example, the feelings of rejection experienced by modern parents when their proffered friendship is spurned and their examples are not followed by their children.

Spock has probably done more to help such parents in their acute dilemma than anyone else. He has restored to them a confidence in their own behaviour which had been undermined for the previous generation of parents. Also it is now generally appreciated that factors other than parental handling have a strong influence upon the development of a child's personality. What these factors are is examined in this book.

The developing personality

(a) What is personality?

Although it can be said that personality *is* behaviour, the two are differentiated in this book for the purposes of study: in this section we consider the various *reasons* which may determine how a child's personality will develop, whereas in section two we review ontogenically how a child's behaviour *changes* with age, and consider also the factors which influence the changes which occur.

Personality has been variously defined, but it can be distinguished as 'that which characterizes an individual and determines his unique adaptation to the environment' (Harsh and Schrickel, 1950). Thus 'personality' includes social and individual factors, the latter comprising a study of the intellect, the emotions and the will.

The direction in which each of the various theories of personality has developed has depended on the interest of each theorist, so that individual theories are predominantly concerned with, *inter alia*, explaining the dynamics, the development, the determinants, the description or the measurement of personality. Although some workers have used a combination of research methods, the two basic methods of studying the personality have been the clinical and the experimental.

In this chapter three theories are reviewed which have probably been more influential in child guidance and education than any others. They are:

(1) Freudian psychoanalytic theory,
(2) social-learning theory, and
(3) Piaget's theory of child development.

Freudian theory with its variants has probably had the biggest influence of all on child guidance work, but the three theories taken together provide a rich insight into the development of the whole personality. Freudian theory is considered in some detail, and the other two theories, aspects of which are also discussed in subsequent chapters, are described less fully in this chapter.

(b) Freudian psychoanalytic theory of personality development

Freud's psychoanalytic theory of personality takes into account the structure, functioning and development of the whole personality from a conception of man as a biological organism with energy for functioning present in the 'Id'; the 'Ego' and 'Superego' develop through the need of the human organism to interact with the real world and with other people. The human being desires release from tension, and through primary and secondary processes such release is obtained either vicariously or in actuality. How the Id, Ego and Superego interact with one another depends partly on biological factors and partly on how the child experiences life, particularly during the psychosexual stages of development in early childhood.

The theory of psychosexual development can best be understood as a way of explaining how the sexual drive, postulated as present from birth, but unable to express itself until maturity, seeks expression in infancy and early childhood through behaviours associated with the self-preservative drives, and with those parts of the body—the oral, anal and phallic areas—which provide satisfactions (or frustration) through such behaviours. The emotions evoked at each of the psychosexual stages are also present in the child's developing social relationships and in the manner in which he deals with the world around him. The concept of 'critical periods' used by ethologists to describe certain early and specific experiences which are crucial to later development, can be evoked to explain in part Freudian ideas of 'fixation' during these psychosexual stages.

The various satisfactions which are obtained by the baby and young child at the psychosexual stages of development cannot continue to be obtained in the same manner later in life. How the psychic energy invested in such pleasurable tension-release is displaced has, according to Freudian theory, an important bearing on personality development.

Another influence on the formation of the personality is the manner in which the Ego deals with the various demands made upon it by the Id and the Superego, as well as how it externalizes aggressive feelings, though in psychoanalysis there is no unified, completely accepted theory of aggression. The kind of defence mechanisms adopted, and the strength and extent to which such mechanisms are used to deal with anxiety, with threats to the personality, and with aggressive feelings, in part also determine behaviour and the formation of the personality.

According to Freud the personality is formed by the manner in which the child experiences his psychosexual stages; by the way displacement takes place; by the kind and strength of the defensive mechanisms adopted; and by biological determinants. Many of the powerful influences which together form the personality exert their effects at an unconscious level.

Much observational work on children has, since Freud's death, confirmed many of his ideas, though whether the personality is affected by psychosexual experiences as powerfully and irreversibly as Freud suggested is doubted by many students of child development. Writers such as Erikson and White and other Neo-Freudians have reformulated a number of Freud's ideas in a manner more acceptable to modern thought than Freud's own formulations. Sears and Farrell and others have also discussed the clinical validation and experimental testing (where appropriate) of psychoanalytic theories. Freud's influence on child rearing and on the thought and culture of our age has been immense.

(c) Social-learning theory

The foundation for social-learning theory was laid by J. B. Watson, who considered that all behaviour could be explained by invoking principles of conditioning, that is, of learning by association. Modern learning theorists who interest themselves in child development are not concerned with the total development of the child, but investigate specific areas of development which can be the subject of controlled experiment and observation. Through 'classical' and 'instrumental' conditioning paradigms and the concept of 'drives', including secondary drives, they seek to explain the formation of complex human behaviour patterns.

Social-learning theory accounts for the development of dependency, anxiety, aggression and conscience formation by learning (conditioning) principles. Through satisfaction of his basic needs the child becomes dependent on his parents' presence, and anxiety is evoked by their absence, or threat of absence. Parental disapproval is felt by him as a threat to their presence, and so disapproval becomes anxiety-provoking. Thus the parents by capitalizing on their child's dependency on them, and on its related anxiety, and by selectively reinforcing the child's behaviour, restrain and encourage his behaviour appropriately.

It is suggested that aggressive behaviour is caused by the baby's angry 'signalling' behaviour, arising from frustration or distress, bringing relief as well as disapproval from his mother. Consequently the conflict situation which thus arises for the baby implies that he obtains relief from distress through the pained or angry responses of another person, so that, through secondary reinforcement, his aggressive behaviour will in due course come to have a rewarding value.

A small child will usually inhibit a disapproved act in his parents' presence, but conscience formation rests on such inhibition becoming internalized. Social-learning theorists suggest that this occurs because the tempting thought to act in a disapproved manner brings anxiety through dependency. In time even the thought of behaving in a disapproved manner brings feelings of guilt. Social-learning theory explains how it is that parental disapproval shown before a child is about to commit a 'naughty' act is a more powerful way of helping internalization than punishment following a committing of the act. It is doubtful, however, whether the various aspects of moral growth, such as conscience development, feelings of guilt, and other related concepts, develop in the same manner in every person.

Social-learning theory has been established through short-term experimental work with children, and by relating what is known about learning to child development. There have been too few long-term studies to enable one to feel confident that the hypothesized causes always operate in the development of social learning in the manner suggested. However, social-learning theorists have undoubtedly made a valuable contribution to our understanding of child development.

(Other aspects of learning, such as imitation and identification, and learning in the context of school achievement, are considered in chapter 4.)

(d) The theory of Jean Piaget

Piaget has concerned himself primarily, though not exclusively, with the child's cognitive development, seeking to clarify how the child's perception and understanding of the world changes with advancing age. His work is not easy to understand, and in this chapter only his theories will be discussed. (The ontogenetic process of cognitive growth is discussed in chapter 4 and Piaget's work on the child's moral growth and on the importance of play are considered in chapters 5 and 6.)

Piaget is concerned with such problems as how 'logical necessity' emerges in the child. What are the processes involved in taking in new experiences (assimilation), in adapting the existing mental structure or schema to such experiences (accommodation), and in gradually lessening the conflict which exists between perceptual information and increasing, but unstable, knowledge about the world? Mental development is, for Piaget, 'an ever more precise adaptation to reality'.

At the baby stage thinking is, for Piaget, wordless, internalized action, and Piaget attempts to account for the developmental process by which this early form of thinking is transformed by adolescence into stable thought processes which are capable of dealing with all manner of abstractions, and mathematical and related problems.

In Piaget's theory development takes place due to

(1) maturation,
(2) learning and experiences of life, and
(3) 'organization'.

The child has to organize his thoughts in relation to his experiences and activities, and this organization is called 'equilibration'. Young children are more advanced in action than they are in language or thought; their explanations of causality are in terms of 'intuitions' because they still lack the ability to co-ordinate percepts and actions into a logical structure. The young child is percept-centred and egocentric; he is unable to practise reversibility of thought, but about seven years of age when he enters the 'concrete operational' stage his thought processes are better structured and less rigid. He is able to carry out an act in the imagination (an 'operation') but usually only in the presence of 'concrete' objects. He has to await a further maturing process before he is able to indulge in abstract and entirely logical thought. The small child *acts* on objects; the older child can *think about objects and act on them in their presence*; the child over twelve can *reflect* about objects and actions. At this stage equilibrium is near to being achieved and the schema is a stable mental structure.

Piaget's work has been, and is still being, criticized. It is considered that his research appears to lack precision, is usually based on small and possibly unrepresentative samples, and is seldom supported by statistical analyses. Other workers also consider that, among various contradictions of Piaget's findings, children can be taught the concepts he says they cannot understand; cognitive development is not invariant and sequential; and that Piaget appears to be studying the child's use of language rather than his successive conceptual structures. However, other workers again have been able to confirm many of Piaget's basic discoveries; for example, while young children can indeed be taught to perform specific skills involving quantities, it does not follow that they can grasp the concept of conservation of quantities, while, in another context, Piaget himself admits that a child's process of inevitable cognitive growth can certainly be affected by the quality of the teaching he receives.

The fact remains that the changes in cognitive growth which Piaget describes do occur; that he has thrown fresh light upon the qualitative changes in children's thinking processes; that he has generated much research, and that he has put forward the most comprehensive scheme for the understanding of a child's mental development which has ever been proposed.

Influences affecting the formation of personality characteristics and the development of intelligence

(a) General considerations

In a consideration of the various factors which are influential in determining how the personality and intelligence of any one individual are formed, it is reasonable to assume that a relationship exists between inherited physical characteristics and behaviour, and some evidence is available linking temperament to such characteristics.

(b) The formation of the personality—genetic influences

Studies of twins, for instance, appear to show that there is a genetic contribution to the degree of extraversion exhibited in behaviour. Various longitudinal studies also indicate that a trait which can be called 'outgoingness' shows remarkable persistence from childhood to adulthood, though this is by itself not necessarily an indication of a genetic contribution. Another longitudinal study purports to have discovered nine 'primary reaction patterns' of behaviour which appear to persist from early babyhood, and selective breeding experiments with animals indicate that animals can be bred to exhibit more or less 'emotionality'. In general investigations show that genetic factors may play a greater part in the development of the personality than had been thought likely until recently. (The influence of the environment on the developing personality is considered later in the chapter.)

(c) The development of intelligence

Although 'intelligence' is difficult to define, there is no doubt that it shows itself most clearly when man is engaged in relational thinking. A presently held hierarchical view of intelligence regards it as being comprised of a 'g' or 'general' factor, as well as of 'group' and 'specific' factors. 'g' accounts for the biggest source of variance between people, and intelligence tests, which test for 'g', are still the best single predictive instrument of a person's suitability to engage in intellectual or educational pursuits. The IQ is a measure of a child's intelligence in relation to his age, and is a sample of his intelligence obtained at a particular period in his life; it is not to be confused with intelligence itself. (A number of different group and individual intelligence tests are described in this chapter.)

The findings of various studies, including twin, consanguinity and sibling studies, indicate that there is a considerable genetic element in determining intelligence. Indeed, both Burt and Jensen ascribe 80 per cent of testable intelligence to genetic factors. Hebb's 'Intelligence "A" ' cannot, however, be assessed in any one individual person, and the degree of variance of the genetic factor when comparing individuals in different cultural and social groups with one another will depend on the homogeneity of the groups concerned.

(d) The role of the environment in relation to the formation of the personality and the development of intelligence—general considerations

(Various environmental influences on the development of personality and on the formation of intelligence are referred to in this chapter, but are treated more fully in chapter 5, chapter 4 and chapter 8, where the social and emotional development of the child, his growing ability to use language, and the adult's role in relation to the developing child are discussed.) Cultural and social-class norms and values influence children's *behaviour*, if not necessarily their *personality*, and may also effect the development of different temperamental characteristics in members of the two sexes. Such different cultures can also influence the type of intelligence displayed by their members.

The influences of social class, particularly on achievement, on motivation, on moral development, on the ability to use language effectively, and on intellectual development, is not inconsiderable. It appears that the quality of parent-child interaction in middle-class homes is such that a child from a middle-class home usually has a much better opportunity of maximizing his innate intellectual potential than a child from a working-class home, and that the difference between children from the two social classes in this respect is already evident in babyhood. Consequently compensatory schemes of education for underprivileged children should start very early in life. Pre-natal and familial influences, together with the influence of parental characteristics, all affect the growth of personality from babyhood onwards. (This subject is, however, discussed in greater detail in chapter 8.)

The baby's brain develops very greatly during the first two years of life, and animal studies indicate that stimulation early in life affects the growth of the brain. Babies appear to be maximally sensitive to certain stimuli at specific periods in their lives, and research is required to attempt to discover the signs by which observant adults may detect when a *particular* baby is entering a specific 'critical' period.

There is evidence to show that a child's *educational achievement* is much more affected by environmental circumstances than is the score he can obtain on an IQ test. Therefore, even if the genetic contribution to tested intelligence is very high, society must act *as if* the environment were of crucial importance in order to help each child to develop his full potential in a manner particularly appropriate to him.

Studies of so-called 'maternal deprivation' experiences including, for example, long periods of institutional life, and also mere breaks in normal mothering, if suffered for a sufficiently long period and occurring at certain periods in a child's life, show that, in addition to the child's initial distress, poor Ego and Superego development can result. Experimental findings from studies of animals appear to corroborate this. However, probably only early and prolonged separation, together with unsatisfactory alternative mothering, is likely to do irreparable harm to the developing personality.

Growth of the intellect

(a) Cognitive growth as described by Piaget

Piaget's theory in relation to child development is considered in chapter 2. In this chapter the ontogenic, cognitive development as described by Piaget is reviewed. At the beginning of the 'sensori-motor' stage—that is, while the child is under twenty-one months of age—much motor activity is of reflex kind, and the child's perceptual and motor apparatuses operate simultaneously. By the time he is a year old he can form intentions and behave purposely. By the end of the sensori-motor stage the baby's thinking can take the form of internalized, wordless action; he can now 'represent' things and actions to himself, which, says Piaget, is what thinking is about. He also now has an *anticipatory* knowledge of causality, but no real understanding of causality as such.

A child has, according to Piaget, to learn progressively to free himself from two influences which are dominant in his early childhood; his percept-centred and his egocentric views of the world. In early childhood his thinking is confined largely to the information produced by his perceptual faculties, and while proceeding beyond this limited appreciation, he also has to learn about the objectivity of things, and about their existence apart from himself. This learning takes place between about two and seven years of age, when he is at the 'pre-operational' stage of development.

Until the child is about five or six years of age, therefore, he will make judgements about quantity or number based on what he sees and not on what is logically right. A child under seven years of age does not usually appear to understand about the conservation of number and quantity, but at that age, when he reaches the 'concrete operational' stage, he is much more free from the dominance of the senses, though these are still influential in guiding his thinking and behaviour. During the next period, between seven and eleven or twelve, his thinking becomes more systematized, and he learns about the truth and value of measurement. The ability to use and understand language greatly helps the process of 'de-centring', though verbal reasoning remains a limited capability throughout the concrete operational period. Before early adolescence children have difficulty in understanding verbal puzzles or proverbs.

Ideas of causality change from 'animism' in early childhood, by which life is ascribed to everything that moves, to a logical deduction of cause in adolescence. This occurs in various intervening stages, described by Piaget, in which effects are progressively ascribed to more and more realistic causes.

Pedagogically Piaget's findings about children's cognitive growth are of the greatest importance, for if action precedes thinking then children must be provided with opportunities for activity using objects which will facilitate the internalization of action. Care must be taken, however, not to alienate a child from learning by seeking to hurry his development; competent teaching at the right time can enable him to understand concepts before the ordinary experiences of life will bring this understanding, though it is doubtful whether conceptual understanding can be brought about entirely by teaching independent of the maturational processes Piaget describes. The child who is under seven years of age usually learns without understanding, whereas the child who is over seven years of age is beginning to learn with understanding.

After twelve years of age new intellectual processes become available to the child and he enters the 'formal operational' period; he can manipulate verbal propositions, entertain hypotheses, build concepts, consider abstract ideas, understand proverbs, etc. Because of these new abilities many other kinds of comprehensions become available, though the extent to which such abilities and comprehensions can be developed and used will depend in part on cultural and social factors; some adults never reach the formal operational stage of growth.

(b) Development of language, and of thinking in relation to language

The study of language development involves considering the role of language in human affairs from a number of viewpoints: *what* happens when a child learns language, *how* does this happen, and what are *functions* of language.

Early voluntary baby babblings give way to 'selection' by the baby of specific, meaningful utterances. This is in part an imitative process, though the baby also responds to the presence or attention of other people by bodily movements and facial expressions, and by non-imitative sounds. To an extent this selection is governed by an 'operant conditioning' process (chapter 4 (c)), though this process cannot adequately explain grammatical speech.

Children obviously understand speech before they can speak themselves, and they are also able to respond non-verbally to speech. It is not only the conceptual meaning of words which has to be learned, but also the affective meaning which is conveyed by the pitch and tone of the speaker's voice, and by her facial expressions. Soon the child's own utterances can evoke responses from others. During the second year of his life a relationship is formed between the baby's speech and his actions, so that, for example, he can tell himself not to do something. During this year also his vocabulary increases greatly.

It is *comparatively* simple to understand how single words are learned and used, but much more difficult to account for children's ability grammatically to structure their speech. It has been suggested that the ability to use language at all, and to use it flexibly, is 'intuitive'. It seems unlikely that the rules of language can be learned merely from what the child hears, because during the process of development a child comes to use an infinite number of word combinations. Possibly some aspects of the rules of language are learned by adults 'expanding' a child's own speech, and the child in part imitating these 'expansions'. Chomsky's differentiation between 'surface' and 'deep' language structure is an attempt to account for the understanding of language rules: it is suggested that all languages may have a common deep structure, which is innately known, and that children learn their own language by relating what is heard to this common deep structure.

Piaget and Vygotsky have both studied the development of speech, and have expressed views on the function of egocentric and social speech in children of different ages. The speech of younger children appears to be more egocentric, and this may be in part due to the fact that the child has not yet learned to differentiate between himself and others. Piaget considers that under seven years of age most children think egocentrically, and that for this reason co-operative play (chapter 6), for example, is difficult, because a sustained relationship can only be maintained through verbal communication, which must be social in character.

A child's vocabulary normally increases tenfold between two and six years of age; by the time he goes to school his speech is usually grammatically correct, and the kind of words he uses indicate the stage of social development he has reached. At this time he is beginning to be able to exchange his thoughts with others. After seven years of age or so his use of language is much influenced by the peer group to which he belongs, and his individuality emerges in part through the verbal reactions of others to his behaviour.

In recent years it has been realized that small children, despite their fluent use of language, often do not understand simple, but in their life not very frequently used, words, such as, for example, the word 'less' when contrasted with 'more'; indeed, they do not understand the diametrically opposed meanings.

Bernstein's work seems to suggest that the two major social classes in Britain make use of two different kinds of language, what he has termed 're-stricted' and 'elaborated' codes respectively, the former being rigid and used mostly by so-called working-class people, and the latter used more frequently by the middle classes, being varied and eloquent, not predictable and capable of making the expression of concepts, ideas and feelings possible. It is suggested that such differentiation in speech patterns reflects a differentiation in what matters in interpersonal behaviour, and that this has important repercussions on child-rearing habits, as well as on moral development. A child from a middle-class home knows both languages, but a child from a working-class home has to learn the 'elaborated' code when he goes to school, which makes the transition from home to school more difficult for him. These limitations imposed on working-class children by their restriction in the use of language may be one reason why such children have greater difficulty with academic work than children from middle-class homes, despite apparently equal non-verbal intelligence.

In order to be able to think a child must be able to make a mental representation of objects in their physical absence. Piaget has termed this internalization an 'operation'. (His theory of cognitive development is described in chapter 4 (a).) He suggests that early thinking is independent of language, but to what extent even later thinking abilities are helped by, or are merely reflected by, the use of language is not yet fully understood.

Bruner considers that children must be able to internalize 'techniques', such as language, if they are to progress to the 'symbolic' stage of thinking, though not all psycholinguists agree with this view. Bruner holds that language, particularly in children between four and twelve years of age, becomes a tool for the translation of experience. He describes four stages of the development of language and of thinking, ranging from, in early childhood, the use of words in speech which the child is unable to use in thinking, to, in adolescence, powers of organization in thought which exceed the child's organizational speech powers. Vernon has written that the achieving of higher-order thinking is totally dependent on the quality of speech models to which the child is exposed. Despite these views Herriot considers that there is great confusion at present in the field of language and thinking, because there is no *absolute* proof which indicates that the quality of language affects thinking processes.

(c) Learning

Learning involves diverse activities relating respectively to the emotional, social and academic aspects of life. In this chapter four kinds of learning are considered: imprinting; imitation and identification; classical conditioning; and operant conditioning.

'Imprinting' is a form of learning by which a human or animal baby responds to specific stimuli provided by the environment at definite and limited periods in his early life. The *ability* thus to respond is most likely inherent. This form of learning is on the whole more applicable to the development of birds and animals than to the development of humans, though there is evidence that human babies are particularly sensitive to certain kinds of experience at specific periods, such as separation from mother between about six and fifteen months of age, when attachment bonds have been formed. Attachment behaviour to one particular person is thought to occur through a process similar to imprinting, and it appears also that certain stimulating experiences early in life are crucial for later intellectual development if a child is to fulfil his intellectual potential.

'Imitation' and 'identification' are potent forms of learning, though it is still difficult to say exactly how imitation occurs. No obvious reward is discernible when a child imitates, though he may well experience a kind of 'empathetic' satisfaction when he does so. Research has shown under what specific conditions and in what particular circumstances children imitate. For example, aggressive behaviour is usually imitated very readily, though less so if the aggressor is punished. Identification is a form of imitation whereby a person models himself consciously or unconsciously on another person, usually someone with whom he has an emotional tie. Freud's Oedipal theory (page 126) attempts to explain sex-role identification and the consequent formation of the Superego.

'Classical conditioning' means that an organism (a human or an animal) learns to respond to a stimulus which has been paired in time and space with a need-reducing stimulus as if it, the former stimulus, were also need-reducing. The baby is excited at the sight of his feeding-bottle, but he will also show excitement in time at the sight of his mother because her appearance is so often 'paired' with need-reducing stimuli. A great deal of learning by this kind of association seems to take place, particularly in early childhood. It is also one of the ways by which children, and adults also, learn to fear objects and happenings.

'Operant conditioning' is a particularly relevant form of learning, both in the school situation and for social development. This kind of learning takes place when an organism performs an action which is part of its ordinary repertoire of behaviour, and which a trainer of animals, or a child's parent or teacher, wishes to encourage. Through suitable reinforcement (chapter 4), such actions are strengthened and are more likely to be repeated. The teaching machine, whose modus operandi is based on operant-conditioning processes, can be used as a model for effective teaching without the use of machines. The situation in the classroom should make it possible for the child

(1) to be more often right in his answers than wrong,

(2) to know at once when he is right,

(3) to progress in learning at his own pace, and

(4) to participate in learning rather than to be a passive attender.

Thus the child is motivated to learn a *specific* task, though his *general* motivation is related to achievement, and this in turn is at least partially dependent on parental and social class norms.

'Learning to think' and 'learning to learn' have been studied by the Harlows, who find that animals and children develop what are called 'learning sets', which enable further learning to take place more easily. In this way 'cognitive structures' are formed.

The child under seven years of age usually learns associatively and mechanically, since he has not developed the cognitive structures which enable him always to understand what he is learning, but as the child matures understanding will come. It is obvious, however, that not all learning requires understanding; many tasks can be learned effectively merely by acquiring the right responses, whereas others require the use of higher-order conceptual thinking abilities. It is probable, though, that many children never develop these abilities on which such great emphasis is placed by the schools. If these children could be taught to maximize their associative learning abilities many more children than now would leave school possessing useful skills in which they were proficient. Some educational psychologists think that systems of teaching and learning appear to have evolved without taking into consideration the limitations, natural and cultural, of very many children who attend our schools.

Moral, social and emotional development

(a) Moral development

As a society we are not really clear what we mean by 'moral' behaviour, although true moral behaviour seems to arise from a consideration of other people's feelings and needs and from an informed conscience. In the study of the development of moral behaviour one must differentiate between moral knowledge, moral feeling and actual moral behaviour.

Piaget has studied the child's acquisition of moral knowledge, both through investigating how children's understanding of the rules of behaviour changes with age, and also how their ability to make moral judgements develops. Between five and eight years of age adherence to rules is very important for children, but after eight years or so they begin to understand that rules can be changed if the participants in a game are agreeable to a change. Concurrent with this changing view about the importance of rules is a growing sophistication in the ability to make moral judgements. Before seven or eight years of age, in keeping with their egocentric and percept-centred view of the world (page 108), children mostly make judgements according to the size of the misdemeanour and not according to the intentions of the miscreant.

Other investigators, such as Kohlberg, have evolved different categories for describing moral growth, such categories ranging from merely obeying rules in order to avoid punishment, to the adolescent's conformity to his own standards in order to avoid self-condemnation. Freud has postulated that moral feelings develop both from 'social anxiety', and also through a resolution of the Oedipal complex (chapter 2).

Basically children are first amoral, when sanctions rest mainly on prudential considerations. They then enter a pre-moral stage, when social and authoritarian factors are the main restraints, and finally they achieve true moral understanding, which is based on altruistic and responsible evaluations. The self-consciousness of the older child will enable him to examine his feelings about forbidden acts, and with most people these feelings become sufficiently strong to act as a restraining force.

An adult person's integrated and mature concept of morality is very different from a young child's tenuously held ideas of moral behaviour, and it is important that adults dealing with children should be aware of this difference.

(In this chapter only the developmental processes of moral growth have been considered; in chapter 8 the factors which affect such development are reviewed.)

(b) Emotional and social development

A mature person should be able to respond socially and emotionally in the manner expected in his society of persons of his age and sex. Not all development of such behaviour is entirely dependent on social learning alone, for the existence of temperamental differences implies that some children will respond more readily to social training than others.

Emotional growth in the child evolves from undefinable excitation to definable emotions; and the way a child expresses his emotions obviously changes with age. The situations which arouse emotions vary also with advancing age, as, for example, the objects and happenings which occasion feelings of fear; older children experience anxieties rather than fears, and these have largely to do with personal relationships, and with their imagined inadequacies as persons. Small children can feel acute jealousy and it is difficult for parents to avoid the occasions for such feelings arising, because the child has a limited appreciation of other people's behaviour and will almost inevitably at times misinterpret behaviour.

Before adolescence children seldom talk about their feelings, but there is some evidence that at about thirteen years of age a child begins to be self-consciously reflective, and at this age he is much more likely to discuss his feelings.

The effect on emotional development of so-called 'maternal deprivation' experiences can be debilitating, but earlier reports of the effects of these experiences were probably unnecessarily pessimistic, and in any case little is known of children who have successfully overcome the results of such experiences. (This topic is discussed in greater detail in chapter 3.)

The child's social development starts with awareness of other human beings as distinct from other objects in his world, and with a growing ability to differentiate between himself and others. This social learning deeply involves the emotions, for the child wishes to please those whom he loves, and as he grows up he also seeks the approval of his peer group. At times his separate desires to please his parents and also to please his peers conflict with each other.

The extent and quality of his interaction with other people indicates the stage of social development he has reached, and through this interaction his self-concept also begins to be formed. Play as such is of great importance in aiding the child's social growth, and role-taking, games-playing and peer-group activities all have their socializing functions.

During adolescence emotional problems, which have their repercussions in social behaviour, can be particularly acute. The adolescent's sexual maturity, his idealism and his increasing self-awareness are often accompanied by a temporary, but nonetheless distressing, estrangement from his parents. At this age he has a newly-found self-consciousness, which is often coupled with an awareness of the many problems which remain to be solved in the world; and often his consequent impatient behaviour is misunderstood by adults. Those adults who enjoy seeing young children behaving independently and creatively, do not equally enjoy seeing adolescents behaving in the 'liberated' manner appropriate to *their* age. Adolescence is not an easy period to live through, or to live with, in our society.

(c) Development of the child's ability to understand other people

We know that, as with cognitive development, the child's understanding of others is limited by his percept-centred and egocentric view of the world. For children under six years of age actions and movements which are indicative of emotional experiences are more meaningful than words and facial expressions. Under about ten years of age the child will tend to take behaviour at its face value, and he is not able easily to *interpret* what he sees; and when he does interpret behaviour, he will be limited largely by short-term considerations and by his limited experience of life. He will also be restricted by his own needs to concentrate upon those aspects of other people's personality and behaviour which relate to such needs. There is some evidence that whereas children are intellectually quite sophisticated at thirteen years of age, they have not yet reached the stage of emotional maturity in relation to their evaluation of other people which has been developed by children only a year or so older. Thirteen years of age may be a special period in the development of the child's understanding of people and their behaviour.

Experience of life has given adult persons the ability to make inferences about other people's behaviour, thoughts, feelings, desires, etc., and to act on these inferences *as if they were directly observable data*. Children up to about thirteen years of age are not able to do this to the same extent as adults, and consequently their manner of evaluating other people's behaviour and assessing their likely responses is generally different from that of an adult. Children use language skilfully and rapidly continue to expand their ability to speak, so that by quite an early age they are able to communicate in the same terms as adults. Adults, therefore, require to use considerable imagination to appreciate that although a child's use of language is so similar to their own, it does not follow that his understanding of other people's behaviour is necessarily similar. As a prerequisite for a good adult-child relationship it is important for the adult to be aware of the child's limited understanding of the behaviour of other persons.

Play

Play in the life of the child is an aid to personality growth. All developmental aspects of a child's life are helped by play activities, although these activities change their character, aim and form as the child grows.

Bühler and Piaget have observed that a baby's first efforts at play help him to learn about the nature of the objects around him; that at eighteen months to two years of age his play helps him to deal imaginatively with objects and with people; and that after about four years of age he needs play in order to cope constructively with the real world. Piaget considers play during this period to be used predominantly to aid social and moral development, enabling the child to recognize the importance of rules in play and in games, and consequently how rules relate to social life. Play for Piaget is an 'assimilatory' process.

Such writers as Piaget, Freud and Isaacs consider imagination and symbolism to be important in a child's play, and although Piaget thinks that in infancy such play is devoid of fantasy, psychoanalytical writers stress the importance of fantasy life for the development of the child's personality. It is possible that the importance of fantasy life on the manner in which life experiences are interpreted has not received sufficient attention by non-psychoanalytic observers. Both psychoanalytic writers and Piaget agree that imaginative play is of great importance in enabling the child (as opposed to the infant) to express and deal with reality. Such play can link the child's inner world to the real world, and can enable him to reconstruct reality to suit his Ego, and so deal with experiences which he might otherwise find painful; this also enables him to indulge vicariously in forbidden desires. As children grow up imaginative play, as in role-taking play, more and more *reproduces* reality instead of being symbolic of reality.

Freud considered that play, while apparently unrelated to reality, has a purpose, and that in play 'children repeat . . . everything that has made a great impression on them in their actual life . . . and so-to-speak make themselves masters of the situation'. Thus Freud thought of play as a repetition-compulsion mechanism, which enables the child to work out his anxieties. Isaacs, from her observation of children, developed Freud's ideas, specifying the variety of anxieties experienced by children, and explaining how these are dealt with in play. According to Isaacs there is a constant interaction between fantasy life and reality which is of great importance to a child's development. Imaginative play also enables a child to test new experiences in safety.

Psychoanalytic writers consider that role-taking has a deeper significance in personality development than merely linking the world of imagination to the world of reality. It is considered to aid identification and to help the child through the Oedipal situation (chapter 2).

With regard to the function of play in relation to social growth, a certain degree of sophistication in the use of language and an appreciation of other children as individual personalities are necessary in order to be able to play co-operatively, and hence such play is not usually possible for children under five years of age. Although at times younger children appear to be playing together, closer observation will show that usually one dominant child is using the others for his own purposes. However, children who are well acquainted with each other often seem to be able to play together at an earlier age.

In early childhood play involving movement helps the development of bodily expertise and skills; play with objects of various shapes, sizes, colours and textures stimulates most of the child's senses as he plays with them, and this is one of the two most influential factors aiding cognitive growth. (The other is having the opportunity in childhood to interact consistently with an adult who has good speech habits and an extensive vocabulary.) A plentiful provision of such play objects and materials in infancy and childhood will also enable the child to contend more competently with reality.

Observing and understanding children

Because of the unique individuality of each child it is desirable that, if this is at all possible, a teacher should understand every child in her care. The several means by which teachers can learn to assess a child's individual characteristics are discussed in this chapter.

The teacher should constantly bear in mind that a child's behaviour is often an expression of inner drives and needs which he cannot easily change, and that these drives largely constitute his temperament. Various studies show that when the demands of home or school conflict with a child's temperamental characteristics he is placed under strain. Situations can arise which cause acute distress to some children, while being quite tolerable to others.

Temperamental characteristics, which make one child lovable and another hard to tolerate, can also affect children's learning abilities. Easy distractibility and a short attention span, for example, adversely affect the learning abilities of otherwise gifted children. Various personality characteristics other than intelligence can also influence academic and scholastic achievement.

Concerning children's use of language, the reader is reminded that young children do not necessarily themselves understand all they are able to say, and there is also the problem of the disadvantage suffered by the child from a working-class home for whom school is the first experience of middle-class 'elaborated' language. Such disadvantages are not confined to scholastic pursuits, but can also cause behavioural problems, for it is probable that the different manner in which language is used by the two major social classes affects the development of conscience in the child, and it also has an influence on the relationship between the teacher and her children.

It is only by appreciating a child's egocentric and percept-centred view of the world, his different understanding (when compared with adults) of the motives and behaviour of other people, and his changing concepts of moral behaviour with advancing age, that adults are able to understand children at different stages of their development.

It is important for a teacher, if at all possible, to know the parents of children in her charge, since by this acquaintance the teacher is enabled the better to understand the child. Certain children may present problems where parent-teacher contact is essential, and these are discussed later in this chapter.

Even children who enjoy the experience of a normal childhood not infrequently suffer distress and anxieties. Most adults and children have to suffer stress at some time in life, and small children learn something about human behaviour by noting the reactions of other people to stressful situations. It is not yet fully understood in what way stressful experiences are either damaging to the personality or, alternatively, may help to establish a suitable resilience, yet in spite of such ignorance decisions are often made about the future of children with insufficient consideration of the possible consequences of such decisions. 80 per cent of all children appear to suffer some form of difficulty in the infant school, nearly half of these being of moderate or marked severity. The teacher of infants should be particularly sensitive to, and understanding of, such difficulties.

Types of children who are *markedly* 'linear', 'round' and 'muscular' in body-build have been found in one study to differ from one another in a number of characteristics, including scholastic achievement, social behaviour and certain personality traits. Although assessment by physical appearance is only one of many ways of making evaluations of a child's characteristics, physical appearance is the most immediately obvious factor about a child. By knowing the likely strengths and weakness of children who are particularly extreme in body-build the teacher can form an approximate expectation of such children's performance; for example, the thin child is more likely to be anxious, and the muscular child will find sitting still for long rather difficult.

In the handling of so-called 'problem' children, the teacher should recognize that the difficulties of most of these children have more than one cause, and that each difficulty must be studied individually before an explanation is attempted. Also to *describe* 'problem' behaviour is not to explain it.

Aggressive children, attention-seeking children, rejected children, withdrawn children, over-anxious children, hyperactive children, rigid children and children who are 'able-misfits'—with high capability but lack of capacity to use it—all these children require each their special consideration, understanding and sympathetic handling, for often their need for help can be very great. (The reader will find in this chapter a detailed discussion of the problems presented by such children.)

Thieving in the classroom among older children presents a very worrying situation for the teacher, creating acute tensions. Small children may have difficulty in understanding the difference between communal, private and loaned property, in addition to their often tenuous hold on moral concepts.

The teacher is often the first person to notice that certain children suffer from minor, although debilitating, physical defects, and who can be viewed as 'bridge' children between those suffering acute physical disability and those with emotional problems, but no physical disabilities. Such defects, including poor visual and auditory discrimination, may cause spelling and reading problems, and a combination of these and/or similar symptoms in a child should cause the teacher to observe him closely.

The problem of a particular reading difficulty called dyslexia has been widely investigated and in one study of 1,900 children it was shown that children of *average* intelligence who were two or more years backward in reading suffered from more involved difficulties than inability to read. Research has shown how important is the teacher's role in relation to the reading and spelling abilities of the children in her care.

The child who is especially gifted also needs special care if his gifts are to mature. Such children are often unusually sensitive and have a need to express their gifts; special educational facilities exist for them.

During adolescence 'problem' behaviour often, though by no means inevitably, occurs in our Western culture. The adolescent may need help from adults at this time in developing both his individuality and his self-esteem, although the important relationship will now be between adolescents themselves and not, as in the child's earlier years, between the child and specific adults. The difficulties which adults have in dealing with this age group are appreciated, but these are seen as often springing from a misinterpretation of the adolescent's behaviour.

At this period young people begin to be interested in human relationships, and the increasing practice of discussing such relationships in the classroom or with the school counsellor provides opportunities, which the adolescent may not otherwise have, to talk about his own feelings and relationships with others.

Formal group intelligence tests, administered from time to time by teachers, prove most useful in discovering the intelligent child who is underfunctioning in his work. Such tests, however, cannot yield as much information as individually-administered tests given by an educational psychologist. Also the psychologist, if called in when a particularly acute problem cannot be dealt with by the school alone, can often also enlist parental co-operation when this has not been possible earlier.

The adult as interactor with the child

Loevinger has suggested that whatever child-rearing methods parents use, children will always seek to circumvent these in order to gratify their own needs and desires. Whether parents basically use rewards and punishments, or teach through insight-learning, or rely on the identification process, children cannot be expected to appreciate their parents' intentions upon which the rearing method employed has been based! This somewhat frivolous approach to a serious problem emphasizes the real difficulty facing the experts when they are asked *how* children should be reared.

There are methodological problems involved in attempting to trace the relationship between rearing habits and personality development, and these are described in this chapter in some detail in order to inculcate in the reader a certain wariness regarding the acceptance of dogmatic statements about child rearing and its attendant effects. Nevertheless research work has established some principles.

Thus severely punished children tend to be either overtly or covertly aggressive, such covert aggression often expressing itself in later life in punitive ideas concerning other people's behaviour and attitudes. Extreme permissiveness when the child is aggressive also tends to increase aggression. Boys in our society are normally permitted to be more aggressive but girls less so, and boys are mostly encouraged to be independent whereas girls are usually not so encouraged.

The terms 'punishment' and 'reward' cover complex happenings in widely varying situations, and the 'commonsense' viewpoint that, for effective control, approved behaviour is to be rewarded and disapproved to be punished is too simple a view. Several investigators have established that the use of physical punishment and physical control is associated generally with the development of a number of undesirable characteristics in children. At the same time the giving of 'unconditional love' in all circumstances does not help the child to discriminate between approved and disapproved behaviour. Psychological punishment, more usually employed by middle-class parents, is more effective in producing a child with a strong Superego, though recent work stresses the 'informative effect' of occasional physical punishment for specific acts. It is important, however, to differentiate between the occasional act of physical punishment and a generally punitive atmosphere, which is not very effective in controlling behaviour.

The use of the 'inductive' method, whereby adults explain to children the consequences to others of their behaviour, was associated in one study with strong conscience formation when this method was used by middle-class mothers. It is suggested by the workers engaged on this study that the bases for internalizing authority and values may well be different for children from the two major social classes, and this finding would seem to be of importance to teachers who have to handle children from both social classes. One worker in this field achieved success in correcting nursery children's behaviour by immediately rewarding approved, and ignoring disapproved, behaviour. Summarizing these findings, one can say that habitual physical coercion produces, among other undesirable characteristics, fear of detection; that expressions of warmth towards the child help him to identify with his parents; that explanations about behaviour can help in the formation of a strong Superego; and that the rewarding of desirable, and the ignoring of undesirable, behaviour encourages the former and discourages the latter.

A number of current studies of the respective effects of permissive rearing on the one hand, and firm but non-authoritarian discipline on the other, in producing desirable qualities in children, suggest that these considerations are less important than whether the adults concerned are loving, understanding, value the child as a respected person, and are generally rewarding and non-punitive. It is also possible that a firm régime suits one child, and a permissive one another. However, not only is the child influenced by his parents' behaviour, but he is also influenced by his, the child's, own interpretation of this behaviour, and by his fantasies in relation to important people in his life. One must also realize that not only do parents affect child behaviour, but children also affect parental behaviour.

Some adults, because of their own personality problems, appear to have special difficulties when dealing with children; they are apt to belittle children, or to use physical force unnecessarily, or in other ways to use their relationship with children to satisfy their own needs. It is tragic when a young teacher is accepted for training whose own problems create such attitudes and behaviour towards the children in her care.

Children themselves at various ages have expressed their views about desirable characteristics in teachers. In the main children consider that a teacher should be helpful, should enable them to learn, should be able to keep control, and should have respect for each child as an individual. Understanding the child is particularly important in the primary school, because unhappiness occasioned by the first experience of school can adversely affect a child's future learning capabilities.

Retrospect

It will be clear to the reader that many traditional ideas about child-rearing have rested on inadequate foundations. Although the influence of the environment on personality development has not been decried in this book, we understand better to-day how difficult it is to define a 'good' environment, and we also know that possibly children vary as much in innate psychological characteristics as they do in physical characteristics. We have noted that children born into homes belonging to the lowest social classes—a high proportion of children in the community—are handicapped in very many ways, and that in order to minimize such handicaps it is important to involve parents in the education of their children from an early age.

The problem of a young child's limited ideas about moral behaviour is considered in connection with adult aims relating to the moral training of children; it is suggested that parents and teachers can capitalize on the desire most children have to please other people most of the time.

Universally applicable advice on child-rearing which disregards the individuality of children is now known to be of little value, but it is suggested that probably most parents would like their children to be able to get on well with other people, and also to develop in such a way that their innate abilities can be used to the full. In order to fulfil these aims children's four basic needs, as defined by Kellmer Pringle, must be met: the need for love and security, for praise and recognition, for responsibility, and for new experiences. It is suggested by Kellmer Pringle that not only parents but the whole of society are responsible for meeting these needs.

I

Cross-cultural and historical review of attitudes to child development and rearing

Cultural variations

The present-day attitude of Western societies to children is unique, both culturally and historically. The concept of childhood, of children's position and role in society, and how children should consequently be treated by adults, has varied from one period of history to another and from one culture to another. The factors which at any time and in any one society determine the attitude of adult persons to children depend on the norms and values of that society, and on the society's state of development. Thus that which is important to one culture will have little relevance in a neighbouring society; and the particular views held about children at one period in time may be of little account in the same society in later years.

Child-rearing practices, and the place of children in relatively primitive societies, are related to the habits, needs, expectation and values of each society, but, as Margaret Mead (1955) has pointed out, if one wishes to study the personality differences seemingly produced by different child-rearing patterns, one must start by considering what it is that all human children have in common. All children must have their bodily needs satisfied, they are all helpless for a relatively long time and they must all learn the culture which is relevant to appropriate behaviour in their society. A child, wherever he is born, must learn to eat on his own, to walk, talk, identify with his own sex, behave appropriately for his sex and age and eventually take on the adult roles assigned to him or chosen by him. It is because of these basic similarities that comparisons can be made between childhood rearing patterns, and also between the varying attitudes adults hold and have held about children in different cultures and at different times.

Problems of discipline and restriction, for example, are handled differently in different communities. The Samoans think of the process of socialization as one of unfolding development: children do not have to be taught to behave properly, but if left to develop naturally they will eventually conform to society's norms. However, they are not permitted to be a nuisance to the group (Mead, 1955). Weaning times and methods also differ greatly from culture to culture: Whiting and Child (1953) compared a great many societies from whom reports about weaning ages are available. In most societies weaning is begun between two and three years of age, although in one Indian tribe weaning does not start until the child is five or six years old. The American children, with whom children from other societies were compared, are normally weaned between zero and seven months. Time of weaning has been of interest as a cross-cultural study, because of the emphasis placed on oral* experiences in relating to personality development in psychoanalytic literature (chapter 2).

If survival depends, as it did for the Canadian Ojibwa family,[1] in trapping alone during the winter months on frozen hunting grounds, then self-reliance is of supreme importance, and the boy is taught by the age of twelve to set his own traps and bring the meat to his sister, who has learned to skin it for him, as his mother skins his father's catches (Benedict, 1955). If, as is believed in Bali, life is seen as a circular stage which includes the returning dead, then the child is viewed as a small human being who, like old members of society, is nearer the spiritual life than the middle-aged members of the community, who are closest in time to the secular life. There is no distinction as such between child and adult, and people do not increase in stature and respect merely because of their position in society (Mead, 1955). Indeed, in many communities the extreme distinction which Western societies make between child and adult is not made. Benedict (1955) quotes Underhill as telling her how a Papago grandfather in Arizona asked his three-year-old granddaughter to close a door. The door was heavy, but she was considered equal to the task and no one helped her. In our own society we think of children as wanting to play and adults as having to work, but in societies where no such distinctions are made children accompany their parents, or other members of the group, to their work, and are given tasks graded to suit their age and strength. The transition from childhood to adult life is thus one of degree and not of kind, though often elaborate initiation ceremonies, mostly at puberty, do mark the child's entry into adult life and adult responsibilities. Thus the gradual adoption of more complex or more responsible tasks, added to a clear conception of his own status in the society, means that the adolescent in the more primitive groups does not have to suffer many of the difficulties which in sophisticated communities afflict both him and his elders as a result of his ambiguous status.

However, these differences between cultures in particular child-rearing habits are not in themselves very important, nor do they alone account for the personality differences which can be observed in members of different societies. It is the dissimilar manner in which the many habits and practices of dissimilar cultures are patterned and made to fit together which account for some of the differences. Weaning habits, toilet training, parent-child relationships, the use of disciplinary methods, the assignment of responsibilities and many other aspects of child rearing, when combined together,

---

[1] Many descriptions of cultural patterns no longer hold, but were part of the culture in the days before the Second World War.

provide a background of learning which enables the adult eventually to fulfil his roles in his society. Children in most cultural groups also have to learn, in relation to roles, what has been termed 'continuity–discontinuity' in cultural conditioning (Benedict, 1955). The boy is obedient: the father authoritarian. The son, first sexless, then seeks sex outside the family: the father is always potent and confines his sexual relationships to within the family. The boy, particularly in our society, has little or no responsibility: the father has full adult responsibilities. As the child becomes the adult one kind of behaviour has to be discontinued and other kinds of behaviour begun; but in addition many habits and ways of behaving remain continuously relevant, regardless of age. Where, for example, the kind of 'age grading' occurs in relation to responsibilities, to which reference has already been made, particularly where ceremonies accompany the transition from one grade to another, children and adults seem able to move from role to role without apparently suffering psychological harm. Often quite different types of behaviour are exhibited by the same person at different stages of life, such as when members of the Arapaho tribe exhibit aggressive behaviour during the head-hunting period, followed by calmness in later life, by which time the role of the elder is to uphold the society's rituals, and it is also proper for him to exhibit peaceable virtues (Benedict, 1955).

Cultural conditioning is not, however, the only determinant of personality. Emphasis has been laid above on child-rearing patterns in order to stress the variety of habits which exist in relation to upbringing, and to indicate that the customs from which these habits are derived are at least in part related to the needs of the society. The more primitive a society and the nearer to subsistence level are its living standards, then the more role-related are its child-rearing customs likely to be. Sophisticated industrialized communities have complex and diverse needs, and there is therefore not the relatively close relationship which exists between the group's need to survive in the face of natural hazards and its consequent child-rearing customs which seek to ensure survival by training the potential adult to act appropriately.

This might be taken to mean that sophisticated communities were homogeneous in their attitude to children. Unlike most primitive groups, however, Western societies are formed from groupings of classes and subclasses, so that one cannot state with certainty that particular customs are applicable universally within a specific geographical area of the society, or that such customs are universal in all classes of the society. In addition the vast social changes which have occurred in the West during the past hundred years have brought about successive and sporadically adopted changes in the way children have been regarded by adults in the community.

Historical variations

There has been for a considerable period an acceptance of the fact that there are obvious and major differences between children and adults, but the appreciation of the nature and extent of these differences has changed. Paintings executed even up to the early fifteenth century (for example, Piero della Francesca's 'Virgin and Child with Two Angels') depict children with the same head-body ratio as adults, and they are depicted in other bodily details also as like miniature grown-up people. For a long time children were dressed like adults and were expected to behave socially and emotionally like grown people, but they were known to be physically weak, with no knowledge, no rights to speak or to have a viewpoint; they were thought of as sexless beings, whose primary duty was to obey. These notions have now given way to a full recognition of the child's legal and social standing in society, accompanied by the view that an adult maturity cannot be expected of him. However, only relatively recently, since Piaget's work on children's intellectual development has become more generally recognized (chapters 2 and 4), has it been realized that children's psychological development, for example, is two-dimensional—progressing *qualitatively* as well as *quantitatively*. Children at different stages of their growth are not only inferior in the *amount* of knowledge and ability they possess, but the *nature* of their cognitive functioning, for example, is different from that of the developed person. Although this difference has been recognized in relation to a wide variety of psychological functioning, the consequences of such a recognition still does not seem to have been fully understood by parents and teachers in their relationship with children (chapter 8).

Newson, E. (1967) has indicated that the greatest concern to parents until fairly recent times was merely to keep their babies alive, and she has shown how the child mortality figures had their inevitable repercussions on child rearing. The mortality rate in England in the 1750s for children under five years is estimated to have been about 75 for every 100 births. In 1865 it was 154 for every 1,000 births and by 1965 it had decreased to 21·8 for every 1,000 births. Once the mortality rate was significantly lowered, attention could be paid to methods of rearing children, though, as we shall see, even when the prospect of their survival was poor, the importance of correct upbringing was nevertheless recognized. Between 1820 and 1860 a large body of literature of child-rearing problems and on the importance of children appeared in the USA. Sunley (1955) suggests some of the reasons for this development, such as that a properly reared child was an asset to ambitious parents because such a child enhanced the parents' position in society. Indeed he is still today considered to do this in middle-class circles where successful children bring reflected glory to their parents!

In addition Calvinistic ideas—the 'religious morality'—prevalent in the mid-nineteenth century consciously related rearing to the ideal type of adult desired: 'A moral, honest, religious, independent individual, who could take his proper place in society' (Sunley, 1955). Susanna Wesley, writing to her son John, advised on child training, and stressed the need for firm discipline even from the cradle. She advised the conquering of children's wills, in order that their 'souls shall live' (Newson, 1967).

The dual influence of the evangelical movement and the impossibility at that time of ensuring a child's physical survival, meant that parents became concerned with at least ensuring the child's eternal survival. Calvinist doctrine was emphatic that the infant was 'totally depraved' and that only the strict guidance of parents could ensure that the child would 'earn Grace'. Dwight in 1834 wrote that 'no child has ever been known, since the earliest period of the world, destitute of an evil disposition—however sweet it appears' (Sunley, 1955). Making the child's will pliant to religious and parental demands was one way of ensuring obedience and submission, which were necessary if the child was to be saved from sinning. Parents saw themselves *in loco dei*, and considered that the proper rearing of their children in order to make them god-fearing persons was a duty they, the parents, owed to God. Failure was seen not only as a failure in the execution of their duty, but might also result in a child's eternal damnation. To ensure his eternal survival the child had to be trained to uphold the moral values of the religious society in which he lived. If, incidentally, one produced a child which was also a credit to one, this was also welcome. So the child was to understand his shortcomings, to acknowledge them and to overcome them. Differences between actual and expected behaviour were emphasized rather than minimized in order that proper humility be learned. It is in the light of these considerations that one must view the very strict, often cruel-seeming, methods of child rearing which were used.

Side by side with strong religious feeling there was also an increasing belief in man's ability to control his environment and to plan his future. It was thus thought highly probable that children could be moulded into acceptable adults, and that the training parents gave was of supreme importance.

It would seem that in such an atmosphere the notion of friendship developing between parent and child was inconceivable. However, Thompson (1969) has suggested that a distant relationship between parent and child was much more prevalent in the middle and upper classes than in the working classes. He recounts memories of persons born of working-class origin at the end of the nineteenth century which tell of the closeness between themselves and at least one parent, and of an absence of physical punishment, which is in marked contrast to the writings then current on child-rearing practices. In discussing the attitude of parents to children, and the behaviour patterns exhibited by both parents and children in the past, it has to be remembered that the views recorded on these matters were largely those of the literate classes. Thus what has been assumed to be customary, and what is often even today thought both customary and desirable in relation to child rearing, is mostly that which is considered proper by the most educated and vocal sections of the community. It is only in relatively recent years that the work of such investigators as the Newsons (1963), Bernstein (1958) and others has concentrated on differentiating not only between classes, but also between classes in different geographical areas.

The strong *paternal* oversight, which had been exercised up to about the mid-nineteenth century, was replaced about this time, particularly in the USA, by the management of children by the women of the home, mostly the mother. The previously harsh discipline, so often involving corporal punishment, gave way to discipline founded on 'conditional love': the mother made the giving of her love dependent on the child's submissiveness (Sunley, 1955). To a large extent this form of rearing is still used by certain sections of the community. In fact, Bernstein (1961) has suggested that until very recent times one of the major differences between the social classes in child-rearing practices of the English communities which he has studied is that the middle-class parent uses psychological 'blackmail' by threatening to withdraw his love, whereas the working-class parent relies on his physical superiority as a means of enforcing desired behaviour (chapter 4).

The nineteenth-century middle-class parent was concerned with moulding the character of his child, and the notion that certain ways of rearing children would strongly affect the adult character was echoed in the twentieth century in the writings of many baby books produced in the 1920s and 1930s, though both the reasons for training and the emphasis on the kind of training to be given were different. The view that a small baby's will should be broken for the health of his soul was no longer prevalent; but the notion of the 'broken will' still survived for other reasons. For instance, unless a child could learn in early babyhood that his desires would not be granted just because he made a nuisance of himself, he would become a tyrant to be feared by all who cared for him. Elizabeth Newson (1967) has indicated how the 'religious morality' gave way at this time to the 'medical morality'; medical science in the form of recommended hygiene had been effective in keeping children physically alive, and it was thought that if one could find the mental equivalent of physical hygiene one would be able to produce a mentally healthy child. By a 'mentally healthy' person the middle classes had in mind someone who was 'self-controlled, obedient and recognizing authority'. These were the virtues admired and to be inculcated into children. Although character training was thought important, the emphasis now was more on mental health, though the two were probably thought of as being synonymous. The main immediate aim was to induce regularity of habits in the baby, for such habits would produce 'all-round obedience' (King, 1937). 'Obedience in infancy is the foundation of all later powers of self-control,' wrote King. Both King and J. B. Watson insisted in an authoritarian manner that it was necessary to replace reliance on 'instinctive' behaviour by well-thought-out methods which were based on a regular régime—'feeding and sleeping by the clock'. Regularity in toilet training was also strongly advocated; if the body could be trained to accept regularity, then the mind too would be disciplined. Such training also made life easier for mother and nurse. To a society which strongly valued cleanliness of all kinds—for hygiene had been shown to produce incalculable benefits—the establishment of regular bladder and bowel movements in the baby must certainly be of value to him! Again, close and frequent proximity of a possibly infectious adult to a weak and vulnerable baby must surely be a danger to the baby. If avoidance of proximity, except when absolutely necessary, had the advantage of safeguarding the baby's physical health *and* providing the necessary character training too by not pampering him and so ensuring mental health, then there could be little doubt that such proximity must be avoided. So mothers were advised not to pick up or cuddle their babies! Thompson (page 41) has referred to the difference in rearing habits between middle and working-class parents at the turn of the century, particularly in relation to physical punishment and friendship between parent and child; this difference was also noted in the manner in which mothers from both classes handled their babies in the 1920s and 1930s. Whilst most working-class mothers appeared to behave 'naturally' towards their chilldren, many middle-class mothers, influenced mainly by Watson (1928) and Truby King, suppressed their 'instinctive' feelings towards their babies. Watson wrote firmly that too much mother love was positively dangerous for the baby, for this does not '. . . help it to conquer the difficulties it must meet in its environment'. Watson was of the opinion that much mother love was erotic, and that it was, consequently, 'unwholesome'. He said that children should be treated as though 'they were young adults. Dress them, bathe them with care and *circumspection'* (!) (author's italics). He advocated no hugging or kissing, but suggested instead a 'pat on the head', 'a morning handshake' and 'a kiss on the forehead'. It seems curious that only just over forty years ago the notion that children were not only *potential* adults, but were also to be treated as *miniature* adults, was so strongly advocated. Again, however, one has to remember that this was primarily a middle-class attitude.

Watson's ideas, and indeed all notions about training in babyhood advocated in the first forty years of the twentieth century, were reinforced by the findings of classical conditioning experiments performed by Pavlov in Russia (chapters 2 and 4). It seemed at the time that an understanding of the processes involved in learning would enable all behaviour to be controlled and modified; Watson actually claimed that he would be able to train a child to become anything he, Watson, chose it to be (chapter 2). Indeed, Watson, a behaviourist, shared with two unlikely bedfellows, the psychoanalytic school (page 51) and the Jesuits, the belief that what happens to a child early in life is of paramount importance to his development. However, whereas Freud himself took individual biological differences into account in addition to laying stress on the importance of early experiences, and the Society of Jesus must have considered the child to be possessed of original sin, Watson laid stress squarely on the early learning processes which, he felt, could be controlled to mould the total personality (chapter 4).

In an analysis of child-training literature in the USA, Wolfenstein (1955) has drawn attention to the factors in children's spontaneous behaviour which seemed important to successive generations of parents bringing up their children between 1900 and 1950. The child was not thought of as necessarily depraved, as earlier writers had stated, but during the first part of this period he was considered to have 'strong and dangerous impulses', which had to be curbed for his own sake. It is noteworthy how much parents were troubled by auto-erotic behaviour, particularly if this expressed itself in thumbsucking and masturbation. Wolfenstein analysed the 'Infant Care' bulletins of the Children's Bureau of The United States Department of Labor, and noted that advice given there for preventing auto-erotic activities included the tying of a child's legs to opposite sides of his crib, sewing the baby's sleeves down over his hands, and being relentlessly watchful against expressions of the child's 'sinful nature'.

By 1929 or so the baby's greatest sin was, apparently, his wish to dominate. Parents had to guard against giving way to his crying, for fear of being coerced into always giving him what he wanted. Part of the aim of rigorous training was to avoid domination of the parents and nurse by the baby, though, as we shall see later, the psychoanalytic writers of this period in England at least were already taking a different view. Wolfenstein writes (1955) that the idea of the baby as, firstly, a sensuous auto-erotic being, and then a grimly dominant one, gave way during the Second World War years to the notion that the baby was, after all, a pretty harmless, sinless creature. Sucking his thumb and touching his genitals were just part of his exploratory activities, and mothers were advised how to handle these situations. Wolfenstein suggests that about this time parents first began to see that there was probably no difference between a baby's needs and his wants. What had previously been considered his 'needs' were very physical, and curiously limited and rigid: he needed to be free of pain, illness, hunger and thirst. If he suffered from none of these then, when he cried, it had been assumed that he cried because he 'wanted' something. The idea that it might be a 'need' and not a 'want' to be picked up and to be cuddled did not occur to the advisers of the earlier time; the emphasis was still so strongly on the necessity of training and the avoidance of a sentimental approach.

Almost simultaneously with the behaviourist influence on rearing came the writings of persons who interpreted Freudian ideas about child development into advice for parents. The Calvinists had stressed the need to save the child's soul, the 'hygienists', as Elizabeth Newson (1967) calls them, stressed mental health through learning good habits in babyhood; but Freud had written about the importance of the child's psychosexual development and of the power of the instinctual forces which seek expression through the life-sustaining drives, and how their expression was linked to the child's social and emotional development (chapter 2). The emphasis was still on mental health, but the link between good mental health and the establishment of a particular, desired character was not so direct; rather it seemed that the child's needs had to be met in a variety of ways in order to avoid his developing neurotic characteristics. The importance of Freud's findings, and particularly of their interpretation for child-rearing practices, cannot be over-emphasized. Their greatest, indirect contribution was to focus attention on the *baby's* needs as opposed to the requirements of *religion* or *society*. For the first time the child was considered *as a child*: the *miniature* adult and the *potential* adult gave way to the child himself, with all his needs, feelings, and problems. Freud's investigations into the adult neurotic led him back into the experiences and fantasies, and thus into the emotional involvements, of children, and he sought to make laws about the developmental process which were applicable to all children (chapter 2). If one could state how a baby developed psychosexually,* and hence emotionally and socially in a normal way, then it ought to be possible to state also what kind of upbringing would aid such development. Though Freud himself gave little advice on child rearing, except to stress the need for tolerance, others made deductions about rearing practices from his writings. Susan Isaacs (1929), writing the year after Watson, suggested that babies should indeed be toilet trained, but she advocated patience and understanding, and she emphasized how natural is the child's pleasure in his own bodily processes. 'If we can really get into our bones . . . the sense of the slow growth of the infant's mind through these various bodily experiences, and the knowledge that each phase has its own importance in development, we are more likely to give him the gentle care and patient friendliness which he most needs. . . .' This is a radically different approach from that advocated by Watson; the early years are certainly important, but for reasons quite different from those Watson postulated. Newson J. (1967) has written: 'At last the dirty, happy, noisy child could also be accepted as a good child.'

It can be questioned, however, whether the influence of the psychoanalysis, beneficial as it has been to an understanding of child development, was entirely to the good. It is true that, whatever the theoretical and clinical reasons for advocating a child-orientated rearing process, the advice given also mostly made sense to a new generation of mothers: at last it was correct to express natural feelings towards one's baby. However, Freud's findings, that severe repression could lead to neuroticism, brought advice from certain quarters which advocated a completely uninhibited upbringing in order to avoid the formation of repressions. Following this advice, parents denied themselves for the sake of the child, but this time they often abrogated most of their normal rights by allowing children to destroy their possessions, and to eat, sleep and defecate where and when they chose. In addition the psychoanalytic emphasis on the importance of libidinal development in the first five years (chapter 2), and the stress on the child's emotionally-laden relationship with his parents, inculcated in parents a sense of overwhelming responsibility for the child's mental well-being. This 'permissive' cult, which has been so prevalent as a child-rearing fashion in the United States, would most likely not have met with Freud's own approval; indeed, the burden of his instinct theory rests on the premise that, by controlling his sexual and aggressive drives, man not only obtains energy for the many civilized activities in which he is engaged, but he receives from society a measure of protection (Freud, 1930). It is not the *repression* of such drives which is harmful, but their *unsuccessful* repression. Another disadvantage to parents who were being given these interpretations of psychoanalytic knowledge was that, feeling so acutely their responsibility, they often became highly anxious to the detriment of an easy relationship with their children. Even writers normally as enlightened as Isaacs (1929) made categorical statements, such as: 'If we follow through the later development of such children [who retain their stool] we *usually* [my italics] find that they tend to be self-willed and obstinate all round. . . . Other children will tend to a looseness of the bowels right through their infancy and childhood, and these children will generally be found more generous and affectionate in character.' There was no observational, longitudinal evidence to support such a statement. Similarly Isaacs painted a gloomy picture of the character defects of the only child, stating that he 'never gains the great comfort and support of real experience . . . making him petulant and hostile to strangers and tyrannical with his mother. . . . [He is] unable to tolerate the least denial of his demands' (ibid.). Such dogmatic statements, for which there was again little reliable evidence, caused great concern to parents of an only child who felt their inability to produce further children to be a great handicap to their one child.

One of the results of the publication of so many baby-books, stemming both from the psychoanalytic and behaviourist schools, was paradoxically that parents became less and less secure in the handling of their children. This plethora of advice was often contradictory, which made for uncertainty, but there *was* agreement on the great importance of early experiences and on the role of the parents in forming the child's personality. This gave parents a sense of heavy responsibility without affording them any certain guidance on how to exercise this responsibility, and consequently a great feeling of anxiety was produced in many conscientious people. A partial rescue from this troubling situation has come in recent years from two sources: firstly from the experts themselves, who have said that dogmatic advice that is applicable to all children cannot possibly be based on sound foundations; secondly from the new 'fun morality', which has suggested that as long as one enjoys caring for one's baby one must also be doing the right thing for him. Wolfenstein (1955) has written about the current fashion of 'fun morality', and in a review of American child-training literature she comments that 'parents are promised that having children will keep them together, keep them young and give them *fun* and *happiness*'. (Author's italics.) Being a parent is no longer to be merely a religious or a social duty, but something to add to the enjoyment of life. Whereas in previous generations the idea of having 'fun' in life was actually something rather reprehensible and to be avoided by responsible people, the new attitude in American culture seemed to imply that if one cannot enjoy life freely then one is somehow a failure. Everything should be made the subject of 'having fun', including one's work and one's baby! It is possible that once more a misunderstanding of psychoanalytic theory was reponsible for this view: that the person who is serious and restrained is repressed and hence not fully normal.

There are, however, two drawbacks to this attitude, as there were disadvantages to all other suggested ways of handling children. One is that 'fun', when it becomes imperative, loses its attraction. Must new parents now feel guilty if they don't find looking after their baby 'fun'? Will they begin to wonder what is wrong with their natural impulses, and worry whether this is likely to harm their baby? The second problem is that children brought up to consider their parents as friends, with whom they play and have fun, may develop an independence which can be very threatening to the parents. Newson, J. (1967) has indicated in what way the 'fun' method may have its own unhappy repercussions for the parents: the 'good' child deferring to his parents' wishes and being obedient does not fit in with the notions of the new, independent 'I-am-as-equal-as-you' child produced by the 'fun' method. Yet parents' 'historical antecedents', as Newson calls them, and the practical necessities of home life, are still strong enough to make them believe in the desirability of producing such a 'good' child, and they hope that friendliness and verbal explanations of why the child should behave as the parents want him to behave will produce a co-operative, reasonable child. However, such a child is as likely to choose *not* to co-operate and to be independent, and then the parents are faced with a revolt which is not against their authoritarian rule, but against the proffered parental friendship! This is a harder cross to bear than if the child could merely be classified as naughty: a free choice has been offered and the parents' way of life rejected.

How then to enforce behaviour which parents feel must be insisted upon, unless they turn once more to an authoritarian mode of rearing which they had earlier rejected? Parents today often find themselves in an acute conflict of roles: are they their children's friend and equal, or their mentor? The desire to be friendly with children is a strong one in most balanced adults, yet the knowledge that socially approved behaviour must also be taught and, if necessary, insisted upon, is also important to them. It can also be questioned whether a friendly equality is precisely what children require. It would seem rather that the physical size of his parents, and the parents' firm handling of him, are both seen by the child as a protective device, at times shielding him from his own impulses. This is not to suggest that parents should return to an earlier mode of behaviour, but that 'having fun with your baby' and being friendly with children cannot be regarded as the whole answer to the child-rearing problem.

Possibly for the first time in history parents today are faced with difficulties in child rearing of a kind which have not been encountered by previous generations. They want to be warm and friendly towards their children, and to be liked by them, but parents know now that such a relationship between child and parent will not necessarily produce children with those personality traits which they, the parents, desire to see in their children. They cannot reconcile themselves to allowing their children's personalities to develop regardless of the accepted social norms and values; some firmness and direction seem necessary, but such an attitude also seems incompatible with equality and friendship! Parents look to the expert for help, but now the experts will not help; they are themselves only too well aware of the complexities of the problems of child rearing and aware too of their own lack of reliable knowledge. They know of the many strands which form the human personality, and that no magic panacea exists for ensuring that one's child will grow up with the kind of balanced, responsible, happy personality one would wish him to have (chapter 8). They seem also to understand better than previous writers on child development that each child has unique qualities which make it impossible for any textbook to give hard-and-fast rules about rearing. In a way this attitude is comforting, for inexperienced parents can feel that, if there is no simple solution, then they cannot be blamed for not applying it; but it does seem to leave parents in a difficulty.

Probably Spock (1957) has done more than any other writer to allay parental anxieties, encourage a 'play-it-by-ear' attitude, and (especially in the later editions of his book) to bring back to parents a sureness in their own actions which was so undermined for the previous generation of parents. Of course it is difficult for parents and teachers alike to achieve the necessarily delicate balance between firmness and gentleness; between authoritativeness and friendliness; between restriction and freedom. However, adults now know that, among other things, they should retain some authority; that the occasional losses of temper won't do irreparable harm; and that they need not feel their floundering actions alone will determine a child's future personality. There is a notion abroad that 'we are all in this together'; that most parents seek to do the best for their children, but that everyone is fallible; and that in the last resort other factors influence personality apart from parental handling. What these other factors are we will examine in this book.

FURTHER READING

MEAD, M. AND M WOLFENSTEIN (eds): *Childhood in Contemporary Cultures* (University of Chicago Press, 1955).
NEWSON, E. AND J. NEWSON: *Infant Care in an Urban Community* (Allen and Unwin, London, 1963).

2

The developing personality

(a) The study of personality

What is personality

This book is entitled *Children: the Development of Personality and Behaviour*. We are concerned to understand how human beings come to possess the personalities they have, and how this determines their behaviour. Personality and behaviour are difficult to differentiate: Eysenck (1952) indeed suggests that personality *is* behaviour. We can, however, differentiate between the *reasons* which determine, as far as we understand them, the kind of personality a child may develop, and *how* his behaviour changes as he gets older, reviewing the factors which influence this change.

The section on the Development of Behaviour (page 103) deals ontogenically* with the way in which children, as they grow older, become normally more able to cope with the social, emotional and intellectual aspects of their lives. In this present section on personality we are concerned with what we mean by the term 'personality', with the way personality is studied by psychologists, with outlining methods of study, and with three theories of personality which have been particularly influential in child guidance and education.

When we talk about 'personality' we know that we generally mean by this how another person impinges on us. Is he pleasant or unpleasant? Does it make us happy and comfortable to be with him? Is he sincere or two-faced? And so on. We think basically of his *qualities* as a person, and of the peculiarly individual combinations of such qualities which makes each person unique. Although such qualities are highly personal they are also social, in that they manifest themselves in interaction with other people. Indeed, it has been suggested that personality is primarily a person's way of interacting with other people. Possibly Harsh and Schrickel's definition (1950) combines the personal and social aspects of personality in that they consider personality to be 'that which characterizes an individual and determines his unique adaptation to the environment'.

Philosophers have interested themselves for a very long time in the human personality. Plato, in his *Republic*, distinguished three aspects of the 'soul', which we might term today the intellect, the emotion and the will. Plato likened these three parts of the personality to the horses driven by a charioteer: the charioteer himself, who directs the horses, represents the intellect, and the horses represent the emotions and the will, thus supplying the energy for personality functioning. Although by the term 'personality' we mean all the attributes of the integrated person in whom these three aspects are joined, man's intellectual qualities have been the subject of investigations independent of the remainder of the personality. It was because Binet (page 84) was so successful in empirically studying and quantifying the intelligence of children that psychologists were encouraged to study, and some to attempt to quantify, other personality characteristics.

The study of personality and theories of personality

The study of the human personality can take a number of forms, depending on the particular overriding interest of the investigator: one might study how the personality functions, that is, the *dynamics* of the personality; or one might be concerned with isolating and *describing* traits and characteristics which are universal to all humans and from which the structure of the human personality can be inferred and the constituents of this structure *measured* in individual people; or one might seek to elucidate the forces which *determine* the personality, that is, what factors—genetic or environmental—influence its development; again, one might be interested in finding how the human personality *develops* from birth to maturity, seeking to understand the changes which take place with increasing age. Dynamics, description, measurement, determinants, and development are all aspects of the study of the human personality. In this book we are primarily concerned with the development and the determinants of the personality, but if we are to understand these adequately we cannot separate them from description and dynamics.

There are two basic methods of studying the human personality, the clinical and the experimental, though some workers, including Piaget, have used both methods in combination. The aim of the clinical method is to *understand* the unique qualities of an individual person; and its studies are focused on the individual. The aim of the experimental method is to arrive at *universally applicable* laws which have relevance in the study of all personalities. This method seeks to *explain* and *predict* human behaviour, and its studies are focused on statistical samples of the population. These two methods of investigating the human personality have developed largely for historical and practical reasons. It is clear that whereas all men are unique, all men also have characteristics which they share with others; therefore, both the study of any one individual person in depth and the study of common human characteristics have relevance.

In this chapter three theories of personality will be discussed: the Freudian psychoanalytic theory, Piaget's theory of child development, and social-learning theory. Freud's theory is considered in some detail, for his theory has probably had the biggest impact on child guidance. The other two theories have also had important influences, but they will be described in somewhat lesser detail than Freudian theory, for their influence on specific areas of development will be covered more fully in later chapters. As Piaget's interests lie mainly, though by no means exclusively, in describing the child's cognitive growth, his description of cognitive development is given in chapter 4. Mention of his work is also made in chapters 5 and 6, when the child's moral growth and the importance of play are, respectively, discussed. Similarly, various forms of learning are considered in the chapter on learning (page 123). Freud's contribution to the development of moral feeling and his ideas regarding play are also described in the relevant chapters.

(b) Freudian psychoanalytic theory of personality development

Freud, who lived from 1856 until 1939, was a medical doctor who specialized in the treatment of nervous diseases. He worked for a time in France, under Charcot, where he was introduced to the use of hypnosis as a possible method of curing hysterical symptoms which manifested themselves as apparent physical illnesses. On return to Vienna he at first collaborated with his friend Breuer and together they began to use the 'talking cure', in which patients talked quite freely, as if talking to themselves; but how this method helped in their cure is not relevant. What concerns us here are the apparent discoveries Freud made about the dynamics, development and structure of the normal personality through his association with many patients over a period of over fifty years.

The structure of the personality

Freud's view was that man was a biological, psychological, and social or moral being. As a biological being he has a body, like other animals, whose needs and drives require satisfying; as a psychological being he is self-conscious, he has to maintain a balance between the needs of his body and the demands of society, and he has to learn also to cope realistically with objects and other people in the world; as a social and moral being he has to develop a conscience and to adopt the ideals of his society. Freud named these three aspects of the personality the 'Id', the 'Ego' and the 'Superego'* respectively. These are, of course, 'hypothetical constructs', that is, they are not actual physical properties of the brain or of the nervous system, as some people have erroneously interpreted them to be, but names given to observed functionings of the personality, and there is no sharp division between them, as there would be if they were separate entities.

Freud suggested that only the Id is present at birth, containing all the energy for the functioning of the personality, and that during the child's first years of life the Ego and Superego develop. The Id and the Superego influence behaviour entirely on an unconscious level—that is, the energy invested in them affects behaviour and the way the personality develops, but one is unaware of the forces which prompt one's behaviour. Only behaviour motivated by the Ego is consciously directed, and then not always entirely so.

Freud thought of man as a biological organism, whose social and psychological self develops from the way physiological needs are met, or fail to be met, by the environment. Freud considered it probable that a young infant is conscious of little other than his bodily needs, and that he is also not very easily able to differentiate between himself and the rest of the world around him. He thought of the personality as a homeostatic* organism which seeks constantly, through the operation of drives, to return to a state of satisfaction, a state of non-tension. Thus, if an infant is hungry or thirsty, he desires food or liquid to relieve the tension. However, the infant has no means of obtaining what he needs; he has no conception of a 'world out there' from which objects are brought which will reduce bodily tensions. Freud, therefore, postulated that the child's first use of mental processes is to produce, in fantasy, imaginings of the tension release he seeks, and that this to an extent, though by no means adequately, at least temporarily reduces the tension experienced. The 'primary process', which is the name given to the use of fantasy for tension reduction, serves the 'pleasure principle', which is the overriding need of the organism to experience 'pleasure', or, in this context, non-tension; but the primary process has in time to give way to the 'secondary process'. The secondary process represents the thinking and problem-solving ability of the personality. As the human personality develops it must learn to obtain *true* satisfaction, not the vicarious and inadequate satisfactions obtained through fantasy. Thus the secondary process serves the 'reality principle'. In order that the child can give up, at least to an extent, the use of the primary progress the Ego must develop; that is, a part of the energy of the Id must split off and must become conscious, and must be in touch with reality, the actual world with which all normal humans have to interact. This is, however, a gradual process and is never fully completed, for fantasy and dreams remain as part of the life of all human beings.

The Superego is formed from the Ego and it represents the social and moral part of the personality. How it is formed we will consider later; it is made up of the Conscience,* which is aware of the kinds of acts which are disapproved, and of the Ego-Ideal,* which knows what is approved by parents and society.

The Id, having no contact with reality and influencing the personality on an unconscious level, seeks immediate gratification of needs. The small child and the immature adult are governed more by the demands of the Id than by the realistic Ego, or the controlling Superego. The Ego is able to postpone action which will bring tension release if such a postponement is in the long-term interest of the personality as a whole. The Superego is seen as an internalized authority which punishes through inducing feelings of guilt, and which produces such feeling even at the mere prospect of behaving in a disapproved manner (page 137).

The inevitable interaction of these three aspects of the personality is dependent on personal constitutional factors, and also on the way in which a child experiences life in reality and in fantasy, and particularly on how psychosexual development in the first five years of life takes place.

Psychosexual development

The account given here of psychosexual development is somewhat broader than a straightforward Freudian view would permit; it is influenced by Erikson's theories (1950). Psychosexual development is viewed by many neo-Freudians*, especially Erikson, as more than a mere account of how the sexual drive expresses itself before maturity; it is seen as part of a total, interacting process, which includes the child's developing sensori-motor* apparatus, and his enlarging social experiences.

Freud suggested that the development of the personality can best be understood if one thinks of the human person as motivated by drives which seek satisfaction through expression in the external world; and of the external world in its turn making demands upon the individual. Man is, according to Freud, born with a drive both to preserve his own life and to propagate the human species. These are the life 'instincts', as the term has been translated from the German, or more accurately, the life 'drives'. Freud's dual instinct theory holds that two drives motivate the psyche*: the life drive (or 'libido', as it is called) and the aggressive drive.

Though there is no unified, completely accepted theory of aggression in psychoanalysis (Rosen, 1969), the idea that there is an innate aggressive drive which seeks expression seems to be accepted by most psychoanalytic writers. Freud postulated that although the sexual aspect of the life drives is not able to express itself directly until maturity is reached, it is nevertheless present at birth. All other bodily functions, such as breathing, excreting, eating, although affected by learning, can be expressed directly from birth. Only the sexual drive has to await maturation for consummatory activity, but meanwhile it seeks expression through other drives, through their functioning, and through the bodily parts through which they express themselves.

By the term 'sexual' Freud did not mean only genital sexuality, but pleasurable experiences and feelings which are aroused through stimulation of various bodily parts or 'erogenous zones', as they are called; and Freud connected the experiences which the child has in this way through his body with the child's social, emotional and even his cognitive experiences. Thus for the very small baby his mouth, or 'oral zone', is of outstanding importance.

Not only is food one of the child's primary concerns in early infancy, but because his various perceptual and motor mechanisms are not yet very well developed, his mouth seems to be the most important part of his body for the purposes of interacting with the world. Recent work has indicated that the newborn baby has a much more highly developed perceptual mechanism than had previously been recognized, but this does not necessarily invalidate the importance of the oral region in early infancy. The small infant will investigate objects by putting them in his mouth, and he also *takes in* much experience visually and tactilely at this stage, just as he takes in food. His contact with his mother is through nearness to her and, very frequently, through a simultaneous feeding experience. The pleasurable or frustrating sensations which he experiences orally are an outlet for, or a damming of, his sexual drive, and they link him emotionally to the people who most frequently give him these experiences. His aggressive drive is expressed at this stage through biting and chewing. He also begins to be aware of himself as a being which is separate from other people and objects. De Monchaux (1957) has suggested that the child's first experience of his own drive processes as externalized in behaviour is when he has contact with his own body; thus sucking his thumb is a substitute activity for sucking at the teat or nipple, but it is also one step removed from, and nearer to reality, than a fantasy image of the teat or nipple. De Monchaux says that the child transfers to his relationships with other people the experience he has, and the fantasies which are evoked, through interaction with his own body. This concept of the influence on development *of the self* through interaction *with itself* has recently been evoked to contribute to an understanding of neuro-biological development (Roberts and Matthysse, 1970).

When later the baby is able to control his bowel movements he not only experiences satisfactions or frustrations related to these functions, according to how he is being trained, but he can use his new power to please, trouble, or annoy other people. Now he is much more aware of his relationship with other people and how he can influence these relationships. At this time —between about eighteen months and three-and-a-half years—his musculature is getting stronger, he is getting better at manipulating objects, just as he is learning to manipulate people; he is easily roused to pleasure or anger, is quickly aggressive, and is both possessive and generous in turn. An example of these developments is shown in his withholding or expelling his bowel motions at will. The fusion of aggressive and libidinal drives can be seen clearly at this stage.

By the time a child reaches the next psychosexual stage at about three-and-a-half years of age he is deeply involved emotionally with those close to him. Now the phallic region of his body is the erogenous zone and the boy, according to Freud, experiences jealousy of his father, because the child's love for his mother has taken on a possessive and sexual nature, though these feelings are not, Freud said, consciously understood. Again the aggressive drive can be seen in the child's dominant and assertive behaviour at this age. This is the time too when, in addition to these intense emotions of love, rivalry and jealousy, he is intrusively curious. Freud considered that such feelings of love and jealousy were a normal part of growing up in ordinary families, and he named these experiences the 'Oedipal situation' (or Oedipus complex*). In Greek mythology, Oedipus, who did not know his natural parents, was destined to kill his father and, later, unknowingly to marry his mother.

At this stage the child's awareness of his relationship with others emotionally close to him is fused to his phallic state* of development to lead to intensely emotional feelings, which, however, have to be repressed, for all societies frown on incestuous acts and feelings. It is suggested by Freud that the Superego develops not only from learning about approved and disapproved behaviour (page 137), but through the repression of the Oedipus complex. The child, unconsciously aware of the impossibility in normal circumstances of having his feelings reciprocated, gives up the struggle and identifies* with the parent of the same sex. In this way he becomes like the envied parent, and so, vicariously, receives what he desires. Through identification he assumes the values and norms of the same-sexed parent, and this results in a boy becoming manlike and at the same time accepting the standards and ideals which are considered right for the men in his society. When this occurs at above five years of age the Oedipus complex is repressed and the child enters the 'latency'* period, during which the expression of his sexual drive, according to Freud, remains latent until adolescence.

The ethologists (students of animal behaviour) have observed that there are 'critical' periods* (pages 97 and 124) during which animals must have certain experiences in early life, in order that they develop appropriate behaviour patterns later in life, and similarly Freud's psychosexual periods are considered to be 'critical'. He suggested that there is an optimum period of time for each child at each of the psychosexual stages, and that if this period is unnaturally shortened or prolonged, then this interferes with experiences at the next stages of development. The term 'fixation' is used to indicate when a child either has had too satisfying an experience, or, alternatively, a frustrating experience at one of the psychosexual stages. Whiting and Child (1953) have termed these fixation periods positive and negative respectively. If the experiences at a particular period have been very satisfying there is a reluctance on the part of the child to move on to the next stage; if the experience has been frustrating then a change to the next stage is anxiety-provoking. Such fixations express themselves in later, often even in adult, behaviour, indicating either the unsatisfied needs of early childhood, or a desire to recapture a very satisfying experience.

Because the sexual drive expresses itself through the activities of the other, life-preserving drives, stisfactions other than the release from tensions which arise from immediate bodily needs are obtained. Thus, for the baby, sucking brings relief from hunger, but it also brings pleasurable sensations through the stimulation of the lips. Freud suggested that the development of the personality depends to a large extent on how the psychic energy invested in such pleasurable activity is 'displaced'* from the original 'object'*, in this example the nipple, to other substitute objects. Thumbsucking is often the baby's first displacement activity. Two influences govern how such displacement takes place as the infant grows into a child: one is that tension release through the original object only cannot always be achieved just when it is needed, and the other is that society expects behaviour to change as children grow up, so that displacement activities which were suitable for the infant are unsuitable both for the child and for the adult. Thus these two pressures on the developing personality to find suitable displacement objects result in the resemblance which successive displacement objects have to the original becoming less and less. In the final analysis the Ego has to make its selection from those displacement objects which are available, and the use of which is also a compromise between the demands of the Id, the Superego and reality. Because displacement is a substitute activity and not, therefore, wholly satisfying, Freud suggested that there is always a residue of undischarged tension in the personality. This energy is used for many activities in which man is engaged, and which have little or nothing directly to do either with the maintenance of homeostatic physiological functioning, or with the expression of the sexual drive. Indeed, it is through displacement that, according to Freud, the development of human civilization has been made possible; he gave the name 'sublimation' to displacement when it takes the form of artistic, intellectual, humanitarian or other activities of a cultural kind.

In normal development the aggressive and libidinal drives act together, and for normal growth to take place the aggressive drive must be externalized, although the prohibitions which are placed by parents and society on aggressive behaviour require that these externalized expressions be limited or displaced. However, in addition to having to deal with aggressive feelings the Ego has constantly to keep a balance between the demands of the Id, Superego and reality. Indeed, Freud considered that internal pressures of this kind were more difficult to overcome than frustrations provided by the environment. One means of externalizing aggression and coping with internal frustrations is through the use of one of the defence mechanisms. Excessive or extreme use of mechanisms of defence is abnormal and their use distorts reality. However, all persons have at times to cope with anxieties, and most normal people employ such defences from time to time to alleviate anxiety.

We may, for example, ease the pressures on the Ego by repressing sexual promptings from the Id; or project the cause of some anxiety on to an external factor; or disguise unsuitable or unbearable feelings by behaving as if, in fact, we had opposite feelings—substituting, for example, love for hate. Whichever of the mechanisms of defence we use, they are all means of dealing with anxiety and threats to the personality, and are means too of externalizing the aggressive drive in a (usually) acceptable manner. According to the defences which we quite unconsciously adopt, so our behaviour is determined and our personality expressed.

Freud, then, suggested that how the personality is formed is in part due to how the child experiences life at the various psychosexual stages; how he deals in fantasy with the emotions which are, so Freud suggested, experienced so intensely during the first five years of life; how displacement takes place, and what mechanisms of defence are used. All the operations of the infantile sexual stages are, of course, experienced at an unconscious Id level, but they influence personality and behaviour nevertheless. So much of what is experienced in life is not consciously recollected, but has its influence on emotional reactions, which show themselves in behaviour which cannot be explained at a conscious level. One has to remember, however, that according to Freud the formation of the personality is only in part due to such experiences, for he recognized biological differences between people which influence their development; thus one person's personality will develop normally following experiences which might cause a breakdown in another person (page 84).

Freudian theory of the development of the personality is much fuller and more detailed than this brief account can indicate; the main features, however, in relation to personality development are: a recognition of the basic biological nature of man, and description of how the human infant, which a non-Christian view can credit at birth with little more than the basic drive to ensure continuity of life, becomes a civilized adult. Freud's analysis of the processes by which a small baby is changed from a 'polymorphous pervert' to a (not infrequently) rational, moral, controlled, creative, loving adult person was the first attempt to account for this process, and in many respects it is a very brilliant account. He showed understanding of the emotions which are experienced by small children as they develop within the family circle, and the feelings which are evoked by their bodily needs expressed within a framework of social relationships. How tensions are created and how they are eased, and the manner in which the personality is shaped, are all fully described in his *Two Short Accounts of Psycho-Analysis* (1910).

Although Freud himself wrote comparatively little about how children should be reared, some of his followers have made deductions from his theories, particularly in relation to 'permissive' rearing, with which he himself would most likely not have been in agreement (page 45). The 'permissive cult' seemed to spring from the idea that repressions are harmful, but Freud specifically said (1910) that 'disagreements . . . between reality and the Id are unavoidable'. It seems from his writings that he might have advocated that children should not be expected to exhibit self-controlled behaviour which is inappropriate for their age, or, to put it in psychoanalytic terms, when the Ego is undeveloped and powerless. That is why so much emphasis has been laid by psychoanalytic writers of baby-books on a gentle and gradual weaning and toilet-training process, as opposed to the firm, habit-training régime advocated by followers of Truby King (page 43). However, allowing the baby to progress at his own pace in relation to these matters is different from allowing the older child unbridled licence. We discuss in chapter 8 the relationship between parental handling, parental personality, and the development of behaviour in children.

Freud's theories about child development were derived from his analysis of adult patients, but since his death much observational work with children has confirmed many of his ideas. Observation of children leaves little doubt that the idea that sexuality is present in infancy and childhood is a correct one, though some psychologists dispute the conclusions about personality development which Freud drew from this observation. Neo-Freudians, too, suggest that possibly he placed too little emphasis on the influence of conscious drives. Erikson has placed stress on the growth of the Ego; and within the eight stages of Ego development which he outlines he gives due weight to the latency period, which held such little interest for Freud. He also carries his 'eight stages of man' on from adolescence to maturity. His scheme relates critical periods, in which the first five years correspond to Freud's psychosexual stages, with Ego qualities 'by which the individual demonstrates that his Ego at a given stage is strong enough to integrate the timetable of the organism with the structure of the social institutions' (1950). Thus he relates the oral, anal and phallic stages with the predominant development of 'basic trust', 'autonomy' and 'initiative' respectively; and during the latency period and in adolescence, young adulthood, adulthood and maturity the 'Ego qualities' of 'industry', 'identity', 'intimacy', 'generativity' and 'ego integrity' should develop respectively ('generativity' meaning the 'establishing and guiding (of) the next generation').

White (1960) considers that Freud's explanations of development are inadequate, and that an adequate developmental theory must account for a child's developing social manipulative skills, and his growing cognitive and linguistic abilities. White argues for motivating forces which are *not* biological drives, and which energize the *persistence* with which children seek to master their environment in a number of ways. He terms this 'effectance motivation': the child's efficacies and inefficacies form his competence to deal with the world and it is this strong desire to be able to deal competently with his environment that, says White, motivates the child's many activities.

Attempts have been made with varying success to verify some psychoanalytic ideas experimentally, both with children and with animals, though it is by no means easy to test clinically-derived ideas in an experimental setting. Work in this field has been reviewed both by Sears (1944) and Farrell (1951). Kline (1972) has produced the most exhaustive review to date of the testing of Freudian theory and his evaluations have in their turn been criticized by Eysenck (1972) and answered by Kline (1973).

It is easy to criticize many aspects of Freud's work, but the fact remains that even if some of his theories have, in the light of further experience, to be modified, even if others have to be radically recast, and some even abandoned, he has nevertheless provided a rich insight into the functioning of the human psyche.* His influence on many aspects of human life

—literature, art, education, child-rearing, child guidance, psychiatry and penology—has been immense. It seems important, therefore, that persons who are going to be in close touch with the developing child should have some acquaintance with his theories, and this is the reason for the outline of his work given in this chapter.

(c) Social-learning theory

General consideration

J. B. Watson (1925), who can be said to have founded the behaviourist school of psychology, laid the foundation for learning theory, though its philosophical basis can be found with the eighteenth-century associationist philosophers, and its experimental groundwork rests on Pavlov's work on conditioning (page 127).

Watson held the the view that:

(1) Human behaviour could be explained by associationist principles—i.e. learning by conditioning (page 127);

(2) genetic factors as determinants of behaviour counted for very little (though this was not Pavlov's view), and

(3) only observable behaviour was suitable for psychological study, so that no account must be taken of such concepts as consciousness, will, desire, goals, etc., in explaining behaviour and the development of personality.

Modern learning theorists who interest themselves in child-development neglect rather than discount genetic factors in their preoccupation to discover how man learns, and they are behaviourist in a methodological rather than in a philosophical sense. Like Watson they pay little attention to such factors as fantasy and the influence of unconscious drives and memories on the functioning and on the development of the personality. Unlike Piaget and Freud they are not concerned with the *total* development of the child, but rather aim at elucidating specific areas of development and behaviour which can be made the subject of controlled experimentation and observation. They are interested in the extent to which the child's development into an adult acceptable to his culture is dependent on learning; in how this learning occurs; and in the terms in which this learning procedure might be explained (Hindley, 1957).

Learning theorists have made, and are still making, the following major contributions in the field of child development: they attempt to account for

(1) how the child's sensori-motor apparatus develops;

(2) how perceptual learning takes place and

(3) how motivated behaviour occurs.

Through the social-learning theories they show

(4) how the development of such traits as dependency and aggression, and the development of conscience and anxiety, can be understood, and

(5) they give an account of such learning processes as imitation and identification.

The importance to human learning of the two forms of conditioning, so-
called 'classical' and 'instrumental' conditioning, are described in chapter
4. In that chapter too imitation and identification are discussed in some
detail. In the present chapter we consider the theoretical aspects of the two
forms of conditioning, and their relevance to the social-learning theory of
personality development.

'Classical' conditioning takes place whenever a natural (unconditioned)
stimulus, such as the sight or smell of food, is paired in suitable conditions,
including appropriate timing, with a neutral stimulus. Pavlov, the dis-
coverer of classical conditioning procedures, caused a bell to be rung about
the same time as he presented food powder to his experimental dogs. In due
course the neutral stimulus (the bell), called the conditioned stimulus or CS,
by itself evoked more or less the same response from the experimental
animal as the original, the unconditioned stimulus, the UCS. The dog's
response to the UCS, in Pavlov's experiments, was to salivate, and once he
had been thus conditioned he salivated *for some time at least* whenever the
bell was rung by itself—that is, without it being further paired with the pre-
sentation of food powder (page 127).

It is usually difficult to condition animals unless the UCS, the natural
stimulus, meets some need. The animal learns to associate the need-reducing
stimulus with the neutral (conditioned) stimulus, and to respond to the
latter as if it were the former. For this reason 'classical' conditioning has
been called stimulus-substitution learning.

The simultaneous appearance on many occasions of the mother's face and
the baby's feeding bottle (the CS and UCS respectively) causes the baby
after a time to respond in the same way to the appearance of the mother's
face only as he previously responded to the appearance of the bottle: he will
make excited and pleased movements and noises.

In an 'instrumental' conditioning set-up an action performed by an
animal in a particular situation will be at once rewarded (or 'reinforced' as
learning theorists prefer to say) by the experimenter if the particular action
is one the experimenter wishes to encourage the animal to repeat. The
animal thus learns that his particular response in a particular situation will
bring a 'satisfying consequence', and will be more likely to make that kind
of response in the same situation another time than to perform other kinds
of action. Thus by a process of reinforcing approved actions, and ignoring
unnecessary or disapproved actions, the experimenter is able to train animals to perform complex behavioural patterns. (The relevance of instrumental conditioning to child learning is discussed in chapter 4.)

When in the presence of his mother the baby makes sounds which approximate to 'Mamma', and when he learns that this causes her to be pleased
with him, which is the 'satisfying consequence', he is more likely frequently
to repeat 'Mamma' than to make other sounds in her presence (at least for a

period of time). The 'satisfying consequence' is normally termed 'positive reinforcement', which is approximately synonymous with 'reward'. 'Negative reinforcement' is punishment for an act.

Learning theorists have sought to clarify the motives for the activity of all organisms, including man. They have postulated 'drives', at least some of which are internal states, such as hunger or some hormonal condition, which lead to behaviour which reduces physical need and is of survival value. Although there are differences of view among experimenters and theorists, many learning theorists hold the view that such drives are innate; that they energize behaviour (that is, they supply the *power* to act); but that the *goal* towards which the energy is directed is learned. However, observation of babies does indicate that drives appear also to have an element of 'goal-directedness' (Vernon, M.D., 1969).

When carrying out conditioning experiments with an animal it is found that a hungry animal will usually pay more attention to food stimuli than to other stimuli. In such a state of deprivation positive reinforcement will be more effective for learning than in circumstances where there is no need for food, and, therefore, no drive to satisfy that need. However, once a *response habit* has been established an animal is usually not very selective: a rat which has been taught to run a maze while hungry will still run the maze, even though it is thirsty and not hungry; that is, it will respond to the stimulus offered by the presence of the maze.

This ability to adapt a habit is particularly useful to humans, who must be able to change their ways of responding to the many and various demands made by their environment, and such adaptation is facilitated by the use of language. According to learning theory, simple habits which are formed through conditioning are built up into ever more complex behaviour patterns.

However, one may ask how such theories can explain the many human activities involving *inter alia* cultural, educational and humanitarian types of behaviour which are neither need-reducing in the physiological sense nor of survival value. The principle of learning by association is again invoked as an explanatory concept (page 127), though this is not too happy an explanation since in due course, without further association with the 'primary' (need-reducing) drive, the associated 'secondary' drive is likely to cease to be active (to 'extinguish'); but this does not always happen in real life, such secondary drives continuing to motivate behaviour after the pairing of the two stimuli has long ceased. One must postulate, therefore, that the secondary drive itself seeks satisfaction through the achieving of *its own* goal. Thus drives are not merely goal-directing energizers, but are themselves subject to learning. In other words, *we learn to have fresh needs*, which probably arise through association with primary needs, but which, as it were, take on a life of their own.

Learning theory is immensely complex and involves many concepts which have been tested experimentally, mostly with animal subjects; only the

barest outline of the relevant theoretical and experimental aspects of learning have been given here. (In chapter 4 learning is discussed in greater detail from the practical point of view.)

Social-learning theory applied to child development

A group of American students of child development, including Mowrer, Sears, Miller, Dollard and Bandura, has attempted to show how the socialization process, the social learning of the child, can be explained in terms of learning theory. Fundamentally they state that the child's dependency on those who succour him in infancy can be shown to be the basis of all social learning. By a process of association the presence of those who minister to the baby's needs brings him a sense of comfort, and hence he becomes dependent on them and their absence will make him anxious. This production of anxiety is, according to the theory, an essential part of social learning, for the child learns by experiencing anxiety what is approved behaviour and what is disapproved behaviour; he learns to associate the satisfying of his needs with the presence of those who look after him, and their disapproval threatens that presence and makes him anxious. In due course, and in addition to his mother's mere presence, other more subtle signs, such as her facial expression, her tone of voice, or her handling of him, and other stimuli, will be interpreted by the baby to indicate approval or disapproval, and so produce corresponding feelings of happiness or anxiety in him.

The mother's approval is positively reinforcing for acts which she wishes to encourage, and through her disapproval (negative reinforcement) undesirable acts can be 'stamped out'. This dependency on the parents makes children susceptible to taking their parents as models for behaviour. The effects of children modelling themselves on the behaviour of their parents 'generalizes' to other adults.

It is difficult to account for aggressive behaviour, although the kinds of circumstances in which it is likely to occur are established (chapter 7). Often it arises as a result of frustration, but this is not an inevitable cause. Social-learning theory suggests that aggression springs from certain kinds of 'signal' behaviour displayed by the baby—for example, the asking for relief from distress of some kind—this signal being answered by maternal attention. The particular signal which is the precursor of aggressive behaviour, however, is an expression of anger by the baby, possibly arising from frustration or some other kind of distress. When the mother relieves the frustration her attentions reinforce the baby's angry behaviour, and so it is likely to be repeated. There are two further consequences of this happening: the first is that the mother's manner, because of the angry behaviour through which the baby obtained her attention, is likely to be hostile or irritable or pained, and if this happens her behaviour will be associated by the baby with release from his own distress and/or frustration. Thus he will indirectly obtain pleasure from another person's pain or discomfort, and hence, even without his being frustrated, through a process of association (secondary reinforcement) his aggressive behaviour will in due course come to have a rewarding value in itself. The second consequence is that the baby will experience conflict. His angry behaviour will be both positively reinforced, as described above, and also punished because of his dislike of the disapproval his mother will have shown.

If the child seeks to inhibit his anger because it brings punishment as well as his mother's desired attention, he will add to his frustration, and this can produce further aggression. (In chapter 4 we discuss the role of imitation in producing aggressive behaviour.)

The development of conscience

(In chapter 5 the nature of moral growth is discussed, and in chapter 8 we review the various parental rearing habits which influence the development of moral behaviour. Here we will discuss briefly how, according to social-learning theory, conscience is developed.)

The term 'conscience' usually includes feelings of guilt arising from an actual or contemplated disapproved act, which implies that resistance to temptation is an important component of a conscience. It is suggested by social-learning theory that when a child is reproved for an act he will inhibit that act. At first this reproval restrains him in his parents' presence. Then he restrains himself, often by first actually saying 'No' to himself. This self-restraint is considered to arise because the tempting thought, evoking recollections of parental disapproval, brings anxiety; this anxiety is due to the child's dependence on his parents, and their disapproval threatens the satisfying of his needs because these are brought about by his parents' presence (page 137). In this way parental disapproval is considered to be internalized, so that feelings of guilt arise even at the *thought* of behaving in a disapproved manner.

The reasons why parental disapproval, particularly when manifested just as a child is *about to commit* a 'naughty' act, is better internalized than when the child is physically punished can be summarized as follows:

(1) The inhibiting of actions in the parents' presence is associated with the tempting thought and also with the anxiety evoked by the temptation, so that the anxiety is likely to be evoked by tempting thoughts on some similar occasion later, even when the parents are not present; this, being associated with the previous inhibition of action, will probably result in the child desisting from doing what is disapproved.

(2) If the child is punished *after* he has given way to temptation, then he will associate the satisfied feeling which follows the disapproved but tempting act with the performing of such an act, and it will thus be reinforced. This punishment, coming after the immediate feelings of pleasure experienced by doing something enjoyable but forbidden, is thus not as effective as it might otherwise be. The child will still feel

anxiety as he gives way to temptation, but inhibition to act will take longer to establish because the initial reinforcing of the disapproved act through the immediate satisfaction experienced by doing it has first to be overcome.

Much experimental work with children has been carried out in an attempt to elucidate different aspects of moral growth (chapter 5). It is clear from much of this work that, for example, conscience development, guilt feelings, dependency needs, achievement need, etc., are in part at least independent concepts, and that the way they combine together varies from person to person.

Although social-learning theory is constantly being revised in the light of new experimental evidence, much of the theory is not based on experimental work *with children*, but is hypothetical, in that deductions about causes of child behaviour are made from what has been established about learning without it really being known whether such hypothetical deductions operate in actually forming the described behaviour. Learning theorists are concerned to be rigorous in their experimental and observational work, and a great deal of their short-term work on imitation is highly relevant to child rearing; yet there have been few long-term studies which directly relate actual child-rearing practices to social-learning theory. In a paradoxical way social-learning short-term research has certainly contributed to our knowledge of what kind of rearing methods are effective, but it has not enhanced the theory itself very much.

Nevertheless, social-learning theorists always attempt to base their theories of child development on empirical foundations, and they aim at the objective study of the child. Undoubtedly they have contributed, and are still contributing, very greatly to our knowledge of how children become social beings.

(d) The developmental theory of Jean Piaget

Piaget's ideas about child development will be considered in the present chapter from a theoretical viewpoint only, because in chapter 4 we discuss in detail the actual developmental processes which take place in relation to the child's cognitive growth according to Piaget's theory. His findings about the importance of play, about the child's moral development and the child's ability to use language are considered in chapters 6, 5 and 4 respectively.

Jean Piaget, who was born in 1896, has concerned himself primarily with investigating the development of the child's cognitive growth, and with his perceptual development, though Piaget has found that these cannot be studied in isolation; the manner in which the child's mental powers develop influences his changing ideas about the world, his notions of morality and causality, and his use of language. Piaget is interested in changes which take place during development in the child's perception and understanding of the world around him. It is not a question of a small child merely *knowing less* than an adult, but that his perception and understanding of the world is *qualitatively* different from that of older children and of adults.

Whereas Freud used the clinical method to make discoveries about the nature of personality development and functioning, and the learning theorists use experimental techniques, Piaget varies his methods according to the particular aspect of development which he is studying. Normally he gives children a task to do and then asks them questions about the task; according to the responses he obtains he frames the next task and the next question, and so on.

Piaget, in addition to being a psychologist, is also a biologist, and he has interests in mathematics, logic, physics and philosophy; terms from these disciplines are used extensively in his descriptions of child development. However, his work has primarily a biological and philosophical, as well as a psychological, basis, in that he is concerned with the way a child comes to obtain knowledge of the real world. How man acquires, structures and interprets knowledge about the world has been a problem of philosophical speculation for a considerable time. Piaget has aimed to discover the processes which enable a child to develop ideas about time, space, mathematics and logic. How does 'logical necessity' emerge in the child's mind? How do concepts about the permanence of objects and the conservation of quantities develop? Piaget himself (1968A) gives an example of the kind of problem which has to be explained: if A equals B, and B equals C, the small child cannot be sure that A equals C, whereas the older child of seven or so is in little doubt, and for the child of eleven and over it is a self-evident truth. Yet how does this ability to understand come about?

'Genetic epistemology' is the term Piaget uses to denote his basic investigation into how the knowledge of what is real and logical about the world develops. Piaget has borrowed the terms 'adaptation', 'assimilation' and 'accommodation'* from biology in order to explain how this knowledge of the world is arrived at. The term 'arrived at' is used deliberately in place of the word 'learned' because for Piaget the process is more than a learning process. By 'assimilation' the child takes in some new action or thought process into his existing internal mental structure, and by 'accommodation' he adjusts his mental structure to accept the new action or thought process. Thus the child achieves 'adaptation' to his constantly changing environment.

A child has to learn to perform many acts, and he has to learn to think many new thoughts. The improvement in the skill of performing any one of these acts, or in thinking new thoughts, is the 'accommodatory process', but once this has been accomplished, then one can say that the child has 'assimilated' the act or thought. Piaget suggests that a child is motivated to carry out tasks which are partly assimilated already. Once a task is fully assimilated then it ceases to be motivating, but the new skill or thought process is available to be used at a later time. Piaget himself considers mental development 'to be an ever more precise adaptation to reality' (1968B).

The 'internal mental structure' into which new experiences are assimilated, and which has to accommodate to change in order to take in new skills and new thinking abilities, is called a 'schema'. A schema can be simple or it can be complex. A simple schema is just a response to a stimulus; a complex schema could, for example, be *all* the processes involved in the infant sucking at the teat or nipple, starting with the head-turning movement and continuing with mouth-opening, sucking and swallowing.

A schema is either sensori-motor—that is, it is an action—or it is cognitive, it takes place in thought. Because for Piaget thinking at the baby stage is wordless, internalized action, the use of the term 'schema' to denote both a skill and a thought structure is not inconsistent. Also the use of such a comprehensive term is justified because Piaget attempts to account for the total cognitive developmental process from the infant's first acts, through the growing complexities of actions and thoughts in childhood to the adolescent's ability to engage in logical, abstract thought.

Although a schema is defined as an 'internal mental *structure*' it is nevertheless a flexible structure, otherwise it could not accommodate new experiences of various kinds. A schema is also 'mobile' in that once a skill or thought process has been mastered the skill can be applied in a variety of ways and the thought process applied to related problems.

Piaget's theory of child development is an age-stage theory. He suggests that all children must pass through certain stages of development, and that with every child the earlier stage must precede the later stages. His theory of how mental development takes place is not an easy theory to appreciate. It is not a learning theory (page 59) nor is it merely a maturational theory, but a third kind of developmental theory. The child is not a passive receiver of impressions from his environment. He *organizes* his thoughts in relation to his experiences and in relation to his activities. Piaget has termed this organization of experiences 'equilibration'. A system in equilibrium maintains a stability, a balance, in relation to forces acting on it, as a thermostat maintains a constant temperature within an enclosed vessel or space despite external temperature changes. It is thus a self-regulating and dynamic system.

Through social learning, through being taught about the properties of the world, such as weights, measures, etc., and the conservation of quantities, and through experiences with his environment generally, through all these means a child builds up a set of beliefs about the real world. These beliefs, however, come into conflict with one another. For instance, a young child can see that water poured from a tall, slender glass into a short, squat glass will look less, and he may indeed think that it is less than it was in the tall, slender glass; but at about six years of age he will also have acquired a belief, at least in relation to some materials which can be quantified, that quantities do not become less unless something is taken away from them; thus to such a child the perceptual evidence, and what has been learned about the conservation of quantities, conflict with one another. This conflict, which is seen by adults as illogical behaviour or as the holding of illogical views, has to be resolved; the child's ideas have to be brought into agreement with one another. In order to do this he must reach a certain stage of maturity, he must also have experience of the world, but over and above this he has to be able to organize his thoughts into a system which is self-regulating. How does it become possible for the small child gradually to organize his thoughts into a logical system?

Mention has been made of Piaget's assertion that a child's thinking before he is two years of age or so is internalized action, but after that age the child has to learn to represent to himself in thought what he has already mastered in action. He is able to be more advanced in action than he is in language or in thought. Consequently what children aged about seven say, or how they apparently think, is far less logical than how they behave. The child under this age is indeed pre-logical. Instead of logical thought he indulges in what Piaget calls 'the mechanisms of intuition'. The child has internalized actions and percepts, but he is without the power to co-ordinate these into a logical structure. His answers to questions which require logical thought are often of an intuitive kind. 'Why does the moon move when you walk?' 'Because it follows me.' 'Why does it follow you?' 'Because I walk', or 'Because it wants to'.

In chapter 4 reference is made to the child's inability at four or five years of age to detach himself from information presented by the senses in order logically to evaluate a situation. If a child of this age is given eight red discs and a handful of blue ones and asked to make a row of blue discs of the same *number* as the red ones, he will make the row of blue discs the same *length* as the red row without bothering about whether the *number* of blue discs coincides. Piaget says that at this stage the child is midway between *actual* experience and *mental* experience. These intuitive actions lack what he calls 'mobility' and 'reversibility'. Action habits, such as performing a task which has a goal, are *irreversible*, because one can only work *towards* a goal, not away from it; but thought processes must be reversible. Thus 4 plus 2 is 6, but equally 6 minus 2 is 4. Because, for the very young child, all thought is internalized action, the thought process at this age is irreversible, as well as being rigid and yet also unstable. However, by four or five years of age some of the rigidity has been lost, and at this 'intuitive thought stage' the child is able to move his thoughts towards reversibility. He is preparing to enter at seven or eight the 'concrete operational' stage of development (page 107).

An 'operation' has been variously defined as an action which takes place in the imagination (Beard, 1969); an act which is an integral part of an organized network of related acts (Flavell, 1963); and an internalized action which has become reversible (Piaget, 1968B). One may best think of an 'operation' as an internalized action which has become organized into a coherent and reversible thought system.

When a child moves from the intuitive thought stage to the first operational stage, the 'concrete' operational stage, it has been found that he is able to manipulate his thoughts, although at seven or eight years of age this manipulation is still very much linked to actual action. For example, if a child under four years of age is asked to put a number of sticks in order from the shortest to the longest, he normally only manages to arrange them in pairs but without comparing the pairs with one another. Only when he is about six or so will he have a sufficiently organized thought system to enable him to look for the shortest first and then move on to put the others in order in the same manner. This ability presupposes an understanding of reversibility, because it must be possible for him to see each stick as both shorter than the next one and longer than the one before. Such understanding of seriation is just one of many kinds of understanding which become available after six or seven years of age. However, operations at this age are still very 'concrete', for the child cannot carry out this kind of thought process without the aid of perception—in this example he is ordering actual sticks. He is still very dominated by perceptions and has no thinking powers at his command which enable him to use words, symbols or other abstractions in the same logical manner in which he handles physical things. The child between seven and eleven years of age has to move from this largely *percept-centred* view of the world to a view which is based on logical deductions; and similarly he has to move from an *egocentric* stand to a more objective viewpoint.

When the child enters the 'formal operational' stages at about eleven or twelve years of age his thought processes are largely released from the influence of perception, and he is much more free to think logically and mathematically. He is now operating on a plane of reasoning where he can think without the support of perception and with the use of language, whether this is a language of words or of symbols. The small child *acts* on objects; the older child is able to *think* about *objects in their presence* and then act on the results of his thinking; but the child of twelve and over should be able to *reflect* about objects in their absence in a propositional sense. Piaget says that at this stage 'thinking takes wings' (1968B).

It is clear that by the formal operational stage the mental conflict between perception and logical structures has been *largely* resolved. The child now has at his command mental abilities of various kinds, but linking them all is the ability to think logically. His cognitive structures are now more stable, capable of being highly complex and organized. Equilibrium has been achieved, and thinking becomes freed from concrete reality. (The actual developmental process from the sensori-motor stage to the formal operational stage is described in some detail in chapter 4.)

Piaget's ideas first aroused interest in the 1930s in the USA, but only since about 1955 or so has his work been considered to be of genuine importance and significance, although it has not survived without criticism. He has worked more as a naturalist than as an experimentalist, which implies that much of his work lacks precision and control, and it is difficult precisely to repeat some of his research. He seldom gives statistical analyses, and he has usually only used small samples. It has been said that children can be taught the concepts he says they cannot understand, so that it is not lack of maturation but lack of experience of the world which causes young children to give wrong answers to some of Piaget's questions. On the other hand recent work by Harris and Allen (1971) which sought to test the prediction that ability to conserve in children under seven was due more to a difficulty in differentiating right from left than to an inability to understand the principle of conservation, was unable to confirm the prediction. Some critics profess to have found that Piaget's theory of age-stage dependence does not hold at all times; others (Bryant, 1971) that the loose design of Piaget's experiments has been responsible for the inferences he has drawn from their results, and that some such inferences, such as children's inability to understand the conservation of numbers, are unjustified. Deutsche (1937), who studied children's ideas of causality, found all levels of understanding present at all ages. Other critics have suggested that Piaget's studies are really vocabulary studies in disguise; they say that what Piaget has studied is a child's growing ability to use words, rather than the child's schema. Another criticism is that the type of answers which children give seem in part to depend on the sort of questions asked. Again it has been said that it is likely that many of the child's characteristics discovered by Piaget are really due not so much to maturational processes as to the culture in which his child subjects were reared. Work with Chinese children (Liu, 1950) has shown that they are more advanced than Piaget's subjects in understanding motives for behaviour, and in understanding causality.

However, many workers have repeated Piaget's experiments, using more controlled techniques, and their findings have been similar. Also, although it is possible that an element of *verbal* non-understanding by children may have clouded some of his findings about apparent *conceptual* non-understanding, there is good evidence that there is some factor additional to verbal understanding which appears to aid the comprehension of concepts. Again, it is probable that although young children can be taught a temporary specific skill to enable them to carry out tasks apparently requiring the ability, for example, to understand the conservation of quantities, it remains doubtful whether they really understand the concept of conservation; and though Piaget places much emphasis on maturational processes, he specifically admits that teaching is influential in aiding the cognitive growth of the child.

It has been established that the kind of changes in children's thinking which Piaget describes do occur. Until his first work was published educationalists were inevitably aware that children knew less than adults, but the emphasis was on a *quantitative* difference between children and adults' mental capacity, rather than on a *qualitative* difference in *functioning*. Young children are more egocentric and percept-centred than older children and adults, and due to this difference in outlook the quality of their thought is consequently different. Also Piaget's findings that a child's mastery of a wide variety of cognitive areas of functioning, such as being able to deal with number, quantity, time, causality, etc., in certain important respects takes place according to a common procedure, and also his linking of the growth of moral development with the development of cognitive structures, were novel discoveries.

Piaget's work has generated much further research, has deeply affected pedagogic ideas, and has given adults a different and illuminating view of how children think, function and develop. His scheme of mental development is the most comprehensive that has been hitherto advanced; and in its analytic power and understanding it has no equal.

(e) Comparison and assessment

The three theories which have been discussed in this chapter differ one from another in a number of important respects. Freudian psychoanalytic theory concerns itself with *emotional* and *motivational* aspects of the personality, whereas social-learning theory views man primarily as a learning organism; and Piaget has interested himself mainly in the qualitative changes which take place in the child's *perception* and *understanding* of the world around him as he grows from infancy to adolescence.

We have seen that psychoanalytic theory stresses the importance of unconscious processes which affect behaviour and the development of the personality, but social-learning theory places no emphasis at all on such processes, and views the developing child as an organism whose behaviour is primarily a response to external and internal stimuli; in Piaget's theory neither unconscious processes nor the responsive nature of behaviour is of supreme importance. The student of child development, viewing these theories objectively, can be forgiven for asking

(1) whether it is at all possible to integrate the theories and formulate a unified theory of child development, and
(2) if this is not possible, whether one can, or indeed should, make an assessment of the relative value of each of the three theories.

Most child psychologists would be of the opinion that it is too soon to expect to be able to formulate a comprehensive theory of child development. Such a theory would have to be descriptive and explanatory, and would therefore have to account for the development of, and change in, all aspects of observable and measurable behaviour, as well as non-observable 'behaviour', such as fantasy, thoughts and feelings, all within a unified theoretical framework. The theory would have to be one of individual personality growth as well as one of social interaction. It is doubtful whether research has progressed sufficiently far to enable such a unified concept to be formulated.

Nevertheless, it is possible to see some similarities in such apparently divergent views of man as those described by Freud, the social-learning theorists and Piaget. For example, both psychoanalytic theory and learning theory see man to a greater or lesser extent as a reactive being: Freud considered man to be motivated at least in part by drives which seek satisfaction through interaction with the external world, and he also thought of man as being subject to pressures from the world; and social-learning theory offers a not entirely dissimilar view of man as seeking to satisfy internal needs by reacting appropriately to those external stimuli which promise to satisfy such needs. Although Piaget's theory of adaptation does not specifically view the child as a reactive being, he says that mental development is an 'ever more precise adaptation to reality', and he describes how this adaptation occurs. It is also unreasonable to suppose that a child's development occurs both through the working out of psychosexual drives *and* through processes of reinforcement, while at the same time the cognitive apparatus is changing qualitatively along the lines suggested by Piaget.

However, the differences of approach to the *study* of child development, and the *contribution* to knowledge made by each of the three theories is so fundamentally different from that of the other two that comparisons are not easily possible. The theorists themselves are, indeed, critical of one another, the Freudians, for example, considering that most other theories, particularly learning theory, are too superficial to take sufficiently into account the deeper-lying influences which shape the personality; learning theorists are sceptical of the interpretations made by Freudians of clinical material, and also critical of Piaget for his manner of sampling and the methods he employs to analyse his data; and Piaget appears to consider that learning theory views the child *too much* as a reactive, rather than a maturing and participating, being.

Taken together, however, one can say that these three theories provide a rich insight into the processes affecting the development of the child's personality. They are complementary to one another, and each theory enables students of child behaviour better to understand the psychological development of children.

FURTHER READING

HALL, C. S. AND G. LINDZEY: *Theories of Personality* (John Wiley and Sons, New York and London, 1957).

FREUD, S.: *Two Short Accounts of Psycho-Analysis* (Penguin Books, Harmondsworth, 1962).

STAFFORD-CLARK, D.: *What Freud Really Said* (Penguin Books, Harmondsworth, 1965).

BANDURA, A. AND R. H. WALTERS: *Social Learning and Personality Development* (Holt, Rinehart and Winston, New York, 1973).

MOWRER, O. H.: *Learning Theory and Behaviour* (John Wiley and Sons, New York, 1960).

BEARD, R. M.: *An Outline of Piaget's Developmental Psychology* (Routledge and Kegan Paul, London, 1969).

RICHMOND, P. G.: *An Introduction to Piaget* (Routledge and Kegan Paul, London, 1970).

PIAGET, J.: *Six Psychological Studies* (University of London Press, 1969).

BALDWIN, A. L.: *Theories of Child Development* (John Wiley and Sons, New York and London, 1967).

KLINE, P.: *Fact and Fantasy in Freudian Theory* (Methuen, London, 1972).

3

Influences affecting the formation of personality characteristics and the development of intelligence

(a) General considerations

The 'nature-nurture' controversy

A discussion of the origins of behaviour, and of the factors influencing the development of the personality, inevitably includes a discussion of the 'nature-nurture' question. Man is naturally interested in whether his dispositions are brought about more by his genetic inheritance than by the influences to which he is subject during life, particularly in childhood. These discussions are themselves affected by historical, political, philosophical and humanitarian considerations. During historical periods when man felt himself to be in growing command of his destiny—for example, during the middle and later parts of the nineteenth century (page 41), and under political régimes which assume that changes in the environment would produce greater equality and opportunities for many persons in all aspects of life, during such periods and under such régimes the role of the environment has been, and is still being, stressed.

Philosophically also the notion that man's intellectual capacities and personality characteristics may be predetermined from birth by his genetic inheritance seems unacceptable to believers in human free will; most sects of the Christian Church hold that man has capabilities which enable him to change aspects of his behaviour, particularly when these are anti-social or injurious to his fellow men. Similarly all attempts at changing the existing social order, whether in the field of penal reform, the treatment of the mentally ill, or the education of children, have relied on the belief that improving environmental conditions would also improve man.

For a considerable time, then, despite the writings of Galton in the nineteenth century (1869), it has been fashionable to stress the importance of the influence of the environment on man's behaviour, and it is only in relatively recent years that, for example, psychologists have conceded that there may be a large genetic component in testable intelligence. Even here, where the evidence is now fairly convincing, recent discussions of this problem have produced more heat than light. The nature-nurture problem is one which touches deeply man's concept of himself, and as such produces strongly held opinions, which often prevent objective assessment of the evidence.

Various formative influences

Psychologists in the past have been interested in the extent to which behaviour and personality are each affected by genetic and environmental factors. It is obvious that both genetic endowment and the influence of the environment are essential for the development of behaviour; without the inherited foundation there could be nothing on which the environment could operate, and without the environmental framework there would be no way in which the inherited factors could express themselves. This 'interaction' concept, as it is called, has taken the emphasis away from the question 'how much' and replaced it by the question 'how' (Anastasi, 1958): psychologists and geneticists are now interested in the *manner* in which the genetic factor has its influence, and *which* of the many kinds of environment has an effect on *what* kind of behaviour. In some ways it is a pity that the emphasis has moved from a concern with the *degree* to which personality is affected by inherited and/or environmental factors, because it is only by knowing to what extent changes can be effected by altering certain aspects of the environment that we can make effective educational and remedial decisions. Jensen recently (1969) insisted that rather than attempt to boost deprived children's intelligence score, remedial work should aim at teaching children according to their specific abilities; this recommendation is based on a (to Jensen) realistic acceptance of the large inherited component in testable intelligence, which, he considers, inevitably limits the level of scholastic performance of many children.

We are interested in the development of children, and such development is not just a matter of an environment impinging on a genotype*. Schneirla (1966) clarifies the relationship between different aspects of development which are at times confused with one another: he points out that the child *grows*; he *matures*, that is, there are qualitative changes with increasing age; and the child *develops*, which includes growth, maturation and also learning.

When we consider the meaning of the word 'genetic' we find that the way this word is used often confuses innate, constitutional, pre-natal and truly hereditary influences with one another. Cattell (1965) shows clearly and interestingly how several terms, which are often loosely and interchangeably used, should be differentiated.

Thus the term 'innate' includes not only what is inherited but mutations which may have occurred in the genes between parent and child; 'congenital' need not mean innate only, for it can include changes which occur in the womb before birth; and 'constitutional' can include changes which occur after birth due to possible physiological changes.

It is important to separate those factors which are definitely due to inheritance from those which are acquired after conception. Such a separation also stresses the fact that the influence of the environment does not commence at birth but at conception; only in relatively recent years has the importance of the uterine environment been acknowledged.

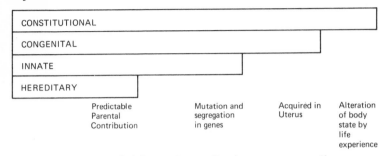

CONSTITUTIONAL

CONGENITAL

INNATE

HEREDITARY

| Predictable Parental Contribution | Mutation and segregation in genes | Acquired in Uterus | Alteration of body state by life experience |

Diagram 1   Definitions of contributions to personality commonly considered 'non-environmental'.[1]

The term 'environment' is also often used as if it were a unitary concept, as if there were only *one* environment, whereas every child is subject to many different environmental influences which contribute in varying degrees to the shaping of his behaviour. These influences range from the chemical and nutritive factors which influenced him before birth, through, inter alia, the culture and society into which he is born; the social class to which his family belongs; the school he attends; his own position in the family; the personality characteristics of his parents; to the peculiarly individual and possibly even traumatic* experiences which he himself has, particularly in childhood, including the products of his own fantasy.

When we consider the influence of the total environment we must also keep in mind the differential effect which it can have on different human characteristics. Thus eye colour, blood grouping and finger-ridge counts cannot be affected by the environment at all, but other characteristics, for instance, intelligence, are undoubtedly affected by the kind of experiences the child has; it is most probable, however, that genetic factors do set a limit to the kind of intellectual achievement which is possible. In this case the environment probably acts as a 'threshold variable' (page 91), making it possible for the genetically determined potential to be reached. However, the environment cannot, as Watson in 1925 thought it could, enable a child to become a specialist in any field in which he might be trained, regardless of his innate potential. Other aspects of human behaviour and personality, particularly social behaviour, are likely to be much more affected by various environmental conditions than by genetic influences.

Consideration has also to be given to the *period* in a person's life when he is subject to specific environmental influences. There is now a good deal of evidence to show that the effects of experiences early in life, even during the first two or three years, may have a more profound and lasting influence than later experiences at least on the development of intelligence

[1] Reproduced from Raymond B. Cattell: *The Scientific Analysis of Personality* (Penguin Books, 1965) by kind permission of the publishers.

(page 97), but probably also on the development of other personality characteristics.

Lastly, it must not be forgotten that although a factor has been genetically caused it may nevertheless be possible to change it. To take an example from work with insects, it has been found that ambient temperature can effect changes in wing size and other structures (Connolly, 1971). Similarly in human children the mental subnormality called phenylketonuria, where the lack of an enzyme causes toxicity in the brain cells, can now be prevented by early identification and by adherence to a suitable diet.

Methods of study

It is difficult to study the relative influence of genetic and environmental factors in humans, for usually the environment seems to support the genetic endowment: for example, a child from a good environment usually has parents who have also supplied him with a good inheritance. For this reason much use has been made in this study of identical twins called 'monozygotes' (MZ twins) who have been brought up apart from one another. The assumption behind their experimental use is that since they are genetically identical, each being developed from one half of a divided ovum fertilized by one sperm, any differences in personality and behaviour must be due to the effects of the environment. One criticism of such studies is that twins are an unusual sample, not representative of the general population, and that any discoveries made about some twins are applicable only to other twins. Another criticism about the use of separated MZ twins is that whenever such separation occurs the circumstances under which the children live, particularly for the child which is fostered or adopted, are unusual. However, we do not really know what a usual or 'normal' family is; also some disadvantages suffered by the adopted twin might be off-set by compensating advantages he may experience. A criticism made more recently (Mittler, 1971) is that since many of the twin pairs who were studied were obtained by means of appeals on the mass communication media they were a biased sample, because presumably only certain kinds of persons will respond to appeals of this kind. It is obviously desirable that the selection of twins for future studies should be carried out by methods which ensure as far as possible a random sample from the twin population, but as the findings from twin studies have by and large been supported by consanguinity* studies and other studies of various kinds, the evidence about similarities and differences between twins cannot be dismissed as valueless. Indeed, since the pre-natal environment of MZ twins is *not* at all the same, one twin, most frequently the younger, being at a disadvantage through obtaining a poorer share of the maternal blood supply and for other reasons, the similarities which have been found between separated MZ twins are somewhat surprising.

Longitudinal studies (page 81), some commencing very shortly after birth, have aimed at elucidating what human characteristics appear to persist from early childhood to adult life. Although the assumption is not necessarily made that such persistence indicates that the characteristics in question are genetically determined, there is again evidence from other sources which not infrequently supports such an hypothesis. Other longitudinal studies seem to indicate the crucially important effects of very early environment.

Another source of information about the respective influence of genetic endowment and environment respectively come from animal studies. It is possible when studying animals to control genetic and experimental variables in a way that is ethically impossible with human children. Although it is admitted that extreme care has to be taken when extrapolating findings from animal studies to an elucidation of human problems, it is possible to make such deductions, particularly when findings derived from animal work are supported by observations on humans.

Attempts have also been made to study the possible relationship between temperament* and body-build. If it were to be found that, regardless of life experience, persons of similar body-build were also of similar temperament, then one could reasonably assume that a relationship existed between body-build and temperament; and, as the final adult human morphological* structure is, except in very extreme circumstances, only marginally affected by the environment, one might surmise that temperamental characteristics too are only marginally affected by the environment.

In addition many cross-sectional studies have been carried out on practically all aspects of child development. Such studies are not usually concerned with elucidating the contribution of genetic and environmental influences, but in seeking to clarify aspects of the environment which have their effect on the development of behaviour. These influences are discussed on pages 92f.

(b) The formation of the personality—genetic influences

Possible relationship between physical characteristics and temperament

Behaviour is displayed and personality expressed through bodily activity. It would seem reasonable to assume therefore that there is some relationship between anatomical and physiological properties and behaviour. Williams (1960) in an article entitled 'The biological approach to the study of personality' outlines the very many anatomical, endocrinic and physiological variations which can be found in humans. He gives many examples of these, such as, for instance, that human stomachs and thyroid glands can vary sixfold in size; that the production of hormones can differ in different persons over a sevenfold range; and that the branching of the trunk nerves is extremely individualistic. It is obvious also that every person has a distinct respiratory, endocrinic and nervous system. Similarly, the brain varies both in structure and in number, size and arrangement of neurons for each individual. Williams considers that the unique equipment which an infant brings into the world must be at least as important in determining his personality as environmental factors. Similarly Mottram (1944) states that 'the endocrine organs are potent in determining our personalities'. Several studies, quoted by Hutt (1972), indicate how psychological differences between people are influenced by sexual factors, so that, for example, men are more susceptible to visual stimuli, but women to auditory stimuli; and women have a lower touch and pain threshold. It has also been observed that boys from birth are more vigorous in their movements than girls.

Mittler (1971), in reporting on examinations of twins in respect of a number of biological factors which may affect behaviour, states that, for instance, intelligence and cognitive skills (to be considered in detail later) 'are built on biological foundations'. He reports on studies of twins which have considered anthropometric data (such as height and weight), motor skills, and sensory and perceptual processes, as well as a number of physiological data, including brainwave functioning, sedation thresholds and the functioning of the autonomic nervous system. The conclusion can be drawn from this data that identical twins are more similar than fraternals in such factors and functions as height, electrical activity of the brain, autonomic functioning and basic sensory processes, and that these functions are unlikely to be affected by the fact that, as Mittler says, 'they [the identical twins] are treated in a more uniform way by their parents [than fraternal twins]'. Although one cannot categorically state that these functions are *not* affected by such treatment (Vernon (1969), for instance, suggests that brainwave activity could itself be affected by the *development* of intelligence), it is unlikely that such functions are in the *main* determined by environmental factors.

Theories about a possible relationship between the body and personality have existed for a considerable time. In folklore there have been assumptions that fat people are jolly people; a vaguely related corollary of this is expressed by Caesar in Shakespeare's *Julius Caesar*, when he says:

Yond Cassius has a lean and hungry look;
He thinks too much: such men are dangerous.

Galen, in the second century A.D., suggested that four basic temperaments, the choleric, phlegmatic, sanguine and melancholic, were related to four different types of bodily 'humours'. In more recent years (1925) Kretschmer reported on a relationship which he believed he had noted between patients suffering from dementia praecox (renamed later schizophrenia) and those suffering from manic-depressive psychosis, and their respective body-builds. The schizophrenic patients were more often taller and of a somewhat thin body type, and the manic-depressive patients were more frequently short and had a 'round' body. From this observation Kretschmer produced a theory of four types of body-build which he related to four personality types, and which were applicable to normal persons.

Later, in 1940, Sheldon developed 'somatotyping' that is, the study of the relationship between body-build and temperament. Sheldon's approach allowed for a large number of distinct categories, rather than the four broad categories postulated by Kretschmer, and he related his physical types to particular temperaments, rather than to personalities as total units. At the time of his death Sheldon was working on a constitutional psychology, for he maintained, as indeed Allport (1937) did, that in examining the human personality one must take into account not only cognitive and affective aspects of the personality, but also physiological and morphological (structural) aspects. Sheldon's three basic types, which are discussed further on pages 171f. in relation to the assessment of individual children, are the 'endomorph', who is relatively round and 'soft' in body; the 'mesomorph', who is muscular and 'hard'; and the 'ectomorph', who is 'linear'. The suggested related temperamental characteristics are, for the marked endomorph, social extraversion; for the marked mesomorph, love of activity, independence and possible aggressiveness; and for the marked ectomorph a retiring intellectualism.

Psychologists may not have given Sheldon the credit he deserves, for his assessments were not made from a random sample of the population as most of his subjects were young males; also his work was carried out from measurements taken from photographs of nude subjects. However, other work carried out since (some additional work with children is discussed on page 172) has, broadly speaking, confirmed many of Sheldon's findings. Thus Cortés and Gatti (1965) have shown significant correlations between self-descriptions of temperament and body-build in boys and girls in late adolescence. The Gluecks (1950), in a well-known study of delinquent boys in New York, found that the delinquent children, who had been matched in a number of important psychological, physical and socio-economic factors with non-delinquents, were nevertheless markedly more mesomorphic in build, and showed Sheldon's associated temperamental characteristics; that is, they were more assertive, impulsive, extraverted and aggressive. However, these delinquents came from homes where they were shown little understanding and affection, and the Gluecks surmised that these environmental factors interacted with the morphological ones to produce the delinquent behaviour.

Sheldon thought that the educational system, at least in the USA, was too much geared to an assumption that all children are more or less alike, and he thought it most important to note that children do differ greatly one from another, largely, in his opinion, because of their different body-builds. He felt that the mesomorph is best provided for in a competitive society where his assertiveness and social extraversion are appreciated.

Constitutional psychology maintains that because there are basic differences between people in their psycho-physical make-up they tend to *interpret* life experiences differently one from another, and consequently react differently to their experiences.

Twin studies, longitudinal studies and work on animals

Another approach to the study of personality is provided by a comparison of specific characteristics as they manifest themselves in monozygotic and dizygotic twins respectively, and in MZ twins who have been brought up together when compared to MZ twins who have been brought up apart from one another. Although such investigations have been concerned with many different kinds of personality traits, two in particular, called 'types' by Eysenck (1959) and 'second-order factors' by Cattell (1965) have been studied fairly extensively. These two are 'extraversion' and 'neuroticism' (or 'anxiety' in Cattell's terminology). In Eysenck's hierarchical view of personality many different kinds of personality traits, habits of behaviour and specific responses can be grouped under these 'types', rather like generations on a family tree. Thus when I am out walking I may see someone I know; my *response* to this is to cross the road. This response arises from a *habit* of, normally, avoiding rather than seeking out other people; and this habit in turn springs from a more general *trait* of shyness, which in its turn comes from my having an introverted personality *type*.

Based on the results of empirical studies and statistical analyses, Eysenck asserts that, by taking specially devised tests (the Maudsley Personality Inventory, or the Eysenck Personality Inventory), every person can be placed somewhere along the scale of an 'extraversion–introversion' continuum and similarly along a scale of a 'neuroticism–stability' continuum as shown in diagram 2 (p. 82). This diagram indicates how groups of persons diagnosed as having character defects or suffering from various kinds of instability can be placed on such a two-dimensional scheme, but it is implied, of course, that all normal persons too can be placed somewhere on such a scheme. Normal persons can be highly introverted or highly extraverted, as well as being 'ambiverts', but they would come low on the horizontal neuroticism scale.

By comparing the places on such scales obtained by MZ and DZ twins respectively, and MZ twins reared apart when compared with MZ twins reared together, it should be possible to say something about the heritability of such personality characteristics.

There is evidence from many different studies, including those by Eysenck and Prell (1951), Shields (1962) and Canter (1969, unpublished), of a genetic contribution to the score which an individual can obtain on the introversion-extraversion continuum, and also on the neuroticism continuum, though the latter is less clear. Canter of the Glasgow Twin Study indeed considers that her work favours strong support for a genetic factor in 'sociability and possibly extraversion, and it would appear that (for separated MZ twins) hereditary influences are most strongly exerted *after* separation'. She found that in some characteristics separated MZ twins were indeed *more* alike than those brought up together. She suggests that when twins are brought up together they 'adopt different roles, at least in the case of social behaviour or social extraversion, to stress their individuality, and that *similarities are only released* when they come to live separate lives'.

If one turns from a consideration of studies of twins to longitudinal studies, there is general agreement that certain personality traits show a remarkable stability over long periods of time even though such traits may sometimes be differently named by different investigators. Thus Kagan and Moss (1962), Tuddenham (1959), the Berkeley Growth Study and the Berkeley Guidance Study have all reported on the remarkable persistence of a trait which, though variously defined, can be called 'outgoing responsiveness versus retractive inward-looking'. Again, several studies have found that 'dependency' in girls, but not in boys, and 'aggressiveness' in boys, but not in girls, are both fairly consistent traits. An interesting finding also is the 'sleeper effect': that is, that certain traits do not appear to run consistently; although they seem to disappear during adolescence, they are present in childhood and again in adulthood. It has been found that a child's behaviour during the period of six to ten years old is usually a better predictor of his adult behaviour than his adolescent behaviour. The turbulence experienced at adolescence probably masks the 'true' characteristics which can be displayed earlier and again later in life.

Thomas, Chess and Birch and Birch (1968) (page 166), in a longitudinal study now more than ten years old, consider that they have isolated nine 'primary reaction patterns' which children exhibit in one form or another from very early in life, and which, they say, exist apparently independently of parental handling and personality. They consider that these 'patterns' are to do with temperamental qualities, and they list them as: activity levels, rhythmicity, distractibility, approach-withdrawal behaviour, adaptability, attention span and persistence, intensity of reaction, threshold of responsiveness and quality of mood. They say that such temperamental qualities can be seen in a child only two months old, and that these characteristics tend to remain constant in quality. Of course the child's *behaviour* is bound to change as he develops, but the instances which the authors give about temperamental consistencies which express themselves in different kinds of behaviour with changing age is shown in the following example: 'If he wriggles at two months while his nappies are being changed, then at a year he is likely to climb into everything.' At five a child which behaves quietly in infancy may dress slowly and be able to sit quietly and happily during car rides. Thomas, Chess and Birch suggest further that certain kinds of 'patterns' of temperamental qualities, when grouped together, make, respectively, for 'easy', 'slow to warm up' or 'difficult' children.

There is some evidence from animal work that characteristics such as 'emotionality' are to an extent genetically determined. Emotionality in rats is determined by the degree to which a rat cowers in its box and by the

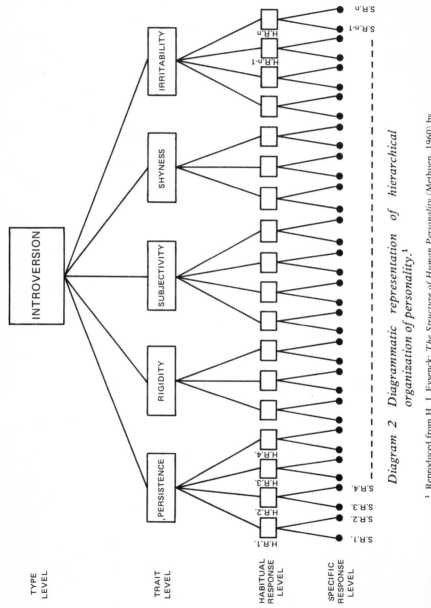

Diagram 2 Diagrammatic representation of hierarchical organization of personality.[1]

[1] Reproduced from H. J. Eysenck: *The Structure of Human Personality* (Methuen, 1960) by

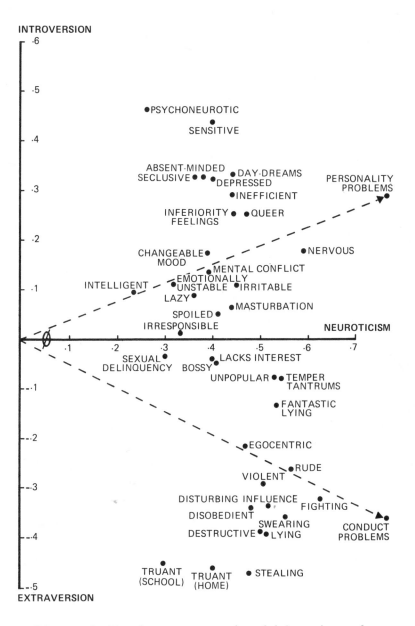

Diagram 3 Two factor representation of Ackerson's correlational study.[1]

[1] Reproduced from H. J. Eysenck: *The Structure of Human Personality* (Methuen, 1960) by kind permission of the publishers.

frequency of its defecation and urination when in an unusual situation. Denenberg (1962) has carried out a series of complex breeding experiments with rats in which babies of disturbed and of normal mothers were fostered respectively by normal and disturbed mothers. Other kinds of variations of the genetic and rearing factors were experimentally controlled, and Denenberg found that the genetic factor seemed to have some influence on later emotional behaviour. He also found that the quality of interaction between the mother and child during the period between birth and weaning permanently affected the adult emotional behaviour of the offspring. Again, Searle (1949) found that it was possible to control the breeding of rats so as to produce some who were more, and others who were less, afraid of the maze apparatuses in which they were tested for problem-solving ability. The results of work with various breeds of dogs (Freedman, King and Elliot, 1961) have shown variations in the seemingly innate reaction to handling by humans of these different breeds. Perhaps more interesting still is work by Lindzey, Winston and Manosevitz (1963) with mice of different strains subjected to 'traumatic' experiences in infancy. They found that the *same* experience had different *kinds* of effects on mice from different strains. One recalls Freud's view that an experience which will harm one child will pass another by without apparent effect (page 57). Infant monkeys display behaviour appropriate to their sex even when reared by surrogate mothers, particularly in relation to aggressive and vigorous (Harlow, 1965).

There is a good deal of evidence, then, to show that certain kinds of temperamental qualities are related to physiological and morphological factors; that they appear to be present from an early age, and that they also seem to be relatively unmodifiable by the experiences of life. This does not mean that the environment has no effect on behaviour, nor that personality characteristics such as, say, optimism are not most probably due to a "combination" of genetic and environmental factors, but it does seem from the evidence from various sources which has accumulated during recent years that innate factors may play a greater part in determining personality characteristics than had been previously conceded.

(c) The development of intelligence

Intelligence and abilities—general considerations

The study of human intelligence, its nature, development and measurement, has occupied psychologists for a longer period than that of any other human trait. Galton (1822–1911) first interested himself in the origin of intellectual ability, and Binet (1857–1914) empirically laid the foundation for the measurement of intelligence. The discussion concerning the nature of intelligence, and also whether it is developed primarily by environmental conditions rather than determined innately, has continued from the time Galton first suggested that inheritance was the prime influence. During the past four years the controversy has been reawakened since Jensen (1969) brought together evidence which seems to many psychologists to support Galton's view (pages 90–91).

There are a number of reasons why 'intelligence', its nature and means of assessment, should be discussed in this book. The measurement of intelligence and the assessment of abilities were fundamental in selecting children for secondary education under the 1944 Education Act, in order that they could be placed in schools which suited their particular intellectual level and their specific abilities. Though this tripartite scheme of secondary education is not largely obsolete in Great Britain, children are still streamed or grouped in various ways according to their intelligence and ability within comprehensive schools. For this reason teachers are from time to time called upon to administer group intelligence tests. Again, in a culture which is predominantly technological, those persons with a good intelligence are more likely to do well in life than those with a poor intelligence. Many parents, particularly from the middle classes, are therefore deeply interested in their children's IQ level and in their scholastic achievement; indeed, they often seem more concerned with this aspect of their children's personality than in whether they are, for example, able to forge happy human relationships!

What is intelligence?

Psychologists do not think of intelligence as if it were 'a concrete entity like bodyweight . . .' (Burt, 1971). However, there are difficulties in trying to say exactly what is meant by the word. The following three definitions collectively state fairly clearly the concept psychologists have in mind when they speak of intelligence:

  (1) Burt (1955) defined intelligence as 'innate, general, cognitive ability'; by 'innate' is implied that the difference between people in the strength or amount of intelligence they display is largely due to genetic, rather than to environmental, factors; 'general' refers to the fact that intelligence is an ability which enters into every form of mental activity; and 'cognitive' means that it is in a broad sense an intellectual quality and not primarily a conative* or affective* quality (pages 49–50).
  (2) Spearman (1923) thought of intelligence as being that capacity which enables man to indulge in relational, constructive, thinking.
  (3) An operational definition of intelligence is that it is the ability to profit from education, it is a measure of a person's educability.

We have, therefore, a trait which involves intellectual functioning rather than the emotions; which seems to enter into every mental activity to a greater or lesser extent; which shows itself most clearly when humans are engaged in relational kinds of thinking; which is a necessary attribute if one wishes to profit from education, and in relation to which there is a good deal of evidence that genetic endowment plays an important part.

The nature of intelligence

There are two aspects of the nature of intelligence which have been the subject of much experimental and statistical work, and also of much controversy. The one aspect concerns the relative weighting that should be given to the genetic factor, and this is discussed on page 90. The other aspect concerns the 'general' quality of intelligence.

Spearman, a British psychologist working in the first four decades of this century, considered that the performance of every intellectual task involved two 'factors': one such factor was *specific* to the task which was being carried out, and the other factor was one of *general* intelligence. His statistical work seemed to suggest that the relative influence of the general to the specific factor varied according to the task, so that, for example, the ability to do mathematics depended more on a higher level of *general* intelligence than did the ability to do music, which required a higher level of specific ability. Spearman called the specific factor 's' and the general, underlying, cognitive factor 'g'. Though he did not equate 'g' by itself with 'intelligence', nevertheless he thought of 'g' as being of prime importance, for it was in his view the one common factor that entered into all intellectual activities to a greater or lesser extent.

Thurstone, working largely from 1935 to 1955, carried out similar analyses of mental abilities in the United States. Thurstone's work led him to the conclusion that one could analyse human abilities without admitting a factor of general intelligence. He postulated seven 'primary' abilities, but as he found later that the scores which his subjects obtained on the tests of primary abilities could be correlated, so that there appeared to be an underlying relationship between such abilities, he admitted that one could extract a factor which might be called 'general intelligence' from the primary abilities.

We have already seen that Burt uses Spearman's 'general' factor as part of his (Burt's) definition of intelligence; but this does not mean that he agrees with the idea of a 'two-factor' theory. Burt (1940), Vernon (1950) and others have shown that one must allow for at least three kinds of factors in the measurement of human abilities, of which the 'g' factor is one, the other two, in addition to an 'error' or 'chance factor,' being 'group' and 'specific' factors. Diagram 4 indicates the hierarchical manner in which it is now suggested that human abilities are structured.

Although we need not concern ourselves here in great detail with this analysis of human abilities, something should be said about the value of such an analysis in practical terms. In administering tests, whether of intelligence or personality, one is interested in the way people differ from one another; that is, in the variance of human abilities, or of personality traits. The hierarchical analysis of human abilities shows that Spearman's 'g' factor still accounts for the biggest source of variation between people; the figure given is between 40 per cent and 50 per cent of the total variance. But people also vary in, for instance, their verbal, spatial, mathematical and mechanical abilities, which comprise the major group factors which represent, for example, such abilities as reading and spelling on the verbal-educational side, and physical abilities on the mechanical-spatial side of the

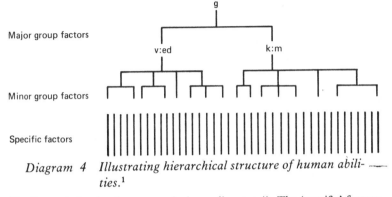

*Diagram 4   Illustrating hierarchical structure of human abili-
                        ties.*[1]

'family tree', (v:ed + k:m respectively on diagram 4). The 'specific' factors are at the bottom of the hierarchy, and they tell us little about a person's *ability,* only how he may perform on a *particular* task or test.

All this implies that if one can find a test which estimates accurately the 'g' factor then correspondingly accurate predictions can be made about a person's suitability for education or for carrying out tasks requiring a fairly high general intelligence.

When we take the measure of a child's intelligence we are, then, not measuring separate abilities, but that quality of intellectual power which enters into all mental activities. For this reason modern psychologists do not claim that an intelligence test is a complete indicator of a child's range of abilities, but that a good test is the best *single* predictor of a child's capability of engaging in intellectual pursuits as far as his general intellectual capacity is concerned. It is a better predictive instrument than school reports or school tests. What it does not necessarily measure is a child's ability to concentrate, his need to achieve, or the other motivational factors which are usually considered necessary to make use of a good intelligence in an academic setting.

The 'IQ' and intelligence tests

When an intelligence test is taken by a child the score which is arrived at through such testing is called the IQ, the 'intelligence quotient' of that child. It is important not to confuse 'intelligence' with 'IQ'. The IQ is a *sample* of a person's intellectual performance, taken at a particular period in such a person's life.

[1] Reproduced from P. E. Vernon: *The Structure of Human Abilities* (Methuen, 1950) by kind permission of the publishers.

Binet first investigated the possibility of measuring children's intelligence when, in 1904, he sat on a committee which had been asked to find means whereby those children in French schools who were in need of special tuition could be discovered. He worked empirically, evolving tests which children of particular ages could do, and he decided that when between 50 and 75 per cent of a large sample of children of a particular age could do his tests, then these tests must be suitable for normal children of that particular age. Thus he arrived at the notion of 'mental age' as a means of assessing a child's retardation or advancement in intelligence compared with other children of the same chronological age.

What is the 'quotient' to which reference is made when we speak of the 'intelligence quotient'? It is the relationship between a child's mental age, (his MA as assessed by tests), and his actual or chronological age (the CA) multiplied by one hundred. Thus

$$\text{(Mental age)/(chronological age)} \times 100 = \text{IQ}.$$

So a child with a mental age of twelve whose chronological age is ten would have an IQ of 120. The multiplier of one hundred was chosen arbitrarily by Stern, the originator of the IQ, so that the average or mean intelligence quotient would be represented by the figure '100'. Obviously a child of ten years of age whose mental age was also ten would have an IQ of one hundred. By using such a method of evaluating intelligence the IQ does not increase as the child gets older. Obviously a child's intellectual abilities increase with age, but this is an increase relative to the child's age, and is what one would expect. The intelligence of adults cannot be arrived at by assessing a mental age, but the scores obtained from adult tests can be transformed into IQ scores. It has been found that for the largest proportion of children the IQ remains relatively stable through childhood and adolescence. If there were to be found an apparently large increase or decrease in any particular child's IQ score then this would be something which the educational psychologist would wish further to investigate.

Intelligence is more or less normally distributed. This means that, as is the case with most measurements which can be made on man, such as height, weight, shoe size, etc., most people fall within the middle range of the scores, with relatively few people at the extreme ends. Diagram 5 shows this normal distribution of intelligence, from which one can see that approximately 68 per cent of all people have scores of between 85 and 115 IQ points, and only about $2\frac{1}{4}$ per cent of the population has a score of over 130 points. The curve is somewhat skewed, as statisticians put it, towards the lower end, and this indicates that there are, due to brain injury and/or pathological and genetic reasons, more people of lower intelligence, but also a very few more people of higher intelligence, than would be expected if intelligence were actually distributed completely normally.

Intelligence tests are constantly being revised and new tests developed, and this work is undertaken with the greatest care. Only when a test is both valid and reliable can it be used to measure intelligence. By 'valid' is meant that the test really measures what it is intended to measure: that is, it meas-

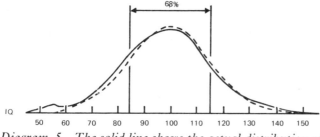

Diagram 5   The solid line shows the actual distribution of IQ scores in the population, the dotted line the 'normal' theoretical distribution.[1]

ures what we mean by 'intelligence'; it does not measure, for example, slickness or knowledge. By 'reliable' is meant that the test will give the same result when administered at different times to the same child allowing, of course, for test familiarity.

Tests of various kinds have been constructed both for administration to individuals and for administration to groups. Some of these are pencil and paper tests, others, such as the Wechsler-Bellevue, involve verbal and performance tests. As an example of the latter children are required to complete and arrange pictures and carry out other tasks, such as trace a path through a maze without entering blind alleys (the Porteus Maze test). The best-known individual tests for children are the Stanford-Binet and the WISC (Wechsler Intelligence Scale for Children). Both these tests seem to be able to predict scholastic achievement fairly well, and they also give an idea of a child's cognitive ability, and even some insight into his clinical condition, which group tests cannot give (page 188), but they take both time and skill to administer.

Group tests can be primarily verbal or non-verbal, and among the former the Moray House Tests and those produced by the NFER (National Foundation for Educational Research) are most widely used. The best-known non-verbal tests are the 'Progressive Matrices', which are made up of sets of patterns, each pattern in a set being different from the others in the series but all having a common feature. The testee is asked to select from a number of additional random patterns the one which fits in with the series given. The tests become progressively more difficult.

Some tests are timed and others not, some are of the multiple-choice kind and others require the insertion of one correct answer.

The inheritance of intelligence

The psychologist Hebb (1949) has suggested that one should think of intelligence as being of two kinds: one kind he termed 'intelligence "A" ', and the other kind 'intelligence "B" '. 'A' is the assumed, innate capacity with which men are born, and 'B' is the intelligence which is displayed by humans when they engage in intellectual activities. Thus 'B' is the product of 'A' *and* the effects of the experience of life, that is, the influence of the environment, on 'A'.

Since the IQ is a sample of a person's intellectual performance taken at a particular period in such a person's life, Vernon (1955) has suggested that one might term the IQ score 'intelligence "C" '.

Recent discussions on the possible difference in intellectual abilities of persons of different races has stimulated interest once more in the heritability of intelligence. A number of psychologists, including Burt and Jensen, consider that the evidence for the heritability of testable intelligence is sufficiently great to enable one to say categorically that by far the greatest single contribution to tested intelligence is made by genetic and not by environmental factors. Jensen (1969), in a long and comprehensive article, has reviewed this evidence.

Twin studies provide much of the evidence for the genetic view, though these have certain weaknesses, which are discussed on page 76. However, such evidence is also supported by other studies which do not involve the assessment of twins.

It is normally found that when twins, who have lived apart from one another since early babyhood, are tested for intelligence, the difference in the IQ scores of such twins is not very much greater than the difference between the two IQ scores obtained from a single person when he is tested on two different occasions (allowing for test familiarity). It has been suggested that as such separated twins are reared in an identical environment until adoption, and mostly in similar environments after adoption, one cannot be certain that the similarities found in their IQ scores are due to genetic factors only. However, reference has already been made on page 76 to the fact that such twins actually can experience very *dissimilar* uterine environments. Also fraternal twins who are brought up together during their *entire childhood* have IQ scores very little different one from another than those obtained from non-twin siblings, and this is exactly what one would expect if the genetic factor made a high contribution. Burt (1970A) has pointed out that when he and others examined the IQ scores of over 150 pairs of siblings, separated soon after birth, who were brought up in a variety of different circumstances, they found that the relationship between their IQ scores was little below the value obtained for siblings brought up together. There is also evidence to show that the IQ scores of adopted and fostered children resemble much more those of their biological parents than those of their adoptive parents. Similarly, when the IQ scores of persons with different degrees of blood relationship are examined

(Erlenmeyer-Kimling and Jarvik, 1963) it is found that the closer such persons are in blood relationship, the closer are their IQ scores, even when they have been brought up apart from one another.

Crow (1969), a geneticist, has written: 'That the heritability [of intelligence] is large is a justifiable conclusion at this stage. . . .' Jensen and Burt indeed claim that there is statistical evidence to support the view that the genetic factor contributes 80 per cent of the total variance of tested intelligence. Vernon has suggested that where cultural and other environmental factors are homogeneous, then apparent differences in intelligence are more likely to be due to genetic factors than to environmental ones. However, where environments are grossly disparate the genetic contribution may well fall below 50 per cent. This means that when one is discussing differences in intelligence between children who come from widely varying cultures, then environmental influences are possibly just as important in accounting for the observed differences as are the genetic influences, though some psychologists would not concede even in those circumstances that the genetic contribution is as low as 50 per cent. However, if one is comparing the intellectual achievement of children who come from more or less similar social classes within the same culture, then the differences in IQ scores are much more likely to be due to genetic factors. Such statements give one, of course, no information about the *absolute* contribution made by either factor in *any one person*. Indeed, Hebb's 'Intellegence "A" ' (page 90) is not measurable in any one person.

Jensen (1969) thinks of environment as a 'threshold variable'—that is, it acts on intelligence as diet does on growth. A bad environment can depress children and prevent them from reaching their potential, but a good environment cannot boost a child's intelligence beyond his genetically-determined ceiling. Some psychologists have suggested that until we know much more about how human beings learn, and know more too about the functioning of the brain, we cannot meaningfully speak of 'ceilings' or thresholds'. One can say, however, that until and unless our knowledge of how to utilize human intellectual ability more fully is increased it is not unreasonable to assume that every person has a potential threshold or ceiling. Another point of importance is that we are normally concerned when applying intelligence tests with *comparing* persons with one another, and the tester is interested in the *difference* in performance between such persons. Such differences, in the normally homogeneous societies in which comparisons are usually made between individuals, seem in the main to be due to genetic factors. However, even if the genetic contribution is a large one the environment still has an effective role in enabling the genetic potential to be realized in order that every child can use his intellectual abilities to the full.

(d) The role of the environment in relation to the formation of the personality and the development of intelligence—general considerations

It has been stated on page 74 that all behaviour is due to the interaction of the genotype* with the total environment. It seems crucially important, therefore, to understand the various environmental forces which affect the formation of different kinds of behaviour patterns, and also the development of personality characteristics, for only thus will it be possible to form a valid opinion about child-rearing methods and educational schemes which seek to enable children to function to the best of their ability.

The effects of various kinds of handling of children by adults is discussed in greater detail in other chapters where the development of language, the child's emotional and social growth, and the adult's role in interaction with the child are discussed. In this chapter the effects of various kinds of environmental stimulation, or lack of such stimulation, will be considered in a more general sense.

It has already been noted (page 75) that the environment is not a unitary factor, but that children are affected by many different kinds of influences which vary in the strength of their effects according to the aspect of life which is being influenced, and the period in each child's stage of development when the influence is being exerted. One can consider the effect of the environment according to the degree of personal involvement in it. Thus each child is influenced by the culture into which he is born, the nation to which he belongs, the social-class membership and the personality characteristics of his parents, and his own experiences of life. These influences are unidirectionally interdependent, so that each 'ring' in diagram 6 to an extent affects the rings inside it.

One could, of course, make other kinds of 'influence' lists, such as, for example, the one suggested by Hebb (1949), which is applicable to men and animals alike.

I   genetic factors
II   pre-natal chemical and nutritive factors
III   post-natal chemical and nutritive factors
IV   pre-and post-natal sensory experiences common to the species
V   sensory experiences which are individualistic
VI   traumatic experiences
      (VI, unlike I–V, is not a *necessary* experience)

Cultural and social class influences

It has been postulated by some writers, particularly by anthropologists, that the temperamental differences found to exist between men and women are solely due to cultural and not biological causes. Some cultures do appear to rear children so that there are no discernible temperamental differences between boys and girls, for example the girls become as aggressive as the boys; other cultures produce boys and girls who are almost the mirror image of men and women in our culture, the men being 'feminine', and the women 'masculine' in temperament (Mead, 1935). However, such cultures are the

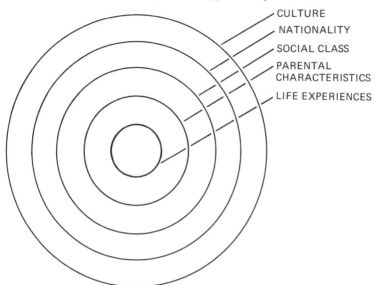

CULTURE
NATIONALITY
SOCIAL CLASS
PARENTAL CHARACTERISTICS
LIFE EXPERIENCES

Diagram 6   Environmental factors which may influence the formation of the personality.[1]

exception rather than the rule, and there is some solid, biological evidence (Nash, 1970) to suggest that the usual temperamental differences between men and women are largely due to biological differences between the sexes, these former differences being most likely strengthened by cultural tradition. Thus we find parents in most societies encouraging dependence in girls and independence in boys; while aggressiveness, if not actually encouraged in boys, is certainly not so frowned upon as it is in girls, though it does seem that boys' greater tendency to aggression has a biological basis.

It is undoubtedly true that while some cultures, nations and societies stress the paramount importance in social conduct of what is considered to be correct behaviour—for example, the Mundugumor tribe in the Western Pacific approves aggressive behaviour, but the Arapesh tribe in the same area gentle behaviour (Mead, 1935)—other cultures are equally insistent on a particular *attitude* to life, such as the accepted Western middle-class Protestant ethic of the need to achieve (McClelland, 1961).

In a general sense, however, the sanctions imposed on disapproved behaviour, and alternative encouragement of approved behaviour, inevitably permit some kinds of actions and inhibit other kinds, although whether or not such regulation of conduct affects the *personality* of the individual as well as influencing his *behaviour* is not clear.

More specifically Vernon (1969) has shown that the style of life of different cultures most likely influences the *type* of intelligence developed by persons who are members of these cultures. In societies where there is an emphasis on conformity and little emphasis on individual responsibility, and where also magical beliefs are accepted, rational thinking and analytical perception are inhibited. Similarly, when the society encourages initiative, more practical-spatial and inductive abilities are found among children than in societies where such encouragement is not given.

There is also a curious relationship between sex, dependence-independence, and the 'k:m' versus 'v:ed' abilities (pages 86–87). Thus girls, who are usually encouraged to be more dependent than boys, are normally better than boys in most verbal abilities; whereas boys, who are usually encouraged to be independent, are better than girls at mathematical, scientific and technical subjects, though it is possible that there may be a sex-linked genetic element involved. It is known also that the distribution of intelligence for males is greater than for females; that is, there are more males who are of low *and* of high intelligence than there are females in these two extreme groups. Similarly males have a better spatial ability which holds across a variety of cultures; and boys score higher on creativity tests than girls (Hutt, 1972).

When we consider the effects of parental membership of a social class, particularly in the English-speaking world, we find evidence that class membership influences a number of behavioural variables, which in their turn affect personality development. Achievement motivation, the development of moral feeling and behaviour, the development of language and of thinking, and the growth of intelligence, are all influenced by social class norms and by class-based child-rearing customs.

McClelland in a number of his writings (1955, 1958, 1961) and Rosen (1956) have shown that the desire to achieve is present much more strongly in the sons of middle-class Protestants than in the sons of members of other classes and/or of parents who are members of the Catholic Church. Again, the difference between the types of moral education which parents of the two major social classes give their children seems to produce a difference between the types of moral behaviour exhibited by the respective groups of children. Thus Hoffman and Saltzstein (1967), whose paper on parental discipline and the child's moral development is discussed on page 196, found that whereas the mother's disciplining method is crucial in the middle classes, the lower-class mother's method of disciplining her child seems less influential on the child's moral development. Bernstein too has written extensively (e.g. Bernstein and Henderson, 1969) on the relationship between the differential use of language and the development of internal moral control (page 117). There is sufficient evidence from a number of different sources to show that both the use of certain disciplining techniques and of certain forms of language in the home affect the kind of morality developed in the child. The use of language both to explain to the child the consequences to others of his disapproved actions, and to point out to him that such actions will usually be disapproved of in other, similar, circumstances, together with the use of a non-power-orientated disciplining technique, tends to produce an inner moral control and a reasonably strong conscience; these are the child-rearing methods more usually used by parents of the middle classes. By contrast, power-orientated disciplining methods, and a 'restricted' code of language used by parents (page 119), which does not enable a child to generalize easily from one situation in which he has transgressed to other, similar, situations, are techniques primarily adopted by parents from the lower working classes. These techniques are not likely to produce moral behaviour which is self-regulating, but a type of behaviour which relies on external sanctions for regulation.

It is likely that the precise kind of language used by parents influences the child's cognitive growth, although to date the evidence of the influence of parental language use is not conclusive (Herriot, 1970) (page 122). Many studies have sought to elucidate the influence of childhood experiences on cognitive processes; Bloom (1964) reports a study in which thirteen variables were found to correlate significantly with the degree of child intelligence. Four of these variables were related to parental language use (two were 'opportunities for enlarging vocabulary and 'emphasis on correct usage'), and most of the remaining nine variables were related to middle-class educational values, such as 'rewards for intellectual development', 'opportunities for learning in the home', and so on. Indeed, when one considers the development of intelligence in relation to the social class structure there is little doubt that the *quality* of parent-child interaction in middle-class homes generally is such that most middle-class children have a much better opportunity of maximizing their innate intellectual potential than most working-class children. Hindley (1971) in a longitudinal study of the intellectual development of children from both social classes has found that by six months of age there is a significant difference between children of the two classes on a locomotor-verbal factor, and by three years of age differences in IQ are highly significant. Hindley suggests that the cultural resources of the home are related to IQ and language differences, and that such factors as the parental use of language, encouragement of speech, emotional home atmosphere, and the breadth of the mother's vocabulary, are all influential. He suggests further that children who have enjoyed a culturally enriched infancy may even have some of its effects permanently embodied in the functional quality of their nervous system. One must also bear in mind, though, that middle-class parents probably hand on to their children a genetically determined higher basic intelligence than other parents.

The genetic basis of intelligence does not, however, preclude the necessity of at least attempting to provide a more stimulating early environment for children who lack such experiences, even though efforts to provide enriched experiences in pre-school nurseries for deprived children in the USA, the so-called 'Head-start' schemes, seem not to have been very successful, or, if initially successful, the success has not been maintained (Jensen, 1969). However, judging by the findings of recent observational and experimental work with both children and animals, it appears advisable to start educational schemes aimed at stimulating a child's natural potential much sooner than has been attempted so far. The Ypsilanti Carnegie Infant Education Project, which was established in 1968, has as its aim the prevention of the kind of intellectual deficit from which deprived children suffer. In a very carefully planned scheme specially trained teachers, with the consent of parents, go into the parental home to work with mothers and babies in their own surroundings, in some instances starting when the babies are three months old (Denenberg, 1970). The importance of early experiences in general is further considered on pages 99f.

Pre-natal and familial influences, and the influence of parental characteristics

There is some evidence that pre-natal nutritive factors have a lasting effect on the intelligence of children especially when mothers suffer dietary deficiency during pregnancy (Harrell, Woodyard and Gates, 1955). Similarly twins are known to have on average a lower IQ than non-twin children, and here again a number of pre-natal conditions are assumed to be responsible for the deficit. There is also evidence to show that, at least within the top level of intelligence, first-born children are more successful in school and college than children who have older siblings (Altus, 1966). Hamilton (1971) has shown that children who are being brought up by rejecting mothers have more difficulty in applying logical, inductive and deductive thinking processes than children who have been brought up by warm and accepting mothers.

Studies which have investigated parental personality characteristics in relation to child personality growth are discussed in some detail in chapter 8. This is a complex area of research in which it is not possible to control influential variables such as the strength and effect of possible innate predispositions in their interaction with the various experiences provided by the environment. However, it does seem that where parents are warm, loving, autonomy granting, respectful of their child as a valued individual, able to enhance his self-esteem, and yet also able to be authoritative (though not authoritarian!), a child has the best opportunity to develop his personality to the full. There is evidence that the behaviour of authoritarian and power-assertive parents tend to inhibit and restrain a child's development, and that such behaviour has a tendency to produce children who, when adult, will be equally rigid and assertive in relation to their children in turn and in relation to persons inferior to them. Adorno, Frankel-Brunswik, Levinson and Sanford (1950) in a study of *The Authoritarian Personality* found that children who had experienced harsh parental discipline, with the giving of love conditional upon behaving in an approved manner, and where the family was structured hierarchically, that such children were often anti-semitic; had a rigid personality; saw personal relationships in terms of an exercise of power by some people over others; and tended also to project* a number of unacceptable impulses on to other persons. Though this study can be faulted in a number of ways, further studies using the authors' 'California F Scale' have in the main supported these findings.

It is relevant here to quote a comment by Burgess and Locke (1956) to the effect that personality qualities 'develop in the interpersonal relations of the family. They arise more or less spontaneously in the social interaction of the child with parents. The earliest distinctive responses of the child to persons in his social environment may be said to be a resultant (1) of his genic traits, (2) of parental responses to him, and (3) of special factors in the situation, such as illness'. Burgess and Locke assume that once these patterns of behaviour are fixed they are not subject to any *great* modification.

Early experiences

Reference is made on page 95 to Hindley's view that children who had enjoyed a culturally enriched infancy may have some effects permanently embodied in their nervous system. It is now known that the baby's brain develops very greatly in the first two years of life. Ritchie (1967) has described how the weight of a baby's brain increases by 350 per cent during this period, and only by 35 per cent in the following ten years. In the first two years there is a rapid growth in the cortical brain cells—that is, of the neurons* also a major change occurs in the interconnections between the brain cells, and by four years of age the last stage of dendrogenesis* is attained. It is, therefore, *not unreasonable* to suppose that experiences which occur during the first four years of life, and particularly during the first two years, might affect the nature of dendrite* growth and consequently of intellectual development. There is evidence from animal work (Altman, Das and Anderson, 1968) that aspects of brain development are affected by environmental circumstances.

Emphasis on the importance of the first two years of life for cognitive development also comes from work on the so-called 'critical periods'*. We discuss on pages 124f. the importance of certain special, early and limited periods in the life of an animal and a baby, and, for animals at least, the important consequences which experiences during such periods have on later social and sexual behaviour. In fact, there is some evidence to show that very young children are particularly sensitive to certain kinds of experience during these periods, although much work remains to be done clearly to define these kinds of experience, and the possible times in a baby's life when they are of maximum importance. There appears to be evidence to show that there are optimal periods for good intellectual and emotional development, and for the forming of basic social relationships (Scott, 1962). It is now suggested that individual babies may have personally specific periods when they are most sensitive to particular kinds of experience, and that research should concentrate on discovering the behavioural signs which would indicate to parents when a particular baby is entering such a period. An example of this is found in the baby's fear response to strangers, which is normally fully established by seven months of age, and seems to herald a period of special sensitivity in the baby's social relationships. Children at this age appear to be most sensitive to emotional disturbance, such as can be occasioned by separation from their parents (page 99).

There is a good deal of work now in progress, some of which has recently been reported (Ambrose, 1969), which is seeking to find the relationship between brain development and early behaviour, and which is also studying the effects of various kinds of stimulation in early infancy on different aspects of development, such as social, emotional and intellectual growth. This is because of the fact that although many theorists of child development in the past have stressed the importance of the child's first few years of life, very little has been known until relatively recent times about the importance of various kinds of experience such as pre-natal conditions, growth of the brain, stimulation of the senses, attachment to a consistently caretaking adult, etc., on different aspects of child and adult behaviour. It is important to discover not only the relationship between certain causes and their specific effects, but also to elucidate the strength and timing of such causes, and, finally, to find signs which will indicate to observant adults when a particular baby is entering any critical stage of development. In addition such work should enable psychologists to advise with much greater accuracy what kinds of early experiences, and, for underprivileged children, what kinds of early remedial teaching programmes are likely to have the best results.

Later experiences, particularly in relation to cognitive development

The emphasis which has been laid earlier in this chapter on the importance in human development of genetic factors and early experiences may give the impression that the influences to which a child is subject later in life are so relatively slight in their effects that beyond providing education in the form of instilling knowledge there is little the teacher can do to help a child towards developing a rich and effective personality.

It seems important to be clear what kinds of influences are at their maximum early in life, and what contributions a good environment, whether at school or at home, can make later in life. Section two of this book concerns itself with the way children learn with advancing age to deal with the social, emotional and cognitive aspects of their lives. Although much of this section is descriptive, outlining the ontogenic growth which normally takes place, it is clear that environmental factors influence to a greater or lesser degree all areas of development throughout childhood. Similarly, in section three, where the role of the influential adults is discussed, there is an inherent assumption that such adults can have a decisive effect on a child's developing personality.

There is some evidence from cross-cultural studies that where children finish schooling at an early age, or where they receive no schooling at all, they make little progress with increasing age as compared with children who have continued their schooling. For example, when Indian children in South Africa, whose entry into school was delayed, were given a number of tests, the investigator reported a drop of 5 IQ points for each year of delayed entry (Ramphal, as reported by Vernon, 1969). Studies among children from Western cultures which have compared the IQs of those who have continued their education beyond the age of fourteen with the IQs of those who have not done so, show that scores continue to rise as education continues, and it has been found that verbal scores of adults can continue to increase well into middle age. Vernon (1969) suggests that possibly the effects which a continuing education has on intellectual development have been underestimated.

When considering the importance of education and other stimulating experiences on child development it should be remembered that even if *intelligence* is largely determined by genetic factors, and to an important extent affected by early experiences, a child's educational *achievement* is much more affected by environmental circumstances than are the scores he obtains on an intelligence test. Mittler (1971) has shown that although separated MZ twins have a similar IQ, their educational achievement marks are often very different, whereas DZ twins who have been brought up together may not have a very close IQ score, but are often similar in educational achievement. What educationalists are primarily concerned with is the *use* to which intelligence is put, and Butcher (1968) has observed that whatever weight may be given to the genetic contribution to tested intelligence, society must accept the responsibility of acting *as if the environment were of crucial importance*. He suggests that even if genes set a limit to performance, the environment in which most people find themselves probably restricts them to an even lower limit.

Deprivation experiences

Child psychology has concerned itself very much with the effects of depriving experiences on child development. Great emphasis has been placed by several authorities on the possible detrimental effects of maternal deprivation upon personality development. However, since in the past no precise meaning has been attached to the 'maternal deprivation' it is important to consider the conditions which the term could be taken to indicate. Thus it has been used to include complete loss of a mother or mother substitute, also multiple mothering in institutions, as well as distortions in the quality of mothering, such as rejection, over-protection, ambivalent attitudes on the part of the mother towards her child, and also temporary separation. The term 'maternal deprivation' also makes no reference to the particular circumstances under which the deprivation has taken place, so that little account was taken in earlier studies of whether the mother left her child, and if so, under what circumstances, or whether the child was removed from home; whether he was healthy or sick at the time of removal; whether he was cared for by a known person or by an unknown person, possibly even by several unknown persons. Often too neither the age of the child at the time of separation, nor the length of separation, was taken into consideration when assessing the effects on the child of such a separation. Investigations of the personality characteristics of children who had suffered such deprivation, and who were resident in institutions, appeared to indicate that separation from the mother was the crucial variable in determining later neurotic and/or criminal behaviour (Bowlby, 1944). However, studies by Rheingold and Bayley (1959) and others seem to indicate that a number of variables, particularly the lack of stimulation which nearly always accompanies institutional care following loss of the mother very early in life, can all combine together in such circumstances to produce problem behaviour.

Earlier studies were mainly concerned with children who had been institutionalized following the loss of their mother or the break-up of the home. Such children, however, not only lacked individual maternal care, of whatever quality, but few institutions were able to provide adequate sensory, affective and social stimulation for the children in their care. If one adult is looking after many children of approximately the same age, her personal involvement in each is inevitably less than if she were in charge of a smaller family. There is a consequent lack of variety of affective expression in her behaviour; a lack of social contact and mothering—that is, of physical contact with the child—and mostly also fewer opportunities for the child to learn. Often, particularly in the past, such institutions were run on a rigid routine which made exploration and the satisfying of curiosity difficult for the child. Also changes in the staff of institutions meant that bonds of affection which had been established between child and adult had not infrequently to be broken to the acute distress of the child, and often causing in him a consequent reluctance to form other affectional relationships later in life.

Institutions vary greatly one from another, but, although not all the disadvantageous variables described above are present in every establishment, children who have had long periods of care in an institution display, more frequently than is usual, such characteristics as intellectual retardation, language retardation, or disturbances in social and personal relationships. This disturbance is reflected, as Anna Freud and Burlingham (1944) and others have shown, either in social apathy, in which little response is shown to other people, such children tending to be insensitive to normal human relationships and unwilling (or unable) to form such relationships, or in a display of 'affect hunger', which expresses itself in showing off, attention-seeking (pages 176 and 179f.) or sometimes in the forming of passionate new attachments, which are nearly always the cause of eventual intense disappointment to the child.

Although when a child is separated from his biological mother many variables can be present which together or independently may contribute towards deficiencies in his personality development, it does seem that even a mere break in mothering by one person can, under specific circumstances, and if continued for a long time, be sufficient to cause poor Ego* and Super-ego* development. Freudian psychoanalytic theory (page 55f.) would lead one to suppose that internalization of the parental image was essential for such development, also that there must be continuity of care by one person, at least for a reasonably long period in a child's early life, in order that such internalization can occur. In addition, acute unhappiness and a feeling of insecurity can also be occasioned by lengthy separation.

We have seen that the critical period for experiencing maximum emotional disturbance (page 98) can be put as early as seven months, and a study by Yarrow (1960) claims that babies placed for adoption as early as three months showed some disturbance and that 86 per cent of babies who were placed at six months were disturbed immediately after being placed. Immediate reactions of infants and pre-school children to separation often takes the form of violent and active protest, followed by a rejection of adults, and finally apathy, withdrawal and lack of activity. When a child in hospital reaches this stage, unobservant adults often comment on the 'wisdom' of not allowing mothers into hospital with their children because, they say, children 'settle down' quite well without fuss after a time; but Bowlby and Robertson (1952) have referred to this stage as 'mourning'. Whether such an experience has a long-term effect will depend a great deal on the age of the child, the length of the separation and the quality of the mother-child relationship before separation. If this has been good the child's immediate reactions to separation are more severe, but the long-term effects are not so bad as they are when the mother-child relationship was poor prior to separation. Robertson's work with children in hospital has shown—and he has vividly illustrated his findings by filming children as they go into hospital and during their stay in hospital, some being unaccompanied and others accompanied by their mother—how strongly unaccompanied children react to separation both immediately after separation, and on their return home.

There is interesting corroborative evidence from animal studies, particularly of rhesus monkeys (Harlow, 1962), where separation experiences and other variables can be artificially controlled, showing how necessary it is for infants and young children to experience continuing attachment to a mother figure, and how distressful and also harmful separation can be for the development of normal social, sexual and maternal behaviour, particularly if such separation takes place at certain ages, and if continued for long.

Studies of children who are cared for by two 'mothers', but not more than two, and where the caretaking adults remain constant, do not show that disturbed personalities develop. Children in Israeli kibbutzim, who are cared for both by their natural mother and by a 'Metapelet', a caretaking adult, develop normal, though in some respects possibly somewhat different, personalities from children who have one consistent mothering figure (Rabin, 1961; Bettelheim, 1971).

It is clear that when a child is separated from his mother other factors, such as illness or death, or a disturbed marital relationship, or some other distressing circumstance, are almost invariably also present. It seems important, therefore, where it is possible to avoid separation such as when it is necessary for a child to go to hospital that this burden additional to his illness should not be placed on him. Sufficient is also known about how a child can be distressed by separation early in life (page 101). However, to date we still understand far too little about the various factors which determine what kinds of psychosocial experiences are likely to be harmful to any particular child. Rutter (1972) quotes Caldwell as writing that research is needed into

(1) the relationship between constitutional factors and susceptibility to certain environmental conditions; it has, for example, been all too readily assumed that all children are equally susceptible to every kind of disadvantageous environmental condition;

(2) what exactly the factors in the environment are which affect human behaviour; so far our knowledge in this area is far too unspecific; and

(3) finding better ways of discovering the constituents of the psychosocial environment; the delineation of influential constituents has probably been far too gross.

Meanwhile it is safe to assume that for *optimal* development most children need continuity of care by not too many, more or less consistently present, adults with whom affectional bonds can be formed; but it should also be noted that probably only an early and prolonged separation period, coupled with inadequate alternative arrangements, such as institutionalization, is likely to have *unfortunate and irreversible* effects on a child's personality development.

FURTHER READING

Butcher, H. J.: *Human Intelligence; Its Nature and Assessment* (Methuen, London, 1968).

Lazarus, R. S. and E. M. Opton (ed.): *Personality* (Penguin Books, Harmondsworth, 1967).

Mittler, P.: *The Study of Twins* (Penguin Books, Harmondsworth, 1971).

Rutter, M.: *Maternal Deprivation Reassessed* (Penguin Books, Harmondsworth, 1972).

Scott, J. P.: *Early Experience and the Organization of Behaviour* (Wadsworth, London, 1968).

Wiseman, S.: *Intelligence and Ability* (2nd ed., Penguin Books, Harmondsworth, 1973).

SECTION TWO
THE DEVELOPMENT OF BEHAVIOUR

4

Growth of the intellect

(a) Cognitive growth as described by Piaget

We have seen in chapter 2 that it is useful for the purposes of study to think of the human personality as constituted of three basic, interacting forces: the intellect, the emotions and the will. In this chapter the development of the child's intellectual abilities will be considered, and in the next chapter in this section the child's emotional and motivational growth and its accompanying social behaviour will be discussed.

In chapter 2 Piaget's work relating to the development of the child's cognitive powers is described from a *theoretical* viewpoint. In this chapter the actual, ontogenic, cognitive development, as discovered by Piaget, will be discussed. Other psychologists, among whom Bruner is an outstanding example, have described intellectual growth; but Piaget's work, both because of its scope and depth, has had a wider influence, particularly on pedagogic practice, than any other comparable theory.

According to Piaget the baby under twenty-one months or so is at the sensori-motor stage—that is, his perceptual and motor apparatuses operate simultaneously. At first much of the motor activity is merely of a reflex kind; soon, however, the baby begins to discriminate between various objects in his world, so that at the end of the first month he will know, for example, what in his immediate environment can be sucked and what cannot be sucked. Co-ordination of hand and eye, of touch and sight, follows quickly, and some time between five and eight months of age the baby is able to act on objects outside himself and he can think ahead, so that he is capable of forming intentions and behaving purposefully. By the time he is one year old he can perceive relationships; he notices events which are not dependent on his own actions, and he begins to have a rudimentary knowledge of causality so that he can make things happen. How often has one seen a baby of this age drop things from cot or pram, in the delighted knowledge that it will fall down for someone else to pick up!

The six months following a child's first birthday comprise a period of rapid learning and experiment, and by the age of twenty-one months he can, within narrow limits, foresee what actions will succeed, *without testing them first*. He is now able to *represent* things and actions to himself—he is 'adapting'—and this, says Piaget, is what *thinking* is really about. It is not necessary at this stage for the child to be able to speak in order to be able to think; his thoughts are really internalized actions; however, the first stages of thinking are thus wordless ideas about actions. The complexities of adult thought cannot, so it would seem, take place without a good language ability.

We will see, as we follow intellectual development through to adolescence, that in order to develop adult intellectual abilities the child has to learn to free himself from two influences which are dominant in childhood but which, with increasing maturity, become less powerful in governing behaviour. These two are

(1) the influence of the information about the world brought to the child by his perceptual apparatus—i.e. his senses—and

(2) the influence of the child's own viewpoint.

Piaget calls these respectively the 'percept-centred' and the 'egocentric' view of the world. (Egocentric is *not*, in this context, to be confused with emotional feelings akin to selfishness.)

We have seen that the small child has first to learn to use his senses in order to interact with people and things; he then has to learn to inhibit some actions and to internalize these, which is the beginning of thought. However, many actions during the first few years of life are novel to the child and have to be carried out before they can be internalized. Great reliance is therefore placed on the information which sight, hearing, touch, taste and motor activity bring to the child about the world. For this reason his interest is 'centred' on information obtained from his perceptual apparatuses, and he necessarily places far less reliance on his thinking processes for obtaining information about the world than do older children and adults.

It is also not possible for the very young child to understand viewpoints which are different from his own. In this context the term 'viewpoint' is not used to refer to an understanding of another's 'point of view', but in the more physical sense of understanding that objects and people in the world have an existence independent of the child's existence. It is thought likely that the newborn baby has no concept of anything being separate from himself; there are no objects, for everything is subjective, an extension of himself. He has to learn first that things exist in their own right, apart from himself. Until this happens the newborn child is entirely 'egocentric'; he lives, as Piaget himself says, 'in a universe without objects' (Piaget, 1968). It is impossible for the young child to understand the most elementary kind of causality, or to appreciate the permanence of things in the world without progressively decentring from his own viewpoint until, eventually, there is some appreciation that other things have an existence separate from himself. He learns to recognize objects viewed from different angles and distances, and so he appreciates his own separateness from other things and their separateness from one another in space. He learns also about permanence and he begins to have some ideas about causality; but all this is a gradual process. A child under seven years of age will find it difficult, as Piaget has shown, to appreciate another's viewpoint from a physical point of view. For instance, Piaget stood a doll on a table and placed before it an object, such as a pencil lying diagonally to the doll's line of vision. He then asked children to choose from two or three drawings the one which represented the doll's point of view. Children under seven or eight years of age found it difficult to deduce the doll's angle of vision.

In a social setting, too, it is possible to observe the child's egocentric view of the world. A boy under seven who has two brothers, when asked if one of his brothers also has brothers, will say: 'Yes, he has *one* brother'—he cannot see himself as the brother of another child, because this would involve separating himself off as an object and seeing himself in another context—i.e. from his brother's point of view.

Piaget gives the term 'pre-operational' to this stage of cognitive development and this stage of development lasts from two to seven years of age approximately. An 'operation' in this context is an action which takes place in imagination (page 67). We have seen that this imaginative process successfully enables a child even before he is two years of age to internalize a selection of simple actions, and also that a child between two and seven is able to internalize his behaviour—that is, he can think to a progressively greater extent. Nevertheless this limitation in thinking is, by adult standards, so marked that Piaget (1968) considers that effective operational thinking does not start until the child is seven years of age. Children between seven and eleven thus learn gradually to internalize more and more of their actions, but even then such thinking, as we shall see later in this chapter, is of a 'concrete' kind; children during this period learn to replace action by thinking, but their thinking is still greatly tied to action.

A great aid in helping the child between two and about four-and-a-half years of age to develop his thinking powers is the child's increasing ability to use and understand language. This may explain why a small child who has much contact with older persons, such as the eldest in a family, or an only child, frequently seems to have better-than-average powers of thinking.

With the first use of language the child indicates that he understands symbolism: that is, that one thing—in this case a word—can stand for something else—for a person or for an object—and the actual use of a word helps him to represent a person or object to himself more easily in his imagination. (The development of language ability as such will be considered in chapter 4 since here we are only concerned with language as a vehicle in the development of cognitive processes.)

Even during the first two years of life the child begins to learn through his use of language to build up a representational world; language enables him to rework, as it were, his internalization of action, so that his previous world of action and of wordless thought gradually becomes a world of symbols and of language. However, because of the slow development of language learning, thinking remains for the nursery child largely wordless, internalized action, and it is greatly affected by what the child perceives.

A child under two years of age can alter his *motor* habit if he perceives *visually* that the habit is unproductive. For example, a biscuit, which the child has found several times hidden under a cup will quickly be retrieved from under a plate if it has been *observed* that the biscuit was hidden under the plate, but, in the absence of this observation, most children under two years of age, even if definitely *told* 'The biscuit is now under the plate', will continue to look under the cup. (One has, of course, to ascertain when carrying out such a test that the child understands the words 'cup' and 'plate'.) Such a simple experiment, and others like it, would seem to indicate that the force of visual experience is stronger at this age than that of verbal information. The Russian psychologists Luria and Yudovich (1960) have carried out interesting experiments of this kind into the relationship between a child's language and the development of his mental processes (chapter 4).

The thought processes of most adolescents and of adults seem to be as stable as the material world appears to be: our thoughts are consistent; we can consider relationships and entertain hypotheses; we can keep a number of criteria in mind when reasoning; we can use powers of thought to order, to classify and to think conceptually; and we can also argue deductively and inductively. These mental abilities in the child have to be developed when he is between about two and twelve years of age. The child under three thinks transductively—from particular to particular; his thoughts are still neither consistent nor stable, and even at a later age they are dominated by what he perceives. Piaget has named the stage from about four-and-a-half to seven years of age the 'intuitive thought' stage; this is still part of a 'pre-operational' stage, but is a substage when children have been observed to make judgements based on their mere perception of a situation and not according to reason. If, in a now well-known experiment carried out first by Piaget, a quantity of water is poured from one glass into a *differently shaped* glass, a five-year-old observer will say that there is now a different *amount* of water in the second glass. Similarly if two rows of beads of equal number are laid out on a table in such a manner that the individual beads in the two rows form pairs, and the equality of number in the rows is clearly visible, when the beads in one row are pushed closely together then a child of five will say that there are now *fewer* beads in this row than in the other row. A six-year-old may solve one of these problems correctly but not necessarily the other. Seven- or eight-year-old children will mostly give the correct answers to a simple problem of this kind.

Children under seven years of age or so do not yet appear to understand the principle of the conservation of number and of property, nor the principle of a one-to-one relationship. Indeed, work by Beard (1963) shows that when the experimental situation is complicated, for example, by the experimenter pouring water from one glass into two smaller glasses, and later from these two into five smaller glasses, it becomes evident that even ten-year-olds not infrequently hold these principles rather tenuously; that is, they assume that more glasses must hold more water!

A child at the same developmental stage (under seven years of age) cannot usually place a number of objects of different quality, or colour, or dimension according to a particular order or category, for example, pencils of differing lengths from the shortest to the longest. If a four-year-old is asked to perform such ordering he will arrange them in pairs first, and then compare the pairs. He cannot carry in his mind a large unit for comparison of individual items within the unit; but when a child has reached what Piaget terms the 'concrete operational' stage at seven or so, he will look at all the pencils, and then order them all from the shortest to the tallest without much, if any, trial and error action. Piaget says that children begin now to have an 'anticipatory' schema.

For the seven- to eight-year-old child thinking is different in kind from that of the four- to five-year-old. The child is now becoming progressively released from the dominance of the senses, though they are still very influential in guiding his understanding and behaviour. However, he is beginning to build up an internal consistency of thought, even if his logical thinking is still mostly based on a consideration of concrete objects.

One of the instances of the difference in thought is shown in the developing ability of the child over seven to classify objects. A child of six is able to make a collection—to pick bluebells in the wood to make a bunch—but he cannot classify according to criteria. Between seven and eleven he learns to hold several criteria in mind, classifying according to shape, colour, size, etc. Because the child is being freed to an extent from the excessive influences of external reality as far as his thinking processes are concerned, he can begin to build concepts—that is, ideas relating to classes, series and numbers; but his conceptual thinking is still tied to actualities—that is, to first-hand realities and not to abstractions. However, his mind is now becoming more systematized, so that he has an increased self-awareness, and he is able to 'turn round on his own schemata' as Bartlett expressed this human ability in another context (Bartlett, 1932). He can now begin to watch his own mind manipulating thoughts, though this ability is not fully evident until the child approaches the end of the 'concrete operational' period at eleven or twelve years of age. During this period he begins to learn not only about the conservation of quantities and to know about measurement of objects, but he also learns about the weight and volume of substances and of containers. Some kinds of measurements take longer to grasp than others, so that the measurement of objects is understood at about six years of age, but weight and volume not until about eight and ten years respectively. It is reasonable to assume that up to about six or seven years of age children have no real conception of measurement (Piaget, 1968), and, from an adult's point of view, they have curious ideas about age: they assume that taller children and taller adults must be older than smaller children and shorter adults! The concept of time is also something which is learned slowly; the four-year-old only understands what morning and afternoon signify; by five he knows the days of the week, and by six or seven he can tell the time.

We have seen how it is only through *action* that the child begins to think; thoughts at first are wordless ideas, but, after the child leaves the sensori-motor period, thinking must be increasingly *verbal*, so that the internalization of actions carried out after the sensori-motor periods has passed requires verbal ability of sufficient extent to enable increasingly complex actions to be expressed in verbal terms. The younger child under seven years of age, owing to immaturity and lack of experience with people and things, has been unable to internalize fully all his actions; the child between seven and eleven years of age increasingly experiences the world, and one would expect the internalization process to proceed fairly quickly, but Piaget suggests that because *verbal reasoning* remains a limited capability throughout the 'concrete operational' period, the process is in fact slower than one would expect. Indeed, children seem to use the same process for *verbal* reasoning at this stage as they did when dealing with *objects* during the 'intuitive thought' stage. For example, at that stage they could only deal with pairs of objects at a time, not with several, and now they can only deal with two verbal propositions at a time. Thus they cannot understand the puzzle which Piaget (1928) set and which appears in Binet's tests. The puzzle set was as follows: 'Edith is fairer than Susan; Edith is darker than Lily; who is the darkest of the three?' Curious replies are received from children under eleven years of age to such a puzzle; children will say things like: 'As Edith and Susan are both fair and Edith and Lily are both dark, so Edith comes in between Lily and Susan.' During this period children also find instructions couched in 'grid' verbal terms very difficult. If one asks, for example, that 'the fourth little girl in the second row should put up her hand', it is unlikely that children under nine will be able to identify themselves by this method. Proverbs too are seldom understood before early adolescence.

It is important to realize that, in addition to having difficulties with rational notions and conceptual ideas, the young child's percept-centred and egocentric view causes him to view happenings in the world around him differently from the way older children and adults view the world. Ideas about causality change from 'animism', in which life is ascribed to everything that moves, to 'artificialism', when children assert that everything is caused by people. As Piaget himself says (1968): 'The young child constantly makes assertions without trying to support them with facts.' Small children think, for example, that the moon moves because they are moving (Piaget, 1951). They cannot imagine an ordered sequence of events, so that, when they give explanations about causality, cause and effect become confused. Teachers will be familiar with the kind of answers a child under seven will give to questions, such as the following, which Piaget (1928) asked: 'The moon grows. How?' 'It [it was a crescent moon] becomes the whole.' 'Why?'

'Because it gets bigger.' 'How does it happen?' 'Because we grow ourselves.' 'What makes it grow?' 'The clouds'; and so on.

At this stage too children consider that inanimate things know their own names and that things which move have feeling. It may well be, though, that these conceptions are due not so much to a maturational stage through which the child is passing, but rather the fault of parents and teachers who, in our society, tend to encourage such anthropomorphic conceptions of inanimate objects. There is some evidence that in other cultures children do not necessarily go through this developmental stage (Mead, 1932).

Pedagogically Piaget's findings about children's cognitive growth are of the greatest importance. If action must precede thinking, then opportunities must be provided for much activity with objects of differing shapes, colours, sizes and textures, particularly for the child of nursery and infant school age. He should have the chance to use sand, water, bricks and other materials; he should have opportunities to learn to grade, to feel and to count. Since it is also the function of speech to replace physical action by verbal 'action', he should have the stimulation of good adult speech. One has to remember, too, when providing materials and opportunities, that already at five years of age the range of abilities exhibited by individual children is very wide. A teacher of five-year-olds might have children in her class who, as far as their cognitive development is concerned, might belong to three different developmental groups—to the 'preconceptual' substage (normally children between two and four-and-a-half years fall into this grouping), to the 'intuitive thought' stage (from four-and-a-half to seven years of age), and some fortunate children to the 'concrete operational' stage (normally from seven years of age). Because of this wide range of development children even in the same first-school class will need different kinds of stimulation and different kinds of materials with which to 'work'.

Piaget's findings imply that although it is possible to teach a child certain *techniques*, such as how to multiply, before he is ready to understand the *concept* of multiplication, nevertheless training in specific skills and concepts within the child's ability range can increase his thinking powers beyond what normally seems possible at a given age. For example, demonstrations of the conservation of quantities can enable a child to understand this concept before such understanding is brought about by the ordinary experiences of life. Nursery-school children tested in 1953 and 1955 could not understand a 'pilot's-eye view', but children of this age tested in 1964 were able to describe such a view (Beard, 1968). The teachers of these children in part explained this by supposing that the children had seen other such viewpoints on television and, in this particular nursery class, they had also been used to seeing diagrams of toys. Even this experience, however, did not enable the children to describe what their schoolroom looked like from a different part of the room from that in which they were standing. It seems possible that certain capabilities are not developed as quickly as they might develop if our teaching were accurately gauged to fit each child's actual developmental stage at any one period of time, but it is unlikely that even such highly specialized training could overcome the natural maturational restrictions of age.

Recent work by Bryant (1971), it is claimed, disproves Piaget's findings that small children are unable to understand the concept of the invariance of number and of quantity. However, it is clear from this work that when a small child is presented with an apparently ambiguous test situation, such as when one of two identical rows of beads, which had previously been laid out in a one-to-one correspondence with the other row, is pushed together so that it becomes shorter than it was before, the child is faced with a conflict. He suffers such a conflict precisely because he does not understand the concepts essential for making the judgements required by the test. What this work confirms is Piaget's view that the young child's cognitive structure is unstable.

From the age of twelve or so onwards new intellectual processes begin to become available to the child. He is now no longer restricted in his thinking processes by 'concrete' operations; he can set up hypotheses and predict what would happen if these hypotheses were true. This ability is in marked contrast to that of the child under eleven years of age who cannot entertain hypotheses which are not actually possible. If one wishes, for example, to demonstrate factors influencing the swing of a pendulum, and asks children to find the time period for the swing in relation to the length of the cord on which the weight is suspended; in relation to the weight itself, and in relation to the push given the pendulum, only children of not usually less than thirteen or fourteen years of age will appreciate the necessity of keeping constant all but one variable during the investigation (Beard, 1968). When a child can understand this kind of reasoning he has reached the 'formal operational' stage. He is now able to reason, using statements at an abstract level, and he can build new concepts. Proverbs are understood, and the relationships of numbers to one another, such as ratio, can be comprehended. The young adolescent is able to entertain ideas relating to the possible, rather than just the actual, and to think of the future instead of the present only.

One can readily understand that with these capabilities many other kinds of comprehension, apart from the rational and scientific, now become available to the young adolescent. A true understanding of history depends on understanding other people's viewpoints, in being able to hold a number of criteria in mind concurrently, and in having a concept of time which extends beyond the immediate past. The anthropomorphic view of God, which young children hold, can now change to one which is less egocentric. As we see in chapter 5 ideas about morality, and also notions about other persons' personalities and their motives for behaviour, are all facilitated by the capacity to be able to deal with abstractions, and to be freed from the percept-centred and egocentric view of life. Such freedom is, however, relative; it would be too bold to claim that even mature adults were totally free from these two influences. The extent to which such freedom is realized depends not only on maturational factors, but also on the values and expectancies of the society in which the child lives. Western culture relies to a large extent on the ability of its members to plan ahead, and to consider the possible as well as the actual, and in consequence conceptual and abstract thinking abilities are much valued. In contrast, members of primitive societies, and persons belonging to subgroups in Western culture where such abilities are not appreciated, may never reach this, the 'formal operational', stage of cognitive development.

(b) The development of language, and of thinking in relation to language

In considering the development of language learning in children we must differentiate between a number of aspects of such learning, many of which present problems which we are far from understanding. We wish, for instance, to describe *what* actually happens between the time when a baby first makes sounds and the time when a young, intelligent adolescent is able to hold an interesting conversation. Then we are also interested in the *theories* of how this learning takes place: is it mainly by imitation or through a process of conditioning (pages 127f.), or through some other means? We are also interested in the *functions* of speech: it is obviously and primarily a tool for communication, but it also serves as a socializing agent, and it also obviously has important connections with the development of thinking abilities.

It is always much easier to describe than to explain, and this is certainly so in the field of children's language learning. Many studies have shown how the baby's early sounds differentiate out to become gradually meaningful vocalizations. Lewis (1963) in particular has made a notable contribution in describing the beginnings of language learning; he considers that unless four necessary conditions are present from the child's earliest weeks, his linguistic growth may suffer: the child must himself make sounds, he must respond to the human voice, his mother must respond to his sounds, and she must also speak to him. Lewis also makes the important point that the meaning which language has for us springs from the meaning which a child's first early distress and comfort sounds have for himself. Lewis comments on the bodily condition of, for example, discomfort, of which the baby is aware, and of the particular discomfort cries which he makes and which accompany the bodily condition, though it is unlikely that he has specific cries for particular states of discomfort. This relationship between physical awareness and accompanying sounds is important in establishing the meaning of language. Babies make quite different kinds of noises when happy or unhappy, and the combination of unhappy, hungry noises and sucking movements of the mouth are responsible for producing that first recognizable sound 'Mamma'.

After about six weeks of age a baby starts voluntary babbling as opposed to the involuntary utterances which he made earlier. It is suggested that the sounds are made because they are in themselves satisfactory to the baby, and that the regularity of pitch, rhythm, stress, etc., which the baby can, shortly, produce at will afford him pleasure. Hebb (1949) says that human beings and primates do enjoy that with which they are familiar, and it is possible that both the pleasure in the exercise of a new-found ability, and the products of this ability, account for the continuation of babbling; and as it continues the baby develops an increasing skill in making such sounds.

It is necessary, of course, to account for the next stage in language development, when the baby 'selects' specific utterances because these have meaning for the people in his environment. The obvious answer is that the baby imitates the sounds made to him, or in his hearing, and it is possible that this may be so; but the difficulty is to explain the nature of this imitation, and the selection of the words which are imitated. We are by no means certain what the principles underlying imitation are (Sluckin, 1970) and all we can apparently do at this stage is to say that 'imitation' occurs. Before the child imitates, however, we know that he first makes involuntary and then voluntary utterances, and Lewis has described how the child can respond to the speech of others not by making sounds himself, but either by ceasing to make sounds or by bodily movements or facial movements which one might call 'smiles'! When he is about three or four months old he will begin to make sounds in response to other people speaking to him, but these are not imitations of what is being said; the imitation lies in responding to the sounds of others by sounds of his own. It is an imitation without similarity, though the similarity may exist for the baby. Slowly, aided partly by parental repeating of the noises the child makes which have some approximation to proper words, he selects for utterance those responsive sounds which are the ones he hears. We have as yet no means of knowing what maturational developments occur at this time to bring about this ability, except that physiologically the child is dependent on the proper development of speech organs and of some brain areas; but this does not explain his ability to make the noises he *hears*. What is important for the child at this stage is that he is in frequent and close contact with his mother, or mother substitute, and this contact gives him the verbal experience which is so necessary to further development.

It has been suggested (Skinner, 1957) that at this stage at least the selection of some sounds and the dropping of others is learned by a process of what psychologists call 'classical' and 'operant conditioning' (pages 127f.): those utterances which approximate to a word in the adult language are 'reinforced'—that is, the probability of their recurring is increased when compared with the probability of other sounds recurring, because the child is in some way rewarded for making the 'correct' sounds. This reward may be merely the pleasure of hearing an adult repeat what he, the child, has just said; or it may bring release from discomfort, or it may bring food or bodily contact, or his mother's presence. Thus, it is suggested, by such 'selective reinforcement' the child's language becomes in time closer to that of the adults interacting with him. This explanation is probably adequate for the early stages of learning to make specific sounds for single objects, but it is not an adequate explanation for the next stage of speech, which will be considered later, when children begin to speak grammatically.

We have seen that in a sense the child's own utterances have meaning for him very early in life; these meanings, however, have mainly to do with his own bodily condition. Now he has to learn the meaning of sounds in relation to people and objects and activities outside himself. It is obvious from quite cursory observation that children understand speech much sooner than they themselves can speak, and the understanding of meaning is first shown by the child when he responds to the speech of others with an action rather than with words. He waves when someone says 'good-bye', or stops doing something when he hears 'no'. In this respect his accomplishment is little different from that of domesticated animals who are able accurately to respond to an (often) large number of verbal commands. It is here, with the growth of meaning, that emotion enters into language learning. Both child and animal are emotionally primed, as it were, to act or to desist from acting when they hear certain words. This requires not only some appreciation of the meaning of the word, but also an understanding of the situation in which it is spoken, and a particular affective relationship with the person speaking. It is not the word alone, but the pitch, the tone and the expression of the speaker which affectively convey meaning.

Relatively soon the child's own vocalizations evoke responses from others; he can get others to do things for him, as when he says 'Mamma' and his mother attends to his needs; and he can get them to change their facial expressions, because they are pleased with what he says. At some point in his development he begins to use words intentionally, and the processes which enable him to do this are probably very complex indeed.

During the second year of life the child's speech development progresses very rapidly and he passes through a transitional stage where his speech is mainly either an approximation to the adult speech he hears or an attempt onomatopoetically to give a name to something in his environment. During this year too a relationship is formed between speech and the baby's own actions, so that he himself desists from doing something after saying 'no' to himself. He also learns to use words as substitutes for action.

Although we do not understand how imitation takes place, and although theories which attempt to explain language learning by evoking an operant conditioning paradigm (page 128) have been criticized, yet it is *comparatively* easy to account for the acquisition of *early* speech by some such principle. What is far more difficult to explain is the ability of children to structure their speech grammatically. Human children have the ability first to understand, and later themselves to make, sentences which have grammatically quite different structures but the same meaning. Thus: 'John gave his sister an apple' has the same meaning as 'John's sister was given an apple by him'. Although children do take longer to understand a passive rather than an active sentence (Hayhurst, 1967), passive sentences of this *kind* are understood, and the fact that the grammatical structure of the two sentences is quite different seems irrelevant as far as understanding their meaning is concerned. Similarly children learn the use of inflections, such as the use of 's' for plural words and 'ed' for the past tense. Berko (1958) tested children's ability in this respect by making up words and saying to children: 'This [a weird toy creature] is a wug. Here is another. Now there are two . . .?' Similarly: 'Here is a man glinging. Yesterday he . . .?' Children produce the appropriate 'wugs' and 'glinged', and one knows from common observations where such usage is inappropriate—when, for example, a child says "Daddy goed out', or 'There were two mouses'—that children apparently apply rules rather than merely imitate what they hear.

Everyone who learns to speak learns to use language in an extremely flexible way, and it is suggested by some psycholinguists that we have this ability to understand and use language 'intuitively'. The learning of words and phrases alone is relatively unimportant compared to the ability to *use* language correctly. As we have seen, children use words with inflections that they may never have heard before, and they are also known from observation to use combinations of words which they could never have heard before. It is also obvious that, as he develops, a child must be able to deal with an infinite number of possible sentences. Slobin (1968), while not claiming that this facility can be learned by a process of imitation alone, does suggest that when adults expand a child's own utterances then the child learns something about the structure of his particular language from such an expansion because he in turn mimics part of the expansion. In this way, says Slobin, imitation may play a part in the early learning of language rules. (By 'expansion' is meant taking a child's combination of words—e.g. 'doggie out'—and expanding it to 'yes, the doggie is going out', to which the child might reply 'doggie *going* out'.)

Referring to the observational work done by Brown and Bellugi (1964) at Harvard with two children 'Adam' and 'Eve', Slobin suggests that from this work one can see that at about three years of age the child and mother converse much more with one another than before this age; the child imitates less and the mother also expands less. Slobin speculates that there may be a 'critical' age (page 123), probably at about eighteen months when a child is most helped by adult people expanding his word combinations.

However, it seems unlikely that imitation alone can explain how the command of 'transformational' grammar is acquired. Brown and Bellugi (1964) suggest that a child 'induces' implicit language rules, but it is then necessary to specify how this 'induction' takes place. It is fairly certain that there is no way in which a child could discover the rules relevant to his own language merely from what he hears. Both Russian and American workers have interested themselves greatly in recent years in attempting to elucidate this problem. Chomsky (1957) has differentiated between 'surface' and 'deep' structures of sentences; thus the two sentences 'John is eager to please', and 'John is easy to please', have the same surface structure, but their deep structure is quite different. Again 'John gave his sister an apple' and 'John's sister was given an apple by him' (page 113) have different surface structures but the same deep structure.

It is known that although the surface structure of languages varies from one language to another, there must be sufficient common ground between languages to enable translations to be made from one to another, and it is thought possible that all languages share a common 'deep' structure. It is suggested, therefore, that children may be born with an innate 'idea of language', and that they learn their own particular language by relating what is heard to the underlying structure. Work in Japan and in Russia in recent years has shown that children's speech development follows the same pattern in Japanese as it does in the Indo-European languages (McNeill, 1966), although the surface structures of the adult languages are very different. However, Slobin (1966) observes that the main problem of psycholinguistics is not to state that certain linguistic structures are innately determined, but to discover the exact nature of the learning process which occurs during the acquisition of the use of language.

Language and social developments

Language, as we said at the beginning, is a social tool, enabling communication to take place between people. We know that the baby's cries of comfort and pleasure are different from his cries of discomfort, so that quite early in life the baby is communicating and expressing meaning, but meaning is expanded by the normal concomitants of adult speech, and the manner, gesture and intonation of others all convey meaning. Thus when his mother smells a rose and conveys her pleasure at the scent and sight of the rose, the word 'rose' is not only a neutral sound symbolizing a particular flower, but in addition a sound relating to something pleasant (Lewis, 1963). So learning to speak means learning about the quality of objects as well as learning what the symbolic equivalent of an object is.

From common observation it is known that children usually begin naming objects by using the same word for a number of objects which have some quality in common, so that there are present the *rudiments* of conceptual thinking at an early age. A child under two years of age had been observed for some time to call his cat, whose name was 'Timmy', 'Tee' (Lewis, 1963). Within two-and-a-half months he also called his dog, a horse and a cow 'Tee'; but before he was two years and one month old he had changed his appellations to 'goggie', 'hosh', mooka' and 'pushie' respectively! So children learn quite early in life both what is common about objects, and how to differentiate between them according to their qualitative variation.

It is usually said that the young child talks but does not communicate;

what he talks about are mostly his own needs and he is motivated to use speech to satisfy these needs. To this extent his speech is a kind of communication, but not in the sense in which the word is usually employed. Piaget (1926) considers that the speech of the young child is relatively 'egocentric' when compared with adult speech, particularly when he is playing with other children. This view implies that for the young child communication is not a necessary function of speech; apart from speaking to satisfy their needs, children repeat words and phrases to themselves for the mere pleasure of talking, or a child talks to himself as if he were thinking aloud, or he speaks because the presence of another person serves as a stimulus for his monologue. This does not imply, though, that such speech is non-social. Indeed, Vygotsky (1962) has concluded that a young child's speech has a high social function, but that it *appears* to be egocentric because children do not realize that their private world is not shared by others. He has shown that 'egocentric' speech is social in origin, and that it is thus of help to the child in organizing his behaviour. Vygotsky thinks that Piaget's 'egocentric' speech possibly links speech and thought, because when the child speaks to himself he is thinking aloud. Piaget has agreed with this view in part by stating (1962) that it is possible that egocentric speech may lead to 'inner' speech which helps the development of logical thinking.

It has been established (Smith, 1926) that a child's vocabulary increases tenfold between two and six years of age. Qualitatively this increase implies a deeper understanding of words, which makes their individual meanings more precise and extends the range of meanings available to the child. Between three and four years of age an important stabilization process occurs: speech becomes grammatically more correct, the number of unintelligible words decreases, and by the time a child starts school he has a fairly comprehensive repertoire of intelligible language. The child's social development is reflected in his speech, so that the kind of words he uses changes: more pronouns of the second and third person are added and fewer of the first person are used. Also the number of emotionally toned words decreases (McCarthy, 1954) and slowly speech becomes more and more 'socialized speech', as Piaget terms it. The child now really exchanges his thoughts with others. This exchange of thoughts and ideas cannot occur, however, until a child is able to take a mental viewpoint away from his own, egocentric, viewpoint, and until he can adopt the viewpoint of his hearer, who is not chosen at random but selected because the child wants to communicate to a specific person. Piaget's studies (1926) indicate how the proportion of what he terms 'egocentric' speech to socialized speech decreases with age, and the number of emotionally toned phrases also decreases.

Lewis (1963) has said that 'children do verbal deeds to each other, deeds which matter more and more in their lives'. A child of seven or eight years of age is already something of a social being, and the use of language is part of the continuing socialization process. Between this age and eleven or twelve years of age the 'group' made up of peers normally becomes more and more important to him. His membership of a peer group is one of the two important social forces influencing him, and it is by the use of the right language that he confirms his membership. (The other social force of great importance is, of course, the influence of adults in school and at home.) By belonging to a peer group he realizes that basically language exists in order that people can communicate with one another. Often the language of such a peer group is special and secretive, and the junior child exhibits great loyalty to the group in preserving the secrecy of the group language.

At this time too the child's individuality emerges strongly, and it is shaped in part at least by the reactions of others to him and by his feelings and reactions to others. He forms attitudes which are expressed increasingly by language rather than by bodily movements and by physical activity, such as fighting. Rules of behaviour, whether social or play, cannot be understood without the ability to use language adequately (page 160); rules now become important to the child, and hence through his understanding of rules and his need to have rules at this age, language brings together the child's cognitive and orectic* functions. It does seem, however, that children do not use language to talk about their *feelings* until early adolescence (page 151).

One aspect of language learning which has not been investigated until relatively recently is children's specific non-understanding of apparently simple language. Mention was made earlier of how very young children understand before they can speak, but it has come as somewhat of a surprise to investigators in recent times to find that such words as 'less' are not understood correctly in the context of a sentence. Thus Donaldson and Balfour (1968) found that children under four-and-a-half years at least were unable to give a correct response to the word 'less', and in the set-up devised by the experimenters children up to this age responded to 'less' as if it were 'more'. Similarly Cromer (1970), in seeking to test Chomsky's ideas about the deep and surface structure of language (page 114), found that only children over six-and-a-half years of age were able to understand a sentence such as: 'John is easy to see'; all younger children interpreted this sentence to mean that John was the actor—i.e., that John was doing the seeing! Donaldson and Balfour's work and Cromer's findings do throw doubt on the assumption that small children always understand apparently simple language.

Language and social class

A consideration of language development, particularly in relation to social growth and cognitive development, must include reference to the work of Bernstein. Bernstein (1961 and elsewhere) studied the differences between the language used by the two major social classes in Great Britain—that is, the working class and the middle class—and he considers that these differences have crucial effects on a number of aspects of child rearing, with consequent differences in personality and moral and cognitive development. He put forward the view that these differences also reflect differences in the values held by people in these social classes. Such differences are probably narrowing now as the divisions between the classes are less clear-cut, but they still exist. Bernstein has emphasized that for a child from a lower-working-class background the first experience which he has of middle-class language is when he starts school at five years of age, whereas when the middle-class child starts school he enters a basically similar milieu to that experienced at home. Speech, says Bernstein (1961), 'marks out what is relevant—affectively, cognitively and socially'; so that what is relevant in the lives of members of the different social classes is reflected in their speech. He has suggested that two different forms of language use are current: a 'restricted' code used at times by the middle classes, but all the time by the lower working classes, and an 'elaborated' code used exclusively by the middle classes. The restricted code is rigid; it is predictable; it does not easily differentiate between people; and it does not aid heightened perception or awareness; it exists largely for the present, and it is highly stylized. It is in some respects similar to infant speech, in that it is used to express feelings and enhance social solidarity with the listener. The middle classes use the restricted code when talking to strangers about the weather! It is a language which is descriptive rather than analytic. With the restricted code a great deal of meaning is conveyed by gesture, pitch, stress, etc., whereas the 'elaborated code' emphasizes the exact description of experiences and feelings; allows for subtle discriminations by appropriate adjectives and adverbs; makes possible the analysis of relationships and enables the speaker to sustain concentration on particular themes. Also it is not predictable; it points out differences rather than obscures them; its range is wider; so the number of stimuli to which a listener can respond is greater, and it allows for the *verbalization* of feeling.

A child from a middle-class home learns both languages; the child from a lower-working-class home learns only the restricted code. It is suggested that because the mother from a middle-class background uses elaborated speech in rearing her children, her attitude to her children and the responses she evokes in them will be quite different from the attitude which a mother from a lower social class may have towards her children. There is a difference between being told: 'I'd rather you didn't do that, dear' and a peremptory 'Stop it!' In the former sentence the words express important, but delicate, feelings. Restricted language does not allow for the expression of such subtleties and thus an awareness of human relationships on such levels does not come so easily to the child who is unused to this type of speech. The sentence: 'I'd rather you didn't do that' not only asks the child to stop its activities, but implies that the activity worries or aggravates the mother; that she is asking, but not necessarily demanding, the child to stop; it therefore also implies a degree of respect for, and a granting of autonomy to, the child, which is absent from the peremptory 'Stop it!' Of course all mothers and teachers from all social classes at times say 'Stop it!', but it is not the only or invariable way of asking a child to refrain from an activity, and whereas the child from a middle-class home can understand both ways of being spoken to, the child from a lower-working-class background can usually only understand the one form.

In addition, by normally using elaborated language the middle-class mother uses a particular situation to teach a lesson which is much more widely applicable than merely to the situation about which she is speaking; the kind of words normally used by the working-class mother specifically direct the child to the one instance. So the child's thinking may be more centred on the present and on what is expedient rather than on general principles and a consideration of other people's feelings. The use of restricted language also reflects a lack of interest by its users in long-term aims. Vernon (1969) has said that because the lower working classes in particular normally have little control over their economic future there is little point in their planning or thinking of distant goals (page 168). This lack of interest in the future is reflected in their use of language.

Bernstein has suggested that by internalizing the language, and the feelings which accompany the language, the child becomes more and more self-regulating, and that the type of self-regulation which is achieved depends largely on the language form used. Briefly one can say that elaborated language used by parents tends to lead to the formation of greater inner control and a more acutely sensitive conscience than the use of restricted language does. The use of restricted language also reflects both for the parents and the children a rearing system which relies for the control of behaviour more on strength and dominance than on inner restraint. In chapter 7 more specific consideration is given to the question of how a child coming from a linguistically deprived home background is affected by being spoken to in elaborated language when he enters school. However, it seems clear that the expressions used to indicate what kind of behaviour is acceptable, the feelings which are subtly expressed in sentences longer and, in structure if not in word use, more complex than the child has heard before—these are all relatively strange to the child and they make the receiving and giving of communications difficult for him. An older child will thus experience a correspondingly greater difficulty in expressing himself in English, and his thought processes may not lend themselves so easily to logical, clear, deductive thinking (page 120). Because linguistic ability is basic to educational success, such children are quite severely handicapped from the beginning of their school lives. Evidence exists from a number of studies (Bernstein, 1958, 1960; Jahoda, 1964) that when young adults from working-class backgrounds are tested on verbal and non-verbal intelligence tests, their verbal scores are always grossly depressed when compared with the scores on non-verbal tests, a difference not found when young adults from higher social classes are tested. The result is that a potentially high intelligence is to a greater or lesser degree unable adequately to use the medium of words in which scholarship is expressed.

Language and thinking

It is necessary before thinking can take place for a child to be able to make a mental representation of objects and relationships in their physical absence. When a child thinks, he must be able to evoke an image of a kind without direct sensory stimulation. Although the child at the early, sensori-motor stage of development (page 103f.), before he is twenty-two months of age or so, is beginning to be able to think in this way, his understanding of the world is so limited that he is not even quite sure that objects exist if they cannot be experienced sensorily. For this reason it is very important for young children to have a great deal of sensory experience with many different kinds of objects, materials, colours and textures. At this level thought is internalized action, and only through action can the early thinking processes develop. This internalized action Piaget has called 'an operation', and his theory of the development of thought is outlined in chapter

Piaget has suggested (page 104) that the beginnings of thought during the sensori-motor period are independent of language. When the child first starts to represent actions to himself (page 103) and thus 'short-circuits' movements, he is using the power of thought. There is some disagreement whether thinking beyond this stage of development is dependent on language development. Flavell and Hill (1969) state the view that 'linguistic ability does not appear to be either synonymous with, nor a necessary precondition for, cognitive processing'. They say that this applies to the 'middling levels of developmental maturity' as well as the sensori-motor state of development, though they also state that it is uncertain whether the ability to engage in the more advanced forms of thinking is independent of linguistic ability. They suggest that linguistic symbols provide one kind of material, suitably coded, for thinking, and that this serves as an '*intra*personal communicative function', as opposed to the usual *inter*personal function of language. However, the notion that even the 'middling' developmental stage of thinking, that is Piaget's 'concrete operational' stage (page 68), is not dependent on language would seem difficult to maintain, though psychologists other than Flavell and Hill are undecided whether language is *necessary* as opposed to being *useful* in aiding the developing thought processes (Herriot, 1970). Although it may be possible to understand concepts of conservation and causality without using words such as 'more', 'less', 'alive', etc., the ability to manipulate such concepts in order to develop a certain and sophisticated understanding must, one feels, depend on the ability to be able to express this understanding in the appropriate words. It has been found that five-years-olds who understood the word 'middle-sized' were better at discriminating between three shapes of increasing size than the children who did not understand the word properly (Spiker, Gerjeroy and Shepard, 1956). Britton (1970) comments on the need to be able to classify and to form concepts of classes in order to name objects. He says that there is an 'hierarchical relationship between word meanings which has the most far-reaching influence upon thinking'. Thus a child will know the colour red, but then learns to distinguish between scarlet and crimson, and later to subdivide the scarlet into vermilion and pillarbox, and the crimson into blood-red and wine-colour. It is certainly difficult to understand how the comprehension of the abstract terms which are used by adolescents and adults who have entered the 'symbolic' stage of thinking can be developed without language, for there is no equivalent to these terms in the material environment.

Bruner considers that children must be able to internalize 'techniques' such as the language of their culture if they are to progress to the symbolic thinking stage. He confesses (1964) that he cannot suggest how language becomes internalized as a programme for ordering experience, but suggests that it probably depends on interaction with others: one might venture to speculate that the 'intrapersonal communicative function', to which Flavell and Hill refer, can only come into play if the *inter*personal function of communication takes place fully and in a stimulating environment. Bruner indeed lays great stress on the role of language in enabling the child to progress from 'enactive' to 'symbolic'* thinking. He suggests that the role of language becomes increasingly powerful as the child grows, particularly between the ages of four and twelve. During this period language becomes a tool for the translation of experience, for once language can be used in this way the child is no longer tied to the immediate, but can represent the past and speculate about the future. Language, says Bruner, has 'features of remoteness and arbitrariness' (1964); and these features enable an integration of behaviour and of thought to occur, which, he suggests, is not possible without such a tool. Bruner has also put forward the following ideas about the development of language and thinking, which he divides into four stages:

During stage 1 the child speaks a language which embodies a power of organization he cannot achieve in thought. (By this Bruner presumably means that children use words in speaking which they cannot manipulate in thought.)

Later, during stage 2 the child achieves in thought what he can achieve in speech.

During stage 3 he extends the range of his power of organization by first verbalizing more complex experiences and then contemplating these verbalizations.

Lastly, during stage 4, his powers of organization in thought come to exceed his powers of organization in speech (Britton, 1970).

Examination of the thinking powers of deaf children should help to establish whether or not language and thought are as intimately related as Bruner suggests. Research work with children who became deaf before the period of language acquisition indicates that many kinds of thinking processes are possible for the deaf, but in Furth's study (1966) nine out of twelve children were inferior to hearing children in aspects of thinking. However, children with such a severe degree of deafness are treated so differently from hearing children in a number of ways that one cannot be completely sure that it is the absence of hearing spoken language which accounts for the difference in thinking abilities.

Vernon (1969) considers that symbolic thinking is totally dependent on the quality of speech models and communications which the child receives from parents, teachers, older children and contemporaries. Many other psychologists also hold the view that more than any other single factor the quality of speech which a child hears acts continuously on the development of his mental powers from the age of six months onwards. Vygotsky (1962) aand Luria (1961) seem to have shown that 'inner' speech is of importance from an early age in helping the child to plan and order his actions. Such internal language abbreviates trial-and-error learning and thus makes problem solving more effective. Britton (1970) has put Vygotsky's view in this way, that in 'inner speech words die as they bring forth thought'. Language is, according to Vygotsky, an internalized regulator of behaviour, but it seems clear from experimental work that such regulation by language can only occur after considerable experience with language. Luria gave children of three years of age a rubber bulb and told them to press it whenever a red light was flashed, but not to press when a blue light came on. Inhibiting the action—i.e., *not* pressing when the blue light came on—seemed impossible for children of this age. Later they were told to give themselves the audible instructions 'Press' or 'Don't press'. The inhibition of the negative function of 'Don't press' was such that the children didn't press at all to either light, or they pressed all the time regardless. By four-and-a-half years of age children were able to give themselves instructions overtly to press or not to press, and to obey these instructions, and finally, at five, they were able to give themselves instructions silently. Burke (1966) has said that the 'essential distinction between the verbal and the non-verbal is the fact that language adds the peculiar possibility of the negative', and it can be seen from Luria's experiment that action and not words is predominant in a young child's life: the force of language which enable the *negative* command to inhibit action is not sufficiently strong before about four years of age to prevent *positive* action from taking place.

Herriot (1970) says that 'the present condition of the field of language and thinking is utterly confused'. There seems to be no *absolute* proof at present to indicate that the quality of language which a child hears affects his thinking processes; it may be that language reflects but does not necessarily determine cognitive growth, and that other factors, such as an increasingly long short-term memory span, may be as influential as language in affecting thinking processes.

(c) Learning

Harry and Margaret Harlow have posed the following problem (1949): 'How does an infant, born with only a few simple reactions, develop into an adult capable of rapid learning and the almost incredibly complex mental processes known as thinking? This is one of psychology's largely unsolved problems.' During the past twenty years the Harlows have attacked this problem in their own way, but before we consider the value of their work for an understanding of human learning we must look at the various kinds of learning which have been identified.

Children come to school in order to learn, and teachers hope to help them to learn: this is what teaching is about; but we have to think of learning as being an activity which is much wider than school learning. From the time a baby is born he begins to learn; indeed man is par excellence a learning animal. He comes into the world far less well developed than other animals, and he is forced to rely on his ability to learn, for he has few, if indeed any, inherited modes of behaviour. This ability enables him to develop greater flexibility of behaviour than any other creature, and this flexibility expresses itself in all aspects of his behaviour. A theory of personality development based on the view that man is primarily a learning organism is considered in chapter 2.

We can understand, therefore, that learning involves diverse activities, such as learning to control our emotions; learning to conform to society's needs of us; learning a skill; learning to think conceptually; as well as learning facts. We know that different kinds of learning, sometimes combinations of different kinds of learning, are responsible for different aspects of what is learned. One of the most difficult things to learn is 'how to learn'! This is, possibly, from the point of view of academic achievement, one of the most important things a child can learn, particularly in the primary school, and it is also possibly one of the most neglected subjects of teaching, as well as of research into teaching methods. The emphasis in schools, even in the upper forms of grammar or comprehensive schools, is on instruction; the development of individual learning ability is seemingly neglected both by the schools and by research workers. We will consider later the specific factors affecting a child's ability to learn in school. It is necessary first, however, to look at learning in the broader context of 'learning to live'.

Learning, from infancy onwards, can broadly speaking be of four types, though experimental psychologists may argue that fundamentally all four can be reduced to a classical conditioning paradigm. It does seem, though, that one can distinguish between (1) imprinting, (2) imitation and identification, (3) classical conditioning, and (4) operant conditioning.

Imprinting

Imprinting is a form of learning which has been extensively studied during the past thirty-five years, first in birds, and later in animals and humans. Imprinting experiments and observations seem to indicate that the kind of behaviour which at one time was thought to be entirely instinctive can actually only be displayed if the correct learning experiences occur at 'critical' times; that is, during special and usually short periods early in an animal or bird's life. The basic difference between imprinting and other forms of learning is that it appears to occur without any *ordinary* kind of reward. Behaviour learned as a result of imprinting experiences was at first thought to be irreversible and quite different in many respects from other kinds of learning, though it is possible, as Hinde (1962) maintains, that the differences between imprinting and other forms of learning are due more to the particular conditions in which learning takes place than to any intrinsic differences between kinds of learning, but such learning does appear to be limited to certain periods in an organism's life, and to be dependent also on innate mechanisms of a particular kind. Imprinting is a kind of amalgam of an inherited tendency to behave in a particular way, and experiences occurring at the right time in early life which are necessary to enable this kind of behaviour to be displayed. Thus Lorenz (1935) found that newly hatched ducklings 'instinctively', or so it seemed, followed their mother, but if during the critical period soon after hatching they heard Lorenz making the appropriate 'quacking' noises, then they followed him, and continued to follow him and not the mother duck at all. The importance of these experiences lies not only in the kind of necessary behaviour which the *baby* bird or animal displays, such as following the mother, but in the fact that lack of the appropriate experience in babyhood has repercussions on the later social and sexual behaviour of the adult. Thus Lorenz and others have found that if a baby bird or animal had been imprinted to an unnatural object, it found difficulty in relating to others of its species later in life. Many farmers know the problem which a hand-reared lamb has in assimilating into the flock once it leaves the farm kitchen.

In chapter 3 evidence is reviewed which indicates that humans are particularly sensitive at certain periods of life to particular kinds of experiences, and that their later development may be affected if these experiences are missed. We know from animal work (Scott, 1962) that the greater the effort which has to be made by a baby animal or bird during these critical periods (for example, in making an effort to follow rather than, say, cling to the mother), the greater appear to be the lasting effects of imprinting experiences. Although the human baby is unable to make any real effort to attach himself by physically following his mother or even by clinging to her, as primate babies do, he is able to smile and he is able to follow her visually, and the 'visual following response' may be the human equivalent of the *actual* following response of animal and bird babies. Attachment behaviour to one particular person is thus thought to occur through a process akin to imprinting, and probably occurs before the baby is six months old; at this age he knows well and smiles at familiar persons, but he begins to be unresponsive to, and often shows fear in, the presence of strangers, if a familiar person is not present. It is thought important that babies should have the opportunity during this period of becoming attached to one major caretaking figure.

Because imprinting experiences appear to have greater relevance to the behaviour of animals who must come into the world with more innate drives determining their behaviour and with fewer opportunities for learning than humans, it is not thought that strictly classical imprinting plays much part in human learning, though one should not dismiss the importance for later personality development of imprinting-like experiences in early life which have been enjoyed, or, more important, have *not* been enjoyed. Yarrow (1960) has collected evidence from the observation of ninety-six babies placed with adoptive parents at different ages during the first year of life (page 101), and it appears that 86 per cent of the babies placed at six months of age showed some disturbance. To date no information is available about long-term effects, but the disturbance after placing is thought to be due to the attachment which had already been formed before adoption, and to the distress which a break in the relationship caused the baby. It is too soon to know how crucial such early experiences are for humans, though we do know (page 97) that stimulating experiences of various kinds early in life seem to be important for later intellectual development.

Imitation and identification

When we consider imitation it becomes difficult to say what exactly takes place when a child imitates, beyond saying the obvious, that he can be observed to mimic the actions of another. Some psychologists have stated that the ability to imitate is innate, others that imitation can be explained in terms of learning theory. Thus several theories of imitation have been put forward, and it is clear that to account for the occurrence of imitation is very difficult, particularly when no obvious reward is given to either the child or the person on whom he is modelling himself. As we shall see later, though it is maintained by some psychologists that learning without any kind of reward can and does take place—and indeed imprinting appears to be a form of learning of this kind—most psychologists consider that in more ordinary forms of learning a reward of *some* kind is always present even if this is not overtly discernible.

Aronfreed (1968) has suggested recently that affect* has a strong mediating role in influencing the occurrence of imitative responses; Bandura's latest ideas (1968) include a reference to the need of the child to see that the act he is about to copy is an appropriate guide for behaviour for himself. If one sees this awareness of 'appropriateness' as a kind of affective reward, that is, that the carrying-out of a new but appropriate act brings a feeling of satisfaction, then it is possible to see the place of rein-forcement* in imitation. This view is not unlike Mowrer's (1960), that imitation is a kind of 'empathetic' learning: the child experiences 'intuitively' the satisfactions experienced by the person on whom he is modelling himself. This assumes that the child will not only be aroused by these feelings, but that he will also anticipate that he too will be rewarded by such desirable feelings if he imitates. Although this theory *describes* the kind of anticipated satisfactions that may initiate imitation it does not *explain* what occurs; indeed it may not be possible clearly to define the affective features which bring about an awareness of 'appropriateness', or the 'empathetic' feelings which seem to suggest that satisfaction will be experienced if another person's behaviour is imitated; and it is possible that imitation of acts for which no obvious reward is given cannot easily be distinguished from 'identification', which is a form of imitation.

Identification is a kind of behaviour whereby an individual models himself unconsciously, or partially unconsciously, on another person, incorporating part of that person's personality into himself. When a child identifies with another person then that person is usually someone with whom the child has a close emotional tie, and in early life such a person is normally a family member who ministers to the child's needs. Freud's 'Oedipal'* theory attempts to explain both sex-role identification and how, through such identification with the parent of the same sex, a child adopts the values, ideas and ideals of the parent. In this way identification aids the development of the personality, and the formation of the Superego (chapter 2). Freud has also postulated that this is indeed how societies are able to pass on their cultural norms from generation to generation (page 55). Sears (1957) has suggested that in the absence of a nurturing adult a child, by imitating the actions of that adult, 'reinstates' her, even though she is physically absent; and also by such imitation a kind of self-administered reward is obtained. Although in early childhood identification will be mostly with close and nurturing adults, this process continues in later childhood, when the child may identify with an admired teacher or a loved peer.

Identification is an extremely complex phenomenon to test experimentally because, whereas one can offer a child *behavioural acts* for imitation and then observe the extent to which such acts are imitated under various conditions, one cannot for experimental analysis offer the more subtle aspects of a model's *personality* for imitation.

A great deal of experimental work with children has been carried out to try to discover under what conditions children will imitate, what kind of actions they will readily copy, and whether they learn other people's behaviour even though they do not imitate such behaviour immediately. There is good evidence that learning through imitation takes place extensively in childhood.

Although we do not yet fully understand thee processes involved in imitative learning and identification (Sluckin, 1970), some practical advantage can be taken of the outcome of experimental work with children. Thus Bandura (1962) found that children will copy aggressive behaviour very readily, though less so if the model being imitated is seen to be punished for his aggression. This finding would appear to have some relevance to the kind of TV material which children see, where the hero is often shown to be as aggressive as the villain, and he is never punished but always rewarded in some way for his successful violence!

Classical conditioning

Classical conditioning, which was first discovered by Pavlov in Russia, is a form of learning in which a natural response to a normally natural stimulus, such as the sucking movements a baby makes when his mouth comes into contact with nipple or teat, is, either fortuitously or through a deliberate training procedure, evoked by an unnatural stimulus, because the natural and unnatural stimuli are closely associated in time and space. Thus if, for example, a baby is regularly picked up just before feeding, as indeed most babies are, then he will after a little time begin to make sucking noises and particular movements of the mouth on being picked up and before the bottle or breast is presented to him. The baby has become 'conditioned' to make the response of sucking to the 'conditioned' stimulus of being picked up, and he will continue to make such a response, at least for a time, even if the teat or nipple is not always presented after he is picked up. The situations under which classical conditioning may take place have been fully studied in many different kinds of conditions, and it seems irrelevant here to say more than that there is little doubt that babies through a process of classical conditioning do learn about the sequences of events in their lives, particularly about those events which relate to their needs. (In chapter 2 the social-learning theory of personality development, which is based on conditioning paradigms, is explained.)

Fears

The classical conditioning paradigm can also be invoked to explain the development of fears. Although the problem of how fears develop in animals and humans is a complex one, there is clear evidence that children, and animals at times, learn to fear people and objects through a process of classical conditioning. They learn to associate a person or an object not inherently frightening with something which is naturally frightening. For instance, a strange person looking suddenly and closely into the pram of a six to twelve months old baby may cause the baby always to associate this person with the surprised fear which he experienced when he first saw him. (Hebb (1958) has suggested that fear can be experienced when the unexpected appears in place of the expected.) Again, a child may be frightened by the sudden movement of an animal introduced to him as a pet, and he may associate the fear experienced by the sudden movement not only with the animal itself, but perhaps also with other similar animals, or even with similar objects, such as furry objects. In a now classic experiment Mary

Cover Jones (1924) was able to cure a boy called Peter of his great fear of a white rabbit by gradually associating the presence of such a rabbit with Peter's favourite food. Indeed, Peter's cure was the first attempt at 'behaviour therapy', which relies in part on classical conditioning techniques to cure phobic patients of their irrational and exaggerated fears. However, such cures are not as straightforward as this description may indicate, and parents and teachers cannot easily and without expert advice themselves cure children of such fears. (Classical conditioning is also discussed on pages 59f.)

Operant conditioning

Operant conditioning employs a different paradigm: here a part of a baby or animal's existing behavioural repertoire is used in a new and particular situation; in an experimental set-up this situation is selected by the expeerimenter. The behavioural act is not a natural response to a natural stimulus, as in classical conditioning, but it may be any quite arbitrary piece of natural behaviour which the experimenter, or, if we are considering the social training of a child, the parent or teacher, is interested in encouraging. The natural behavioural act is 'reinforced', which in most circumstances means that it is rewarded; and consequently the likelihood of that piece of behaviour being displayed again is increased. In our discussion of language learning (page 111) we show how those natural early sounds which a baby makes, and which approximate to 'Mamma' or 'Nanna', are reinforced, mostly because the adults in the baby's life show pleasure when he makes them, or because the baby is rewarded in some other way when he repeats the sounds. As a consequence these sounds are more likely to be repeated than other sounds. Notwithstanding the fact that the training of animals and the socialization of children through a system of rewards (positive reinforcement) and punishments (negative reinforcement) is usually based on aspects of operant conditioning techniques, for various complex reasons the methods employed in such training programmes meet with less success than parents anticipate, particularly so far as punishment is concerned (chapter 8).

The two forms of learning most applicable to the child as far as social and school learning is concerned are probably imitation and operant conditioning, and of these two operant conditioning is of the greater importance in relation to teaching. Although no contemporary psychologist would today state with certainty *exactly* what effects reward has on behaviour, it is possible to make some general statements which may be of help to teachers. Skinner (1938) has shown how an animal can be trained to perform complex acts (he has taught pigeons to play 'ping-pong'!) by waiting until the animal performs a particular act which the experimenter knows is to be part of the final act he has planned for training, and then when, quite by chance, the animal performs this act, immediately rewarding it. The act is thus reinforced. The training schedule continues in this manner until progressively a succession of acts has been established by rewarding those pieces of behaviour which fit the predetermined pattern, and ignoring those which do not fit it. It has been suggested that this 'selective reinforcement' is as effective in the home and in school with human children as in the laboratory with birds and animals. Teachers must be 'observer-detectives' and if possible reinforce immediately those aspects of a child's behaviour which the teacher wishes to strengthen, ignoring as far as possible those aspects which are not desirable. The question of rewards and punishments in relation to social behaviour is discussed on page 193; here we are more concerned with the strengthening of a child's school learning ability.

If one considers the principles underlying operant conditioning as they are applied to teaching-machine programmes one can learn a great deal about how these principles might be used in classroom teaching without the use of machines. The programme on a machine is designed to teach a subject in very small steps. There are at least two reasons for this: one small step in a process of learning can be understood more easily than several steps explained in quick succession; and by making sure that one step is understood, and telling the learner that he was correct in the answer he gave to the machine, the learner is being positively reinforced. We know from animal work that this strengthens the response just emitted; in other words, learning has taken place. The principles underlying teaching-machine programmes also show how important it is for learning that children be allowed to progress at their own pace; in addition the active participation in self-generated learning, rather than being passively attentive at an instruction session, seems to be a relevant feature of learning. So by observing the four principles of

(1) contriving a situation in which a child is more likely to be right than wrong,

(2) telling him immediately that he is right,

(3) allowing him, with supervision, to progress at his own pace, and

(4) ensuring that he actively takes part in the learning procedure,

the teacher is maximizing the child's chances of learning. Successive positive reinforcement is also cumulative as far as motivation for learning is concerned.

Adherence by the teacher to these four principles motivates the child by giving him success in learning through enabling him to understand what he is doing. His interest and attention must, however, be continually aroused and he must be able to memorize what he learns; but a poor memory may mean a lack of interest in the subject learned, or a lack of attention, or both, for what has not been attended to cannot really be remembered. So interest, attention, memory and motivation are all linked. It is easier, of course, to interest a child if something new he is required to learn is linked to some everyday experience he has had in his life outside school. Most primary schools teach with this principle in mind, but, although more difficult to put into practice with secondary-school subjects, one feels that more could be done to bring academic subjects to life in this way for older children than is at present being done in many secondary schools.

Sears and Hilgard (1964), in an article on the teacher's role in the motivation of the learner, say that a good teacher utilizes and arouses in the child three different motives for learning: he seeks to arouse curiosity, he stimulates a child's desire to achieve, and he uses the child's wish for a warm relationship with his teacher to activate his learning abilities. Of course only a basically affectionate teacher can do the last, and only a teacher who is himself interested in the subject he is teaching can do the first. Although a good teacher can also stimulate the child's wish to achieve success by learning, this is possibly more dependent on social class and cultural factors than on the school situation. Undoubtedly the need to achieve is present in children from quite an early age when they find they have a competence in the performance of some task (Heckhausen, 1967). Indeed, White (1959) has suggested that the need to master the environment directs persistent behaviour, and one may assume that children experience a *need* to become increasingly competent in dealing with their environment. In addition, Western middle-class values place great emphasis on the need to achieve, and many studies have found that the drive to achieve, particularly in children from middle-class homes, acts as a powerful impetus to learning (McClelland, Atkinson, *et al.*, 1953). The findings from a number of investigations indicate that children from such homes show more responsibility in school, and a higher degree of aspiration than children from working-class homes. It is, therefore, likely that children whose parents set a value on achievement will be able better to take advantage of the teaching they receive in schools, and this may be *one* of the reasons why children from middle-class homes in Great Britain have in the past won grammar-school places out of proportion to their number in the population.

Learning to think and learning to learn

Thinking in relation to language development is considered on pages 120f. and the development of cognitive processes from birth to maturity is reviewed on pages 103f. We must, however, consider here how the *ability* to learn to think develops. Harry and Margaret Harlow (1949) (page 125) trained both monkeys and children to choose small objects on a board by showing them a sample of the object and they then rewarded them by enabling them to find something edible if they chose the right object. By elaborating the training series it was possible for monkeys and children to learn that the relevant clue was, for example, not the shape of an object, but the colour, or the size. They were shown a blue object and they had to select all the other blue objects regardless of how they might differ from one another in other respects. The next test might involve not the colour of the objects, but their shape; thus all the round objects might have to be selected regardless of other criteria. One test consisted of nine objects on a tray; monkeys were given a sample similar to one of them and they had to pick out *only* those objects, but *all* those objects, which were in some relevant way like the sample. In a more difficult test they were given a sample which had nothing obviously to do with the objects, such as a triangle which *represented* the colour red and a circle which *represented* blue. At least one animal learned this sign language almost perfectly. Thus both the monkeys and the children in the Harlow experiments were not learning to solve *one* problem only, but they developed what have been called 'learning sets'. The first solution is based on a random, trial-and-error method of discovery; but as opportunities for learning continue to be provided, random choices cease and deliberate choices are made. There is good evidence to show that what has been learned in this way is retained for considerable periods of time. By these methods children 'learn to learn'. The Harlows suggest that children build up learning sets by learning to solve increasingly difficult problems. At first they try previously learned habits and also new ways of responding, then they discard those responses which are unsuccessful, and retain the useful habits which have been formed. As children continue successfully to solve many problems of a certain kind, new habits are established which are then brought into operation whenever they appear to be relevant. Thus the ability to solve problems is established and a 'set' is built up which enables further learning to take place more easily and rapidly. Humans have the advantage over animals in that they can use language, and words have the function of calling forth particular learning sets which are appropriate for certain problems.

At the beginning of this chapter the cognitive development of the child is described, and in particular Piaget's scheme of how this development takes place. It is suggested both by Piaget and by Bruner that the highest stage of thinking is reached when a child in early adolescence comes to be able to think conceptually, and Piaget and Bruner both describe how this stage is gradually reached. Psychologists are not agreed whether all learning, including the ability to learn to think conceptually, is basically a form of simple conditioning—that is, learning ever-increasingly complex response 'sets' by association—or whether some kinds of learning are of the conditioning-association type, and other kinds of learning are due to insight or understanding which, presumably, depend on the development of cognitive structures. Thus simple rote learning would be an example of the former kind of learning, and complex problem-solving an example of the latter kind of learning.

There is little doubt that the young child under seven years of age finds all kinds of abstract and conceptual thought difficult, and that when he learns he learns 'associatively'—that is, he learns the correct *responses* to make. He has not yet developed the cognitive structures which enable him to *understand* what he is doing: indeed, his learning abilities exemplify the difference between learning with, and learning without, understanding. He can at this age do many schools tasks, such as simple arithmetic, by learning the correct procedures; for example, he can learn his multiplication tables and so multiply, but he may not at all know what is meant by multiplication! Gradually, as he matures, increasing understanding will come.

However, whether someone learns with or without understanding depends not only on the age of the learner, but also upon the *type* of learning which is taking place. Most learning involves a mixture of habit and insight, and diagram 7 below shows how learning tasks can be scaled from those which depend entirely, or almost entirely, on acquiring the right responses which become habitual, to those which are entirely, or almost entirely, dependent on the ability to form concepts.

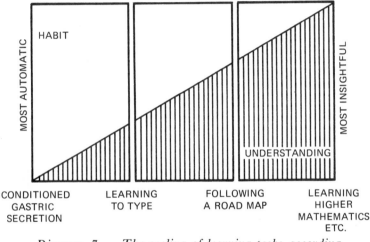

Diagram 7   *The scaling of learning tasks according to degree of understanding involved.*[1]

It is obvious that a great deal of what we have to learn in life does not depend on using conceptual thinking powers.

We have considered two factors in relation to conceptual learning: one is that its development can be seen as a result of developing *maturity*, and the other that the use of such learning powers is dependent on the *kind* of material being learned. There is, however, a possible third factor which we have to consider when discussing conceptual learning, which is that the power to think in conceptual terms may well be an ability which some children simply do not possess, or possess only to a very limited degree, and that this ability, at least at certain limited levels of intelligence, may be independent of intelligence.

[1] Reproduced from E. R. Hilgard and R. C. Atkinson: *Introduction to Psychology* (Harcourt Brace Jovanovich, 1967) by kind permission of the publishers.

Jensen (1969) has suggested that not only is there evidence that this may be so, but that if such evidence were to be fully substantiated this could have important implications for educational practice. Jensen and others have produced fairly convincing proof that some children have a high *associative* learning ability—that is, they are good at rote learning—but these children also often have a low *conceptual* learning ability: they have difficulty in learning material which requires insight and understanding. Jensen considers that children who are disadvantaged either because their home life is unstimulating or because they lack particular abilities, or for both reasons, are not able to take advantage of the traditional classroom situation which puts great emphasis on cognitive learning. However, many basic skills necessary in life can be learned by associative learning methods, and Jensen suggests that if children, who find this method easy but who find the cognitive learning method difficult, could be taught suitable basic skills, they would leave school conscious of having been able to take advantage of what the school offered, instead of feeling inadequate and helpless. It is undoubtedly true that many children leave school feeling hopeless about their scholastic abilities and probably as a result generally depressed about the kinds of abilities which they may be called upon to exhibit in their subsequent life.

Jensen believes that the traditional system of learning has evolved without taking into consideration the natural endowment and cultural backgrounds of many of the children who are now receiving education. Teachers must, he suggests, find ways of teaching children who find the traditional, cognitively orientated method too hard. He feels that schooling takes too little advantage of the great diversity of abilities which children exhibit, and that a good educational system should tap the abilities of each child and maximize these.

FURTHER READING

BEARD, R. M.: *An Outline of Piaget's Developmental Psychology* (Routledge and Kegan Paul, London, 1969).

RICHMOND, P. G.: *An Introduction to Piaget* (Routledge and Kegan Paul, London, 1970).

LEWIS, M. M.: *Language, Thought and Personality in Infancy and Childhood* (Harrap, London, 1963).

SLUCKIN, W.: *Early Learning in Man and Animal* (Allen and Unwin, London, 1970).

HILGARD, E. R. AND G. BOWYER: *Theories of Learning* (3rd ed.), (Appleton-Century-Crofts, New York, 1966).

BRITTON, J.: *Language and Learning* (Allen Lane The Penguin Press, London, 1970).

5

Moral, social and emotional development

(a) Moral development

It has recently become obvious (Wilson, Williams and Sugarman, 1967) that as a society we are by no means clear what we mean by 'moral' behaviour, nor are we able definitely to say what kind of moral attitudes and behaviour we wish to inculcate in our children. In chapter 1 it was shown that previous generations were much more certain both about what they meant by 'moral', and how to produce moral people. They were probably wrong about the latter though certainly convinced about the former. Today we are uncertain whether some behaviour, which was previously considered moral, is in fact moral at all; often in the past people were just obeying rules which it suited the society or the class to which they belonged to make, and this kind of rule-following had little to do with what is normally considered to be true moral behaviour. Nor do we necessarily know what causes moral or immoral behaviour to take place. It is important, therefore, to examine what is meant by the concept 'morality', and to study how children develop morally before anything can be said about how to attempt to inculcate moral behaviour. Some teachers may feel that, except for the purpose of ensuring discipline, it is not their task to morally educate the children in their care; but Burt (1970B) has recently suggested that character training is of even greater importance than intellectual training, and that the teacher's role in this training is particularly relevant; but he also says that 'the questions of character training, moral education, and discipline are questions of bewildering complexity'.

A discussion in depth of philosophical definitions of morality and of moral behaviour is out of place in this book. The reader interested in such concepts in relation to education is referred to either Wilson, Williams and Sugarman (1967) or Kay (1969). However, it is important to discuss here what is meant in practice by 'moral behaviour'. *True* moral behaviour seems to arise from a conception of morality which is based on a consideration for the feelings of other people, an appreciation of their needs and rights, and it stems from an informed conscience. *So-called* moral behaviour can stem from a mere knowledge that certain acts are disapproved of, and to this extent the behaviour becomes a crude, rule-following type of activity; or it may come from a fear of punishment, or it may be purely imitative.

In order to understand the development of behaviour which displays true morality one must, according to Brown (1965), differentiate between moral *knowledge*, moral *behaviour* and moral *feeling*. These three aspects of morality do not necessarily develop or exist together, and they each appear to be learned in a different way. Also these different aspects of morality sometimes support one another, and at other times are not closely related. Thus moral feeling, which in itself can arise either from conscious understanding, or from having a conscience or feelings of guilt (the reasons for which are not necessarily cconsciously understood), can influence moral behaviour. However, a number of studies have shown that there is no consistent relationship between resisting temptation and feeling guilty (Bandura and Walters, 1963). Similarly, moral knowledge may influence moral behaviour, and though there is usually some relationship between these two factors, it is not necessarily a close one (Hartshorne and May, 1928–1930). How do these three aspects of morality relate to the developing child?

A number of psychologists have investigated the acquisition of moral knowledge. There are two ways in which Piaget has approached his study (1932): one was to see how children's understanding of *rules* of behaviour become modified with age until, as Piaget says, genuine moral development has taken place; the other was to see how children learn to understand with increasing age the *reasons* for behaviour where a question of morality is involved—that is, how well they are able to make moral *judgements*.

The young child under four-and-a-half years of age does not usually play co-operatively, but he plays often in parallel with other children (chapter 6). As he approaches five years of age he begins to be aware that other children, whom he sees at play, have rules by which they play, but these rules have no importance for him. Moral growth cannot proceed faster than language understanding (chapter 4) and the *idea* of rules having to be enforced cannot be comprehended without the language structure which explains this. After five years of age, or so, children begin to become keenly aware of rules; indeed, rules assume a great importance, being thought of as 'sacred and untouchable, emanating from adults, and lasting for ever' (Piaget, 1932). The child does not know how the rules are formed or who formed them, but he appears to think that rules, even of childish games, have always existed. Children at this stage find a certain security in the seeming unchangeability of rules, and this is the age when they play a lot of games with rules.

After eight years of age it becomes permissible to alter rules, provided that the other players in the game agree. Piaget considers that this final stage, which arises from mutual respect and co-operation and from a consideration of the rights of others, is the phase which represents the achievement of a true understanding of the nature of rules, and the one which is the most relevant to the question of genuine moral development.

Children are not, of course, consistent in their handling of rules, just as they are not consistent in their comprehension of the conservation of quantity or number (chapter 4). There is little doubt, however, that just as they become released from the dominance of the senses at about seven years of age, they also somewhat later become released from the necessity of a slavish adherence to rules.

Concurrently with the child's changing view about the importance of rules is a growing sophistication in the ability to make moral *judgements*. Piaget has investigated children's ideas of justice and fairness, how they view punishments, and their understanding of such concepts as lying. He has asked children what is bad about telling lies: before eight years of age children say it is worse to lie to an adult than to a child; also the enormity of a lie is directly related to its size, so that a lie about a completely improbable happening, which would most likely not be believed and be treated as a joke, is nevertheless considered before this age to be naughtier in the young child's eyes than a lie about something which is possible.

Young children under eight are also mostly concerned with fairness and retributive punishment, rather than with people's needs and an assessment of intent. Piaget has suggested that before seven years of age children do not judge the gravity of an act by the intentions of the agent, but by the amount of damage done. This percept-centred view of life means that for such children it will be more naughty to break a big jug while helping mother to lay the table than to break a small jug while trying to steal some cream from the larder. Again the size of the damage done, like the size of a lie told, is important, and not the intention behind the evaluated action. Because children under seven are so percept-centred, most of their evaluations will be dominated by what is immediately visible. It is difficult for them to understand motives for behaviour which cannot be easily and actually perceived, so that only what is quite obvious can enter into consideration (pages 104f.). After seven years of age children begin to judge more by intent and not so much by consequence, and at twelve years of age Piaget considers that there is a real change towards concern for motive and intention. It has been said that this ontogenic development mirrors the phylogenic* development of man's ideas of jurisprudence.

Other investigators have evolved different categories for describing the differences they have noted in aspects of moral growth, and such categorization does not normally differentiate between the acquisition of moral knowledge and moral feeling. Thus Kohlberg (1963) has isolated six stages which range from the obeying of rules to avoid punishment, through conventional role conformity, that is—the child conforms in order to avoid censure and feelings of guilt—to the highest form of morality, when conformity to his own standards enables the adolescent to avoid self-condemnation. Kohlberg's work and that of Kay (1969) provides evidence of the child's need to pass through definite developmental stages in relation to moral growth. Kay has described these stages as follows:

In the *first* stage children are prudential and authoritarian in their view of moral behaviour—that is, they are restrained from behaving in certain ways because they know that an authority figure says a certain act is wrong, and they may get caught. *Later* they apply the principle of reciprocity, when they don't want others to do to them what they are tempted to do themselves, and at this stage control by social sanction enters into consideration. *Next,* social approval is important: what would a child's friends say if they knew he had done a certain act? This attitude indicates that the child has now arrived at a self-concept. In the *final* stage a moral maturity is reached, which rests on personal sanctions: the child has developed a moral feeling that it is wrong to do certain things. Kay makes the point, however, that to an extent conscience-derived factors and sanctions which spring from religious ideas can be detected in some children at every stage of development. It can be questioned, however, whether 'conscience' is a suitable word to use for children in an early developmental stage, and whether Freud's term of 'social anxiety' (1930) might not be a better term to use.

One can, then (Kay, 1969), think of moral development taking place approximately in three stages: the first is an *amoral* stage, which involves hedonistic, egocentric and prudential considerations. The second is a *premoral* stage, which involves reciprocal and social considerations; children at this stage have developed an ego-ideal* which serves as a sanction. The third is the *moral* stage proper, when considerations are personal and independent, altruistic and responsible.

Although these stages of development have been described, no attempt has been made so far to say how or why moral *feelings* come about. Freud (1930) has suggested that the helplessness and the dependence of man on others makes him fear 'loss of love', and this is particularly so when a child is young. This fear engenders 'social anxiety', which is not a true conscience, and this is the force which motivates a child to forgo a desired possession or experience. For the young child the fear lies in being discovered. However, as the child grows the external threatening authority becomes internalized so that the Superego (chapter 2) feels the guilt associated with a tempting thought as soon as it is thought and so the child is 'found out' even before acting out (page 55). This is why an innocent child sometimes looks guilty when a wrongdoer in school is asked to own up: it might so easily have been the child himself who committed the misdemeanour, and the mere thought produces punishment in the form of guilt feelings from the Superego (page 55). Freud also considered that the child's need to identify with the parent of the opposite sex at the Oedipal stage of psychosexual development was instrumental in the formation of the Superego. So for Freud both the fear of loss of love—that is, 'social anxiety'—and the desire to take on the norms and values of the same-sexed parent, contribute to the development of the Superego. (These ideas of Freud are discussed more fully in chapter 2.) In one of the few remarks which Freud made about child rearing he states that the strength of the Superego has little to do with the severity of parental upbringing, but that innate constitutional factors—for example, whether a child is more or less prone to be anxious —combined with environmental factors and the resolution of the Oedipal situation, form the Superego. (Parental handling in relation to child personality characteristics is considered in chapter 8.) The idea that proneness to anxiety is, to an extent at least, a constitutional factor would be supported by Eysenck (1960), but he would also consider that a person with an introverted personality is likely to have a stronger conscience than a person with an extraverted personality, the degree of introversion-extraversion also being determined in part by constitutional factors.

As the child develops he will be able self-consciously to review his thoughts, and then the mere thought of acting in a prohibited way will produce feelings which would be aroused in anticipation of punishment had the forbidden deed been already committed; these feelings become sufficiently strong in most people to act as sanctions, so that moral feelings as well as moral knowledge become restraining forces. Some adults can never develop moral feelings, and in its acutest form the absence of all moral feeling results in psychopathic* behaviour, the psychopath having been defined as a 'moral imbecile'.

One can see then that moral knowledge, moral behaviour and moral feeling only come together when the child has fully developed, though it may be doubted whether even in mature adults these three aspects of morality co-exist in an integrated manner at all times.

In this chapter the *maturational* development of morality in the child has been considered, but in chapter 8 the forces which possibly guide social and moral development in different directions will be reviewed. However, it may be emphasized at this point that the more or less integrated adult way of looking at moral responsibility is quite incomprehensible to the young child, particularly a child entering primary school, and that in this area of psychological development, as in others discussed in this book, it is essential for adults to try to view life from the viewpoint of a child if they are to understand the children in their care.

(b) Social and emotional development

What precisely do we mean by social and emotional development, and what is involved in such development? The socially and emotionally mature person is a competent member of his society and before any child can reach this competence he has to learn many skills and habits. He has to learn how to differentiate between approved and disapproved behaviour, and he also has to learn both how to understand others and how to react appropriately to their behaviour. He finds that he feels guilt, love, anger and other emotions, and he learns that some of these feelings may be displayed and others must be controlled. The sanctions which operate to control and shape his behaviour change as he gets older, and as this occurs his awareness and appreciation of the world in which he lives become wider and keener. With increasing age he becomes more involved with other people; his feelings can be assailed more easily and his emotions aroused more readily by what people say and do. In comparison the baby who appears to be aware only of his own needs cannot be offended, and even though he may be very hungry he will only be aware of his acute need for food; he will not think malignly of the adults who seem to be denying him his need, whereas the eight-year-old who is thwarted will most likely feel resentment and hostility.

We will consider later (pages 147f.) how children learn with increasing understanding to interpret other people's behaviour, and also review in subsequent chapters how adult handling may affect children's development (chapter 8). In this chapter children's social and emotional development will be studied in rather more general terms; we shall be concerned with reviewing what is known about the development towards social and emotional maturity of children growing up in our culture, and also consider the various factors which influence this development.

Heredity and environment

When we look at the origin of the kind of social and emotional behaviour exhibited by any one child we have to take into account both the congenital and the environmental factors which influence behaviour. On pages 77f. the congenital influences on temperament are reviewed; in any consideration of social behaviour assumptions must not be made that only the environment shapes behaviour. Thomas, Chess and Birch (1968), in their longitudinal study of children (page 81), have observed that in the first few weeks of life children show an individuality in temperament which seems to be independent of parental handling and personality. They also observed that this individuality persists over the years. Temperamental characteristics are modified by the influences of home, school and society generally, but such environmental influences play upon unique material and so produce unique effects.

Consideration of these influences involves separating not only early experiences from later experiences, but also appreciating that social influence may well be a two-way process—that is, that the child may influence the parents as well as the parents influencing the child. Bell (1968) makes the point that a correlation between parent and child behaviour only indicates that a relationship exists, it does not show the direction of the relationship; and too often the assumption is made that the influence can only be directional—that is, from parent to child. In chapter 8 (page 192) we discuss the question of how different children in the same family may each evoke different behaviour towards them from their parents, and there seems little doubt that the characteristics of any one child have some effect on the behaviour of the adults, both parents and teachers, with whom he has to do, and this in turn affects the child; extremely assertive children, for example, will evoke responses from adults which are normally unusual for them. Another example is provided by children who are primarily interested in material things and in being active; such children are not as susceptible to social training as those who are more concerned about their relationship with other people and who are more desirous of pleasing others. That this may well be a congenital factor is discussed by Scarr (1965), who comments on children's differential social responsiveness and sociability from an early age.

The processes of emotional development.

The direction which socialization and the development,of the emotions takes in any one child will, then, be dependent at least in part on the child's innate temperament, and also on the effects on others of his temperament, as expressed in his behaviour. What, however, is the usual process of this development? It has been suggested that emotions are exhibited when a human or an animal moves towards something which is joyful and away from something which is hurtful, and when, subjectively, feelings are involved. Very small babies exhibit 'emotions' but most psychologists prefer to describe such behaviour as 'undifferentiated excitement'. Both the psychoanalytic and the behaviourist schools presume that certain specific emotions exist at birth, but all one can say with certainty is that a small baby's emotions are related to his needs, and that definable emotions cannot really be said to be established before three months of age. Bridges (1932), who was one of the first psychologists to observe emotional growth, considered that such development takes place in three ways:
  (1) definable emotions differentiate from undefinable excitement;
  (2) the expression which emotions take changes slowly as the child develops mental and physical skills for expressing feeling, and
  (3) differing situations are capable of arousing emotional responses at different ages.
After three months of age a baby can express delight and anger in relation to feeding, and he becomes increasingly more vocal in expressing his emotions instead of expressing them with a variety of bodily movements. Fear of strangers begins to develop at about six months. It has been suggested that by about this age a child has established a social relationship with the people who look after him regularly, and as soon as he is able to recognize these people and differentiate them from strangers, then fear of strangers begins (Scott, 1962). This fear can last a considerable time; babies over six months of age who cry in their mother's absence are too often thought to be 'making a fuss', but their distress may well be as acute as it appears to be to sensitive adults.

By eight months or so a child can exhibit reciprocal affection, and by thirteen months of age spontaneous affection. From this time onwards anger at being disappointed, affection for other children, and temper tantrums when things don't go right for him can all be displayed. Although a child of eighteen months may well show his annoyance with other children by hitting and pulling, there is very little hostility in his actions. By this age too he is likely to be jealous if the occasion warrants it. It is often particularly difficult for parents to understand why an older child should be jealous of a new baby when even more attention than usual is paid to the older child in order not to make him feel neglected; but such a child's limited appreciation of the world around him—that is, his egocentric and percept-centred view of the world (pages 104f.)—implies that he can only understand what is important to him and what he can perceive; and what he perceives at any one moment in time is that another child is receiving attention. This is because only a very much older child can take the past into consideration when making evaluations of the present, and, therefore, feelings of jealousy will inevitably arise between children in a family, however much the parents try to allay such feelings; nevertheless every effort should be made to minimize the occasions when such feelings may occur.

We do not know certainly at what age and at what stage children can think about their own feelings, though Jersild (1955) observes that children seldom mention before adolescence that they wish they could learn to cope with their emotional difficulties. Biber and Lewis (1949) have suggested that small children use language more to express ideas than to express feelings, and it is possible that before seven or eight years of age the affective and cognitive aspects of experience are not fully differentiated. Certainly Wood (1968) found that when she asked children under thirteen years of age to describe others they seldom mentioned how they felt about other people, but at fourteen years of age children were remarkably more willing to discuss the feelings evoked in them by other people. It is possible that children develop cognitively more rapidly than they do affectively (page 151) or, alternatively, that in our Western culture they feel themselves to be prevented for subtle reasons from expressing their feelings before they are about fourteen years of age.

Variety of emotions experienced

By the time a child is two years of age he can *experience* a large range of emotions, although he may not be able to reflect on these emotions. It is now established that at all ages children differ very much in the amount of emotion, including fear, that they can experience, and many happenings, such as hearing a loud noise, or being introduced to new and strange objects or situations can arouse fears when the child is alone or with strangers, but not when he is with a familiar adult. Fear of the dark and of being left alone are very evident by the end of the second year.

It is difficult to differentiate anxiety from fear in a small child, anxiety being a 'painful unease of mind concerning impending or anticipated ill' (Jersild, 1955). The fear of a dark room, for example, is a fear of what the dark holds, not of the darkness itself; new situations too can produce an acute feeling of 'unease'. Slater (1939) has shown how children new to a nursery school are apprehensive at first, and on page 170 the many anxieties which the majority of five-year-olds experience when they first start school are discussed. Obviously many such fears are overcome in the normal process of growth, but it is difficult for adults adequately to assess such feelings, and the degree of emotion revealed by children is probably only a poor indication of their true feelings of fear and anger, for we possibly make it difficult for children to express their feelings freely in other ways (page 151).

Children's fears obviously change with increasing age; a junior child's greater experience of life makes him more susceptible to anxieties which are necessarily unknown to the younger child. At this age there seems also to be some discrepancy between conceptual fears and external danger; what children fear is not necessarily a repetition of what may already have happened to them, but they fear something imagined. The older a child gets the more anxieties replace fears; older children report fears of being ridiculed, of loss of prestige, of inadequacy and of failure in school (Jersild, 1955). Much anxiety too is caused by children's relationships with their parents. As the pre-adolescent begins to feel himself to be critical of his parents, but does not yet feel free to express this criticism (page 150), and as he also begins to feel that his parents are more critical of him, the previously happy relationship between himself and his parents appears to be threatened, and this produces feelings of anxiety which the younger child cannot experience.

Up to ten years of age a child mostly seems to lead a happy and balanced life: he is approaching the climax of the 'latency period', as Freud termed it, during which period neither the earlier disturbing pregenital drives, nor the even more disturbing later genital drives, affect his emotions and his attitude to life (pages 53f.). At twelve years of age this balance is beginning to be upset. Previous physiological changes have been largely changes in growth only: now hormonal sex changes occur which have their counterpart in the changes which occur in emotional feelings and social attitudes. These changes cause some anxieties, and new feelings of insecurity arise from an inevitable greater knowledge of himself and of other people, but the twelve-year-old still tends to retain the poise and social charm of his earlier years. However, he is beginning to discover himself and needs to understand his experiences, but it appears that not until he is about fourteen years of age can the young adolescent fully reflect on his feelings.

Much has been written about a child's need for love, but little about its ability to give love. The ability to give and feel affection is largely dependent on the amount of affection a child receives, particularly in the first months and years of his life. Many studies have shown the importance of receiving warmth and love, and the anxieties, depressions and general emotional impoverishment which follow when children are denied the experience of such affection. The development of feelings of affection has largely been studied in the negative; children who have been deprived of such affection have been observed, and the early work of Bowlby (1944) and others appeared to indicate that 'maternal deprivation' had powerful and unfortunate effects on the developing personality. (The effects of depriving experiences are reviewed in some detail in chapter 2, page 99.) However, later work has shown that the long-term effects may not be as disastrous as earlier workers had indicated, and that, in any case, the term 'maternal deprivation' could cover such a wide range of experiences over a long period of a child's life that it is a somewhat meaningless term by which to describe such experiences. What one can say is that deprivation of a certain kind and of a certain quality must occur at certain stages and last for particular periods for it to have a *lasting* effect. Harlow (1962), in a charming but also somewhat pathetic article, has described his work at Wisconsin University with rhesus monkeys, with whom it has been possible experimentally to set up maternal-deprivation situations of various kinds. He has found that unmothered infants, once adult, become 'helpless, hopeless, heartless mothers, devoid, or almost devoid, of any maternal feeling'. It would not be wise to deduce exclusively from this work that all humans who do not experience consistent mothering with the same person, or who are cared for physically but neglected emotionally, inevitably become bad parents; but it seems probable that in order to develop fully and spontaneously, both cognitively and affectively, all but the most unusual children must experience a loving, warm and consistent relationship with a mother or a mother substitute. A close and consistent relationship with a group of peers, though, has been found both by students of animal behaviour (Harlow, 1962) and by observers of human children (Faigin, 1958; Anna Freud and Sophie Dann, 1951) to be a good, though by no means totally adequate, substitute for consistent and warm mothering. One must say also that little is known of children who have had acutely depriving experiences but who nevertheless have appeared to grow up to become normal, loving persons.

  It has been mentioned earlier that the child of eighteen months of age or so will show his displeasure if he is frustrated, but that any attacks he makes against other children are not hostile in intent. Nevertheless, as his feelings develop and as they express themselves in actions, he must learn, at least in our culture, to control such actions if they are likely to hurt others. The young child is mostly angry because *things* don't behave as he wants them to, and there are consequently frequent occasions when he feels frustrated. However, by the time a child is about eleven years of age most angry feelings are engendered not by frustrating objects but by people. Being teased, unfairness, siblings taking their property, people lying to them, sarcasm and bossiness, all these are factors which make the pre-adolescent angry. Children seem to vary greatly in the amount of frustration, leading to aggression, which they are able to tolerate.

  In addition to learning about his feelings and how to control and display their expression, the young child has to learn how to interpret other people's feelings. Probably a quite young child can differentiate between a pleased and an angry voice, but the junior child in play with others learns from the epithets applied to him by other children whether they feel friendly or hostile towards him. He becomes aware how acceptable he is to them, and so his individuality emerges as he forms a picture of himself through interaction with others. It is not suggested that this is in any way a conscious appraisal, but it *is* suggested that constant interaction with adults and with other children provides opportunities for adjustment of behaviour in order to try to please others. Of course some children are curiously insensitive to the feelings of others, and they are, consequently, much more difficult to socialize (pages 139f.).

The processes of social development

Many writers, Mead (1934) and Horney (1950) among others, have emphasized the importance of the development of the self in social relationships. It is considered most probable that the very young baby has no clear differentiation between himself and objects and people around him, and that learning to differentiate himself from others could be said to be the child's first social act. Piaget suggests that the child under two years of age has difficulty in establishing a limit between himself and the outside world. Slowly differentiation takes place, and as this happens other 'significant' people become important to him. According to Sullivan (1947) the self is made up of 'reflected appraisals', the origins of the self being in the hands of 'significant' persons, such as his mother and others who are intimately connected with the child. Sullivan further suggests that there is a close relationship between attitudes towards the self and attitudes towards others, and the clinical work of Rogers (1951) and others seems to support this view. If the predominant attitude towards the child from people who are important to him is one of hostility and disapproval, then this may well become his attitude towards himself and towards the world. Trasler (1967) has stressed that the socialization process implies both relating to people *and* learning modes of behaviour, and therefore social and emotional development progress hand in hand.

 Social learning is different in kind from the learning of skills, or learning by rote, or learning to solve problems. The young child has to learn by a process of association which deeply involves his emotions; he has to learn to associate parental disapproval with certain types of behaviour, and his emotions are evoked because he feels unhappy if his parents show their disapproval, whether by physical punishment, or verbally, or by their attitude towards him. It has been suggested that middle-class parents in order to discipline their children sometimes exploit both the child's need for, and dependence on, his parents, and also the exclusive relationship which he has with them. There is some evidence, however, which will be discussed later, to show (page 196) that this way of socializing a child is not as effective as had previously been thought.

 It is certain, however, that the socialization process starts in the family, and through the child's relationship with his parents. It seems that in our efforts to train children to be acceptable members of our society we may succeed in making them feel over-anxious and guilty at the thought of acting in an unacceptable way. Children don't always anticipate punishment, nor do they necessarily fear it, but they become worried and uneasy when contemplating carrying out a disapproved act (page 53). The development of such feelings inhibiting disapproved actions rests in part at least on the child's dependence on his parents, and on his desire to please them. In chapter 8 the effects of rewards and punishment in 'shaping' behaviour are considered.

Although socialization of the small child starts in the family and through his relationship with his parents, the role of the peer group soon begins to be influential and we have already considered this influence in relation to the formation of the self-concept. Certainly too social development takes place increasingly through a child's interaction with other children, and for this reason the social growth of children is often studied through observing them at play. The extent to which children interact with one another, and the quality of their interaction, indicates how far they have developed socially. The role of play in the development of children will be considered later (chapter 6). Here we will only look at play as a socializing agent.

Under two years of age or so a child's ability to relate socially with others of its age comes to little more than an awareness of other children. Because the young child has not differentiated himself fully from others he cannot co-operate in play, and the beginnings of co-operative play are, therefore, an important landmark in social development. However, co-operation obviously cannot take place until communication can be established, and this depends, at least for children who are relative strangers to one another, on the development of speech. Psychologists have observed a number of earlier play stages, which indicate an increasing awareness with increasing age of other children. Indeed, very young children, under a year, look at and smile at other children, and babies enjoy games, such as 'peep-bo', which means that they are already engaging in a form of social play. An interest in the activities of other children leads successively to 'looking-on' play, then to 'parallel' play and then to 'associative' play (page 160) before true co-operation can begin. This is relatively rare under three years of age, indeed most psychologists would say that children do not co-operate usually under five years of age, and Piaget considers that only after seven or eight do children play truly co-operatively, though, as described in chapter 6, there are special exceptions. Playing with others means that children learn to share toys and they learn also, regrettably, to compete with others.

As the child enters junior-school age play becomes more complex and later turns into the playing of games. With better co-operation, complex schemes can be organized, and these are influenced by what children read and by what they see on TV. It is unfortunately true but inevitable that the usually dominant and submissive children fill the respective roles in such games which their temperament dictates, and the responsive behaviour of other children will reinforce them in these respective roles. It is possible that through subtle social influences of this kind initial temperamental differences between children are crystallized to form the major personality differences we note among adults. It is difficult to know how adults can influence the role-taking of children in games without spoiling the children's enjoyment and without killing spontaneity.

The emphasis on games and on group activities implies that children become interested in the rules by which they play, and learning about rules is part of their moral development (pages 135 and 161), but it is also the beginning of their understanding of the need for order and for regularity in social life.

One of the social functions of play is not only to help the child to learn how to co-operate with others, but also to enable him to act out social roles. Play is, in this respect, a kind of 'trial run', whereby children can practise the behaviour of adults whom they observe, whether they are parents, or other adults whom they may admire, or whom they may even fear. For this reason playing at being 'mothers and fathers', or driving an engine or a car, being a cowboy, a policeman or a nurse are favourite and recurring themes. We consider in chapter 6 (page 161) what additional significance such playing may have, but the observation of children at play when they are taking the roles of adult persons leaves little doubt of the importance in social development of such behaviour.

Other features of social development which are closely bound to emotional development are: learning to interpret other people's feelings; developing empathy for others, and also understanding the relationships which people have to one another, whether in the family or in social and work life. The development of social awareness, together with a consideration of how children learn to understand the behaviour and intentions of others, is considered separately, and in some detail, on pages 147f.

Adolescence is an age stage which, more than any other, at times presents difficulties both for the adolescents themselves and for the adults who are in contact with them; it is discussed on page 187. Emotional and social development in adolescence is different in kind from such development in earlier years. The hormonal changes which have taken place or are taking place with the younger adolescent produce changes also in emotional feelings, and have their counterpart in social behaviour.

The adolescent is much more self-aware, and much more aware too of the impact which other people's personalities make on them, than is the younger child. In part at least this increased awareness accounts for the moodiness of which adults so often complain. All aspects of the adolescent's emotional life are now intensified: sexual feelings become strong, localized and directed heterosexually at another young person, though in early adolescence, especially among girls, homosexual interest in a somewhat older young person is not unusual. The adolescent's need for social activities outside the home increases, and it becomes most important for him to feel that he belongs to a peer group. Now the 'significant' persons are not so much his parents but his contemporaries, and he needs *their* approval. When at adolescence young people begin to have some understanding of national and world problems their sense of idealism is offended, and they begin to be aware for the first time of how much suffering is being experienced by other humans. The desire to help others can be very strong, and this, coupled with an impatience with the ordinary machinery of political and social change, is, partly at least, responsible for adolescent rebellion. In addition, because the adolescent is aware of himself in a way in which the junior child is, seemingly, not aware, he has an ability to reflect on his own feelings, and this new level of self-consciousness makes him, socially and emotionally, a different kind of human being from the kind of being he was when he was younger. Just as the three-year-old's temper tantrum is an assertion of his new-found *self* now differentiated from the rest of the world, so the adolescent's rebellion is an assertion of his new-found *self-consciousness*, his awareness of himself as a personality. It is often difficult for parents to adjust their behaviour to meet the behaviour of an almost different human being, and when the adolescent's way of behaving forces such an adjustment, it is often resented by parents. In addition, many parents, feeling so acutely their responsibility for the children who belong to them, are not infrequently frightened by the apparent loss of control they experience. Often, too, acute anxiety is felt both by thoughtful and sensitive adolescents and by their parents at the inability to communicate with one another at this stage.

The modern adolescent has, it seems, many more problems in adjusting emotionally to his maturity than his parents had a generation ago. Our society is even more confused now in the values it propagates (page 134) than it was in the period before 1939. Additionally, the more modern method of primary-school teaching, which has done away with serried ranks of small children sitting in a school room, and has substituted group and individual teaching, has as its aim the encouragement of initiative, independence and creativity. Unfortunately many adults who enjoy seeing such 'liberated' junior children, do not like dealing with equally liberated, but much more verbal and critical, adolescents. They would like to see the pleasant, curious, intelligent child change overnight into an equally pleasant, intelligent and mature adult, but the emotional and social adjustments which have to be made by developing adolescents in our society cannot be made easily or suddenly.

(c) The development of the child's ability to understand another person

Kelly (1955) has pointed out that we are not the victims of our history, but only of our construction of that history; what influences us is not so much what actually happens to us, but how we *interpret such happenings*. We are also constantly making interpretations of other people's *behaviour*, and indeed, the ability to make such interpretations reasonably accurately is a necessary social skill. However, until relatively recently little attention had been paid to how such causal inferences are learned, nor have we known much about how children perceive other people, nor how they interpret behaviour at different ages. An adult who decides to punish a child, or who decides to abstain from punishing him, because either way he hopes to teach the child something, cannot be sure that the child will construe his action as he, the adult, wishes it to be construed (page 190). It would seem of prime importance, therefore, that adults should try to know how children of different ages are likely to interpret the actions of adults, and how the children understand them as persons. The fluent way in which quite young children use words misleads adults into thinking that they have a comprehension of concepts and an understanding of persons which is not usually warranted.

Infants first have to become aware of the existence of other persons, for although one cannot know for certain, it is doubtful whether the very young baby is aware of his own separate identity. However, from a relatively early age (that is, from about six to eight weeks of age) the human voice and the human face evoke greater interest in infants than other sounds and sights (Bühler, 1933; Fantz, 1961), but it is not until the baby is about eight months old that he will pay some attention to another child placed side by side with him in a cot. Social awareness proper only begins when, at about fourteen months of age, a child engaged in solitary play will take note of another child, particularly if that other child has a toy with which he himself wishes to play! Effective social *responsiveness* does not come about until about two years of age, though even at this age play is largely solitary (chapters 2 and 7). A child of this age is aware of his own sex, though it is not until he is three years old that he is aware of the different social roles which distinguish the sexes.

As the opportunities for social interaction increase with increasing maturity so children begin to understand that other people are both similar and different from themselves with regard to sex, age and social roles. Piaget (1929) has referred to the young child's conception of his position in the world as absolute; his notion of causality is often related to his own behaviour, such as when a young child describes the apparent movement of the moon, as he walks along, as 'following me' (chapter 4). This egocentrism remains to a greater or lesser extent throughout the 'intuitive thought' period (chapter 4), and it limits the child's understanding of others to those situations where definite 'sign stimuli' are present; for example Murphy (1937) noted that children of three years of age were able to feel sympathy for another child who had incurred an accident, but only if that child were bandaged! Gage, Leavitt and Stone (1956) refer in their work to an 'assumption of similarity' which is made by young children when assessing others: by this they mean that a child will assess how another child feels by what he himself would feel, rather than what that particular child may actually be feeling. Indeed, it would seem from more recent work that the ability to feel true empathy is not developed until relatively late.

In an interesting investigation into children's understanding of facial expressions Honkavaara (1961) found that children learn first to understand *actions* and then *expressions*, so that they understand the significance of laughing or crying before they recognize a happy or sad expression; Frijda and Philipzorn (1963) found similarly that movements and actions rather than expressions convey emotional meaning to a child under six years of age. It is only when a facial expression is accompanied by the appropriate action or by definite signs, such as a bandage, or situational cues which are well understood, that children under this age can understand emotional expressions. We can see, therefore, that young children do not gauge the feelings of other people by their facial expression, as adults largely do, but that the ability to understand facial expressions and relate these to feelings is learned, presumably, by associating meaningful action with the coincident expression.

What are children's concepts about other people, and what characteristics are important to them? When children are asked to describe other people, the words and phrases used by them are indicative of, and limited by, three factors:

(1) the importance to them of certain personality characteristics in the people they describe,

(2) their ability to understand such characteristics, and

(3) the range of their vocabulary.

In most investigations into children's person-perception these three variables have not been clearly differentiated by the experimenters, but some conclusions can, nevertheless, be drawn about the satisfactions in interpersonal relationships sought by children of different ages, and also about their ability to understand other people.

The outcome of investigations of children's ideas about their parents has been somewhat contradictory; but Koppitz (1957) suggests that such contradictory findings can be explained if it is assumed that attitudes formed early in life towards other people are fairly enduring; a strong perceptual 'set' is built up which appreciation of real facts may be unable to overcome. It would seem also that sex-identification, sexual jealousies, familiarity, and particularly the mother's nurturant qualities, play an important part in children's feelings for their parents, apart from what realistic assessment they may be able to make of their parents' personality characteristics. Kagan (1956) reports that the same-sex parent is usually considered by children under ten years of age to be the less benevolent and more frustrating, and the opposite-sex parent is usually rated the higher in 'disposition and character'. Despite this most of the children in this study regardless of sex expressed a *preference* for their mother, but it was clear that a majority of them wished to *resemble* the parent of their own sex. Hawkes and Pease (1962) found that children between five and twelve years of age tended to evaluate parents by comparison of the fairness of the treatment they received from them with that received by their friends from their parents. Children of this age also long for admirable traits in their parents (Sowers,

1937). Five- and six-year-olds in a study by Wood (1968) commented frequently on their parents' willingness to play with them; the seven- to nine year-olds' comments also indicated that they found satisfaction in joint activities and a happy relationship with their parents; children of the ten- to twelve-year age group spoke less of joint activities, but referred to the kind of discipline parents upheld; by thirteen years of age the term 'understanding' was used, and helpfulness of parents to the child now again became important in descriptions of them. It seems that parental unselfishness and help with school work and with hobbies, and the taking of an interest in the child generally are all appreciated and regarded as valued characteristics in parents. In fact at this age (thirteen) a good parent-child relationship seems particularly important to the child; and the needs which influence younger children's assessment of parental characteristics no longer stand so much in the way of relatively realistic evaluations being made, with one exception: in this particular study children of thirteen years of age were *less critical of others* than any other age group, either younger or older. The five- and six-year-olds particularly commented on their dislike of people who shout; the middle age-group also referred to their dislike of shouting, but commented too on unfairness, bad temper and excessive strictness; children of fourteen and fifteen spoke of sarcasm, selfishness, bad temper, moodiness and unhelpfulness as parental characteristics which they particularly disliked. However, the thirteen-year-olds were quite uncritical. It is possible that at this age children are still very bound by parental standards, and although the peer group is becoming increasingly important, the two groups —parental and peer—have different value systems, and it may be that a child of thirteen is generally insufficiently sure of his peer-group membership to be critical of parents. It is also possible that, since our culture disapproves of the direct expression of dislike, children of late junior age and those of pre-adolescence are too bound by fear of disapproval to contravene this norm. Older children, having developed greater emotional independence, are possibly more free to express negative feelings, and younger children are not sufficiently aware of the cultural restriction to be hindered by it.

How do children learn to appreciate the personality characteristics of others, bearing in mind the complexities involved in the study of adult person-perception? In a child's perception of persons, cognitive, social and emotional development interact, for the child's needs in part at least dictate what he will note about other people's characteristics. His social relationships determine his contacts with others, and the increase in cognitive development with age is accompanied by increasingly 'free' thought (in the Piagetian sense) regardless of present perceptual information. Wood (1968) investigated cross-sectionally the ability of children from five to fifteen years of age to understand other persons' characteristics. Her findings regarding the manner in which this ability develops can be seen in Piagetian terms. Thus children under seven years of age are egocentric and percept-centred (chapter 4), and people were described largely in terms of their outward appearance—that is, their dress—and also by their names and their helpfulness to the child. List-like descriptions were also given of other people's activities. It seems that at this age persons and objects are scarcely significantly differentiated, for no feelings about the persons being described enter into their evaluations. Livesley and Bromley (1967) found that when testing children under seven years of age 50 per cent of the statements made about other people dealt with their appearance, identity, possessions and family, as well as including some simple evaluations. They comment that a seven-year-old's concept of another's personality seems to include persons and animals attached to the described person, as well as his environment and his possessions. Many teachers will be familiar with this kind of description: 'I used to like her, but I don't now because her dog bit me!'

Wood (1968) found that by nine years of age children commented more on personal physical characteristics, as opposed to dress, and they understood that people vary in mood and exhibit different traits at different times. At this age people were no longer seen as if they were objects; also a person's behaviour was described *as if* children were aware that it is an indication of his personality, but few conclusions were drawn about behaviour as an indicator of underlying personality characteristics. Children in this age group —seven to nine years of age—are less dominated by a percept-centred view of life, and they are also less egocentric. However, such children still referred frequently in this study to the help they received from others as an indication of other people's personality characteristics, but very few comments referred to the feelings which other people aroused in them. Biber and Lewis (1949) have observed that children at least up to nine years of age use language to express ideas and not feelings. It might be profitable to reflect how much this could be due to our educational system which stresses the development of the intellect but seems curiously unconcerned in helping children to learn to cope with their feelings. In Wood's study (1968) the ten- to twelve-year-olds talked of the personal attractiveness of described people, rather than about less personal features, such as clothing worn by them; they referred to the described person's attitude to others and not only towards themselves as younger children did; only occasionally did children of this age speak about the feelings which other people evoked in them. By thirteen years of age there was a marked change in emphasis when describing people: children spoke twice as frequently as the ten- to twelve-year-olds about the feelings they had for other people. At this age, and in this study, the children were able to comment on how people are able to understand other people's behaviour, and they understood the relationship between personality attributes and behaviour. Indeed, the thirteen-year-olds' descriptions were not dissimilar to those of the fifteen-year-olds in sophistication of words used and in the range of attributes described, but they differed remarkably in expressing very little criticism of others, to which reference has already been made. However, they were aware of their parents' criticism of them, while also appreciating good parental qualities.

At fifteen children appeared to be much more self-critical, and also more critical of others, including parents. Jones (1943) has referred to a growing and critical self-awareness at this period, and this awareness extends seemingly to other persons too.

Understanding other people's personality characteristics is linked to an understanding of psychological causality—that is, an understanding of the *motives* which govern the behaviour of other people. Piaget has investigated children's conception of physical causality (chapters 2 and 4), but *psychological* causality has been relatively little investigated. Piaget asked such questions as: 'Why do the clouds move?', but it seems equally important to obtain answers from children to such questions as: 'Why was she angry with him?' Since as adults we are constantly making inferences about the causes of other people's behaviour, it seems important not only to know how the ability to make such inferences more or less correctly develops, but also to know what inferences about other people's behaviour children of different ages are able to make, so that we can the better understand their view of the world.

Whiteman (1965) investigated children's conception of psychological causality, comparing two groups aged five and six, and eight and nine years of age respectively. He found a greater difference between the two groups in their 'formulations of psychological causality' than in their formulations of physical causality. Also Laurendeau and Pinard (1962) had already noted a pronounced change at seven years of age in the explanations given for physical causality. One is justified in assuming that processes similar to those affecting the development of an understanding of physical causality also affect the development of an understanding of psychological causality.

Growth in the development of moral judgement can also be linked to advances in understanding psychological causality; Piaget (pages 135f.), in discussing the basis for moral judgements in children under seven years of age, has referred to their 'objective morality', which is that a child renders judgements which are based on the *consequences* of an act with little regard for the *motives* of the actor, and similarly the external, the overt behaviour of others, rather than their purposes and intentions, is the basis for judgement of behaviour by children under seven years of age. Williams (in Wilson, Williams and Sugarman, 1967) has suggested that the child under seven may have difficulty in separating ends and means, so that there is an undue concentration by him on means. To refer, therefore, largely to people's overt behaviour, without being able to infer intentions, and to concentrate on the observable and on the means, rather than on the motivation and the end, is consistent with Piaget's distinction between the way the child under eight years of age and the child over eight (pages 135f.) view moral behaviour. Piaget comments on the major change with age which occurs in the child's thought processes at about seven years of age when he is able to conceptualize conservation of a substance, despite appearances to the contrary (chapter 2). This is consistent with Whiteman's findings (1965), and also with those of Wood (1968), in a study in which she investigated the development of psychological causality in children between five and fifteen years of age. Children viewed films in which the behaviour of the actors could be interpreted in either simple or in sophisticated terms. It appeared from her evidence that the child under seven is able to draw on his experience of life to link observable means to an observable end, but that he is not capable, by and large, of making inferences about behaviour, feelings, thoughts, etc., which lie outside the *immediate* field of observation.

The increased use of inferences and deductions in explaining behaviour, which takes place from seven or eight years of age onwards, seems to be closely related to the child's increasing cognitive ability to synthesize experiences, rather than, as at an earlier age, simply to see separate experiences in juxtaposition to one another. Piaget has also noted that children at this stage of moral development will base moral judgements on what is observable or measurable (page 136); the same tendency to evaluate motives for everyday behaviour, as opposed to behaviour with moral connotations, was noted when younger children in Wood's study were asked why actors in the films shown behaved as they did. Between seven and eleven years of age the child gains the ability to appreciate that a variety of actions may culminate in the same result, and this seems to enable him also to realize that one action can be seen to have originated from a number of possible causes. Also the child's increasingly accurate concept of time makes it possible for him to look into the past for reasons for any particular piece of behaviour which he is observing. However, until twelve years of age or so the child still seems very concerned with notions of first-hand reality, so that concrete and observable events are uppermost in claiming his attention.

Flavell (1963) has suggested that for cognitive functioning there is a definite difference between Piaget's second and third stage of thought development, in that representational thought at twelve years of age can now be concerned with the *possible* instead of only the *actual* (chapter 4). It would appear from work on person-perception in children that, though this release from actuality is a gradual affair, it reaches an important point at thirteen years of age when the attempt to understand behaviour includes all kinds of inference, conjecture and speculation. By thirteen children's interests are focused on the meaning of other people's behaviour; they make deductions from such behaviour, and they seem more concerned with purposes and intentions than in merely noting what people actually do. It would thus appear that not until early adolescence is the child sufficiently released from the influences of the perceptual world to be able to live in a world of the possible and the future, rather than in a world of the actual and the present.

A striking example of the changing view which children of different ages may take of the same piece of behaviour was provided by noting children's observations on an episode in a film shown by Wood (1968). A boy was depicted in one silent film as showing off at a party. He performed several tricks, during one of which he upset a jug of fruit juice, and his hostess was cross with him. At the end of the four-minute film—some time after the above episode was shown—she is seen saying 'good-bye' to him rather sadly. When the children under seven years of age were asked why she was sad they said: 'Because he is going home', which was the last depicted episode in the film. Most of the eleven-year-olds said that she was sorry she had been cross with him; to children of this age group the earlier episode of the spilling of the juice could be seen as being related to the later expression of sadness. However, the majority of the fifteen-year-olds said that the girl was sorry for the *boy* for having made a fool of himself by showing off. Not only are children of this age able to evaluate behaviour in terms of delayed consequences and antecedent happenings, which younger children apparently find difficult to do, but they can understand the empathy which one person can have for another.

It is, of course, uncertain in work of this kind, which like Piaget's work makes use of children's verbal responses in reply to adult questioning, how much a child's increasing linguistic ability contributes to an apparent increase in his understanding. Not only does the child's ability to use and understand language grow with increasing age, but there is evidence that children actually *use* language age-specifically. For example, Davis (1937) has shown that children up to ten years of age tend to avoid terms with unpleasant connotations, and Richardson, Dornbusch and Hastor (1960) also state that children usually find it more acceptable to express positive rather than negative evaluations of others, though we have seen that in one study at least (page 150) both young children and adolescents seem to have been less restricted in their criticism of other than children of junior and preadolescent age. Regarding the actual use of language, Wood (1968) found that a good verbal ability did not necessarily help a child to describe people better, and an examination of the actual words used by the children in this study indicated that when a child had understanding he was able to express it in quite simple terms.

The methodological problems involved in undertaking valid studies of the kind which have been reviewed have by no means been adequately solved, since most studies have relied on eliciting verbal responses from children in reply to verbal questioning by adults. However, the findings of studies which have used different techniques (Witkin, Dyke, Paterson, Goodenough and Karp 1962; Jackson, 1952) by and large support those which have relied entirely on verbal questioning and replies. One can, therefore, suggest that it is not necessarily the limitations in language ability which prevent the younger child from expressing understanding, but that understanding is probably limited to what is actually expressed.

Piaget's work has shown how different *qualitatively* a child's thought is from adult thought, and work on children's person-perception indicates that this qualitative difference exists also in their comprehension of behaviour and personality. The implications of this are no less important for parents and teachers than the pedagogic implications inherent in our understanding of cognitive development. Indeed, in view of the value to human beings of good interpersonal relationships it is perhaps of even greater importance for adults to make the imaginative leap required to understand children's views of other people than to understand their cognitive functioning. Presumably those people who are 'good' with children have the ability to make this leap without difficulty.

NOTE The developmental aspect of the child's ability to understand other people has been considered in more detail than other aspects of developmental psychology because the subject is somewhat neglected as a research topic. It is not, therefore, easy to find references to it in other texts. However, a recent book by Livesley and Bromley referred to under 'Further Reading' has largely repaired this omission.

FURTHER READING

WILSON, J., N. WILLIAMS AND B. SUGARMAN: *An Introduction to Moral Education* (Penguin Books, Harmondsworth, 1968).

KAY, W.: *Moral Development: A Psychological Study of Moral Growth from Childhood to Adolescence* (Allen and Unwin, London, 1969).

DANZIGER, K.: *Socialization* (Penguin Books, Harmondsworth, 1971).

SCHAFFER, H. R.: *The Growth of Sociability* (Penguin Books, Harmondsworth, 1971).

GRAHAM, D.: *Moral Learning and Development: Theory and Research* (Batsford, London, 1972).

LIVESLEY, W. J. AND D. B. BROMLEY: *Person Perception in Childhood and Adolescence* (Wiley, London, 1973).

6

Play

Millar (1968) has defined play as 'behaviour which, to the observer, appears to be neither the reasonable result of a plan nor out of the person's control'. It is a pity that the word 'play' conjures up ideas of useless activity and carries with it overtones of disapproval. So often parents ask a child in the primary school: 'What did you do in school today?' and the answer not infrequently is: 'We played.' Many parents still feel that the child can play at home, but school is the place for work. However, for the young child there is little difference between work and play, so that when parents ask this question, as so many seem to do, and the child replies that he spent the day playing, this does not mean that he has learned nothing, nor that work, in the sense in which parents may think of 'work', has not been done. Piaget (1924) suggests that for the young child under seven years of age 'play cannot be opposed to reality, because in both cases belief is arbitrary and pretty much destitute of logical reasons. Play is a reality which the child is disposed to believe in when by himself, just as reality is a game at which he is willing to play with the adult and anyone else who believes in it.'

For the young child play activity is of enormous importance; indeed, playing and taking part in games are even for the older child of great value, though Piaget (1951) thinks of games as an activity different in kind from playing. Many of the young child's experiences of the world, of people, and of things, come to him during an impressionable period of his life through play activities.

Philosophers have been interested in elaborating theories of play, for it seemed necessary to account for the apparently purposeless behaviour of both young animals and young humans. Today we know that play is for the young child a proving ground for the serious experiences of life which come later, and we know that it has many important functions in the development of the child. Indeed, it is difficult to name any part of the developmental process which is not helped by play activities. 'Practically every form of psychological activity is initially enacted in play' (Piaget, 1969). Experimental work with animals and observational work with children who have been prevented for whatever reasons from playing with other infants and/or with materials of various kinds, show that such children and animals have difficulties in their social relationships and are also usually retarded intellectually. However, one has to remember, particularly in relation to grossly deprived children, that so many factors in their lives may add to the total picture of retardation that the absence of play facilities may be only one of these.

The exact function of play varies, of course, with the age of the child. The baby feeling a wooden cube with hands and mouth; the toddler building a small tower with three or four cubes; the older child trying to get as many cubes as possible on top of one another; these are all apparently merely playing with cubes, but the exploration in which they are engaged is different for each child. The baby is finding out about shapes, learning to co-ordinate what he sees with what he feels; the toddler is exploring how cubes can be used and so learning to manipulate objects in his environment; and the older child may be attempting to build something which is his own height, and in this way using the cubes to see what his own height looks like—he is learning something about measurement and something about himself. Again, the fantasies which are worked out through imaginative play will vary according to the needs of the child at a particular age; the small child may be establishing his relationship within the family, and through fantasy play he may be learning to cope with his fears and jealousies; the older child, in taking on adult roles, is testing one aspect of reality which he has observed or has had fantasies about, but which he cannot yet know in actuality. From the development of the senses in infancy and during emotional, intellectual, moral and social growth in childhood, play activities aid the processes of psychological development.

Different students of child play have studied the subject from different viewpoints, depending on the aspect of child development which has particularly interested them. Stern (1924) thought of play as being important both to the development of the individual and to his growth as a social being. 'Individual' play includes mastering bodily functions, whereas by 'social' play Stern meant the playing of games, including fighting and imitation. Bühler's studies (1935) concerned themselves with the development of the individual personality; Piaget's ideas on play are linked to his invariant, specified age stages for intellectual growth; and Freud's theories deal largely with the child's fantasies and with the importance of play in emotional development.

Bühler's theory of play

Bühler divided play periods during childhood into:
(1) functional,
(2) imaginative and
(3) constructive play.

As in most theories of child development the particular divisions made are used for convenience and indicate a *predominance* during particular periods of childhood of an activity or a mode of functioning (page 7). Such classifications do not mean that the influence of a particularly predominant period ceases altogether when the child enters the next period. Thus, although

Bühler's 'functional' play is predominant from birth to eighteen months, children continue to engage in such play long after this period. During this period children learn about objects and about people, and each child learns too about his own bodily movements. 'Imaginative' play is at its height between eighteen months and about four-and-a-half years of age, though it continues to be an important aspect of activity at least until the seventh or eighth year. During this period children use objects and people to 'stand for' something else; between four and seven years of age imaginative play loses some of its symbolic characteristics and becomes more realistic, and after four-and-a-half years of age Bühler's 'constructive' play period proper begins. Constructive play is much more purposive and more related to the real world rather than to the child's inner world.

Piaget's theories of play

Piaget's close observations of children playing has led him to propose that the two processes of assimilation and accommodation which together he has termed adaptation (page 65) are applicable to play as they are to all other childhood activities. By 'assimilation' Piaget means that the child uses some new experience or objects in his environment for an activity which is already part of his behavioural repertoire—that is, a new situation evokes a particular pattern of behaviour because it resembles other similar situations in the past which have evoked such behaviour. By 'accommodation' Piaget means the addition of *new* activities to a child's behavioural repertoire (page 65). Piaget suggests that whenever a child in early years *imitates*, the accommodatory process is operating, and whenever a child *plays*, the process of assimilation is being used. Piaget relates the development of play to the child's general growth of intelligence and to his experiences in childhood. The play equivalent of the sensori-motor* period Piaget terms *jeu d'exercice* or 'functional' play; play during the two to four age period he has termed *jeu symbolique*, and for the period four to seven years of age he has given the name *jeu de règles*—that is, play with rules. It can thus be seen that Piaget and Bühler both place emphasis on the same aspects of play during the infancy and early childhood periods, but whereas Bühler considers that play in the four to seven age period has the major function of helping the child realistically to learn how to use objects in his environment, Piaget for this age period places the emphasis on the child's relationship with others in regard to his appreciation of the rules of games and consequently how rules relate also to social life.

Piaget suggests that the pleasure of causing something to happen is the beginning of enjoying play: a baby of under six or eight months will manipulate things for the sheer pleasure of doing this, though since much activity in infancy and childhood seems to arise from a need to explore, one suspects that the pleasure experienced is not the aim of play but is incidental to the activity.

In the next play stage, one activity, according to Piaget, is linked to another, and ritualization often emerges: Piaget gives examples of a child lying down and sucking his thumb as if preparing to go to sleep, but the activity only lasts about half a minute, and it is not followed by sleep itself. This seems to be the beginning of symbolic play. By the beginning of the second year this symbolic activity often includes imaginary objects. The child at first uses himself as the object of his imaginary play, and then he uses other people and objects: he may pretend to drink ffrom something which looks like a cup, or get someone else to do so. Thus the objects and people he encounters are 'assimilated' to the needs of his symbolic play.

Symbolism is of great importance, for once a child begins to understand language, he realizes that one thing, a sound, represents something which is not a sound. Piaget says that symbolic play is not, however, like the symbolism of language, because symbolic play remains, as Piaget puts it, 'an egocentric assimilation'. Whereas language uses symbols in order to communicate the expression of needs, symbolic play is a private activity. Thus for Piaget symbolic play is relatively late in developing, and early infant play is, in his view, without any fantasy content. Piaget suggests that the imaginary people who populate the child's fantasy world at this stage may have an important role in his inner life. Piaget says that fantasy play involving imaginary people is a prolongation of reality, and that the imaginary symbol is used as a means of expressing and extending reality, and not as an end in itself. The psychoanalytic view, that fantasy activity is present from early infancy, is not directly observable in the infant's activities and has thus not found general favour with experimental psychologists. However, this discounting of early fantasy life seems to have had the effect of lessening interest in studying children's fantasies even as far as such studies are possible, and the importance which these creative imaginings may have in life has not been adequately assessed. Frank (page 199) considers that psychopathology may not be caused so much by a child's experience of life as by his tendency to distort reality by fantasy; and it is not improbable that we are affected not only by our interpretation of experiences, but also by the fantasy creations of our minds. Indeed Piaget believes that for the child at this age the division between play and reality is not at all clear, and it is not, therefore, inconceivable that real experiences and fantasy creations become fused, so that the development of the child's personality may be affected as much by the one as by the other.

Fantasy play forms a link between the child's inner world, which is at first inexpressible, and the outer world of experience: the two are joined by investing reality with some of the attributes of the inexpressible inner world, and play of this kind at this age stage enables the child to restructure the environment to fit his Ego. Here Piaget and Freud's views coincide, for it is suggested by them both that the child restructures his environment, partly because by doing so he can cope with experiences which he might otherwise find too painful or threatening, and partly because by such reinterpretation of reality the child is able vicariously to indulge in forbidden desires. A fuller consideration of this function of play will be given later when psychoanalytic views of play are discussed.

For Piaget the main purpose of symbolic play is that it allows the child to relive his experiences in some degree to his own satisfaction; he can exteriorize his thoughts, and through such play his inner speech—that is, thinking in words rather than in actions—can begin. This kind of play continues after four years of age, but due to the effects of socialization Piaget considers that it becomes progressively rooted in reality. Role taking, dressing up, behaving like adults, are all forms of imaginative play indulged in by children after this age, but it is *reproductive* of reality, rather than *symbolic* of it.

Social play

Very young babies can only play by themselves; no playful association with any other child is possible for them (page 135). Theirs is 'solitary' play, though babies between about nine and thirteen months of age will be aware of one another when they are in the same playpen. Soon after this age children are definitely interested in each other, and their play may begin to be 'looking on' play—that is, they watch what others do, and when they are a little older, perhaps about two years of age, they may talk about what they are doing, but their talking will be an 'egocentric monologue'. Indeed, Piaget says that a child even up to the age of seven or so will speak almost as much in egocentric as in social terms, and that he does not communicate in the sense in which adults communicate (pages 115f.). He suggests that for this reason children do not play co-operatively until seven or eight years of age, but Gesell and Ilg (1946) found that American children were earlier in playing together in this manner, which indicates that it is possible that cultural and educational factors which encourage or discourage solitary or co-operative play respectively, influence the age at which such play may take place. Gesell also found that children between two and three years of age play 'in parallel'; they use the same playthings but do not play together. After this age 'associative' play is possible—children involve one another in what they do; they take ideas from one another and borrow toys, but each is concerned with his own interests. 'Co-operative' play begins usually after children are about three-and-a-half or four years of age. However, if by the term 'co-operative' one assumes that meaningful conversation is taking place between children so that they can effectively combine in an activity, then this is not really possible until the child has ceased to speak egocentrically. Often children of five and under, who are relatively strange to one another, can be seen to play together apparently with co-operation, but closer observation will indicate that usually one child is using the others as part of his own private play activity. Frequently one dominant child will in this way incorporate other children into his play.

Isaacs (1933) says that in apparently co-operative play at five years of age a child will note other children but not their personalities, nor will he see that they have a purpose independent of himself. She says that the ego-centric situation is marked by fantasy influencing the aim and style of the play, and other children are given roles in the play set-up; reality enters into such play in this form. Thus Isaacs gives as example children playing at 'shops' where one child is sent to the shop to wait and ask for things to buy.

Children who know one another well, particularly siblings near in age, and other children raised together such as children who are members of the same kibbutz, are able to play co-operatively much earlier. Constant propinquity probably enables them to understand non-verbal communications which they receive from each other and which aid co-operation, whereas children less familiar with one another have to rely on speech with which to ccommunicate.

Co-operation between children can be helped by keeping the play groups small; three-year-olds cannot attend to more than one person at a time, and their power of concentration is limited, so that these factors, in addition to language problems, make it unlikely that small children can co-operate in any meaningful sense.

Co-operative play among children of junior age leads inevitably to co-operation in the playing of games, which Piaget thinks, however, is different from just 'playing'. Games playing implies following rules, and these 'entail certain obligations' (Piaget, 1969). The importance of understanding rules both in relation to moral and social development is discussed on page 135 and page 146. It is clear that social and moral growth imply learning both to appreciate the rights of others, and also that to an extent these rights can be safeguarded by everyone observing rules.

So, when children begin to play with other children they first use them as stimuli for their own activities; later, when co-operation is possible, they are able to extend their own activities by working with others, and they also thereby help others to develop their own skills and abilities. Later again, when rules have to be adhered to in games playing, they learn about the need for regularity in social life. Through playing with others language use is also developed, though this is not so important as having opportunities of talking to and listening to adults who present a good speech model (page 95). Also through play, and the verbal interaction with other children which this brings, a child will learn what others think of him and he will begin to form a self-concept.

Psychoanalytic view of play

Daydreaming and night dreams, art and the experiences of the mentally disturbed, are all aspects of fantasy life. However, they all serve a purpose; indeed, that no human activity is without meaning was one of Freud's most important discoveries. He considered that play, which seems purposeless and is apparently unrelated to reality, is part of fantasy life. Like other aspects of fantasy, however, it is certainly not without purpose, and, again like dreaming, its form and content are, according to the psychoanalytic viewpoint, dominated by wishes. Freud's views about the relationship of reality and fantasy in children's play are not dissimilar from those of Piaget (page 159), for both consider that a child when playing re-orders events and uses objects and people in ways which please him, or at least in ways which are less worrying than they are in actuality. Whenever a child reproduces in a play situation events which are similar to, but in many respects different from, a frightening or threatening experience, he is 'abreacting'* his anxieties—that is, he is reliving in his imagination the actual event he experienced. 'Children repeat in their play everything that has made a great impression on them in their actual life . . . and so to speak make themselves masters of the situation' (Freud, 1920). Thus Freud thought of play as a 'repetition-compulsion' mechanism, which enables a child to work out his anxieties. By re-enacting on several occasions something which has been anxiety-producing, the anxiety is slowly dissipated. This theory seems to account for the curious observation that children will repeat in a play situation experiences which, according to a commonsense viewpoint, one might expect them to wish to forget.

Isaacs has developed Freud's ideas from her extensive experience with children. Though not all her ideas about the origin of behaviour (page 45), are wholly acceptable her observations on the nature and purpose of play, considered partly in terms of psychoanalytic theory, add to our understanding of the dynamics of child development. Isaacs suggests that there are three main varieties of play activity:

(1) imaginative or make-believe play,

(2) play which involves movement and bodily skills, and

(3) play with physical objects.

Part of the purpose of imaginative play is to ease the anxieties and fears which all children feel to a greater or lesser extent throughout childhood. These anxieties arise from a number of causes: there are first the anxieties which spring from recollected experiences, and the abreacting of these through play has already been discussed. Then there are, according to Isaacs, those anxieties which are generated by the child's own fantasy life, such as fear of the damage which destructive feelings and thoughts might inflict on people with whom the child is emotionally involved. By imaginative play these fantasies can be projected outwards, or externalized, and they thus lose part of their force—destructive impulses can be assigned to witches or other imaginary, wicked persons! Aggressive feelings, which spring from jealousy, can be vented on inanimate objects rather than on live persons who have occasioned such feelings; dolls, rather than the child, can be made to be naughty. Thirdly, fantasies can be amended to fit reality. One can say that, in Freudian terms, this view of the function of play assigns to play the role of mediator between the 'primary' and 'secondary' processes (page 52). Through play activity the child is helped to come to terms with reality and there is, according to Isaacs, constant interaction between fantasy life and reality. This interaction is of the greatest importance in child development. She considers that the child's make-believe play is part fantasy, and part thought, that progressively throughout childhood experiences of life penetrate feelings and fantasy, and that for this reason make-believe play becomes more reproductive of reality as the child gets older. A fourth purpose of imaginative play is that it enables the child to explore and test in safety new experiences, and to make the familiar ones even better known. For young children there is a constant approach-avoidance conflict in operation between being attracted to new experiences and seeking to avoid them because of their potentially dangerous unfamiliarity. In play such situations can be postulated and tried out without any danger.

Isaacs, unlike Piaget, ascribes fantasies to the early infancy period and she gives the infant more emotional and symbolic life than Piaget would allow; indeed, she considers that imaginative play derives its energy from repressed infantile wishes and fantasies. There are, of course, no means by which such a theory can be verified by observation. Indeed, there seems to be no need to postulate what the origin of the energy needed for imaginative play might be in order to discuss the purposes of such play.

As the child gets older imaginative play becomes more closely linked to the real world and soon the child begins to explore adult roles (page 160). In psychoanalytic theory role-taking has a deeper significance than merely trying out what it feels like to be adult; it is linked to identification, which is discussed in some detail in chapter 4 (page 55). This is bound up with the taking on of sex roles; with overcoming jealousies experienced for the parent of the same sex, and with working through the Oedipal situation (page 55).

Play involving movement and play with objects

Play which involves movement is predominant in the first eighteen months of life, but the toddler is for ever 'on the go'; later children enjoy planned movements, such as games of skipping or 'hopscotch', which involve bodily expertise and skills. Almost all children, except the most severely deprived, have opportunities for this kind of play. In contrast, play with objects does depend on the provision of the objects; Piaget has shown how the child is 'percept-centred' (pages 104f.)—that is, his evaluation of the world around him is made far more according to the information which his senses bring him than from rational deduction. When he is very young he has to learn to co-ordinate hand and eye, and in his earliest days his mouth probably tells him more about the nature of an object than his eyes! Later he learns that objects do not change their shape though they look different from different viewpoints. The world has to be experienced in order to be understood, and in order that actions involving objects can be internalized. White (1960) has written that 'exploratory play, even in the first years of life, shows it to have the characteristics of directedness, selectivity and per-sistence'. The child is attempting to learn about his world, and the more opportunities he has early in life to experience the world the more compe-tent his handling of his environment will be. It is probably no exaggeration to state that the two factors most potently affecting the development of intellectual capacity in the young child are, on the one hand, the opportuni-ties for listening to and conversing with an understanding adult who has good speech habits and an extensive vocabulary, and on the other hand, the provision of conditions in which he can play with objects and materials which vary greatly from one another in shape, colour, size and texture. It is suggested that stimulating activity of this kind during infancy and early childhood, when rapid growth of cortical neurons and interconnection be-tween neurons takes place, aids the development of this growth and thus helps to lay the foundation for intellectual functioning later in life (page 97).

Continuing opportunities to handle a variety of objects and a variety of materials during nursery and primary school periods will enable the child to move away from his percept-centred view towards an evaluation of the world through reasoning and deduction. This is one of the reasons why 'play' with objects and materials is not a waste of time for the child in the infant school, but an integral part of learning.

FURTHER READING

MILLAR, S.: *The Psychology of Play* (Penguin Books, Harmondsworth, 1968).

7

Observing and understanding children

In chapter 1 it was stressed that experts today no longer give advice about how to treat children. They are reticent about advocating specific child-rearing practices, partly because they are more aware than writers of a previous generation of how much is still to be learned about the development of the human personality and the factors which influence human behaviour, but also because we now know that what is helpful behaviour towards one child may not be helpful when applied to another. The emphasis is, therefore, on trying to understand each individual child and adjusting adult behaviour accordingly. Teachers who are 'good with children' do this quite automatically when they behave differently towards different children in their class. Often they feel guilty and unfair because of this, and often too they are justified in having these feelings, for behaviour towards children is dictated as much by the degree particular children appeal to adults as it is by considerations of what ought to be done; but this does not mean that differential treatment is wrong in itself. What is important is that adults should try to adjust their behaviour according to an understanding assessment of the temperament, anxieties, desires, motivations and other characteristics of children.

Observation of children

Good observation of each child is important if an evaluation of his characteristics is to be valid. Such observation includes not only noting his own behaviour, but also developing a skill in interpreting parental attitudes during teacher-parent interviews. It is important also to be aware of possible anxieties caused by, perhaps, the illness of a parent, the arrival of a new baby or other domestic disturbances, such as the possible or actual breakup of the family. It goes without saying that a child who is already somewhat anxious about life when all is going well may be overwhelmed by the mere threat of such disturbances at home, so that a knowledge of a child's physical and emotional environment is important for the teacher. In addition, however, it is also useful to make an assessment of a child's traits and characteristics in response to daily handling.

Such an assessment can be made by several means, including: observing his behaviour when by himself and when with others; getting to know the parents' attitude to work, discipline and other matters affecting their children, as well as being familiar with the child's family environment generally; noting the kind of work the child does in school and how he does it; and by applying formal tests.

Responsibility for behaviour

As far as behaviour and responsibility for behaviour is concerned, society's attitude towards adults and children alike appears to be based on an assumption that humans are entirely in control of their behaviour, and that when such behaviour conflicts with the needs of society, or, in the case of children, with the demands of parents and teachers, then the offending person is considered to be culpable. To what extent humans are controlled by the genetic and environmental influences which contribute to their shaping, and how much control in the last resort is a matter of a free exercise of will, is, in part at least, a complex philosophical problem.

In chapter 3 we examine studies which seek to investigate the factors which influence the way the human personality develops. These include studies which relate body-build and temperament; observational work starting at two months of age which noted the persistence over at least ten years of behavioural factors such as activity levels, distractibility, adaptability, etc.; and longitudinal studies which investigated the persistence of definite personality traits such as dependency and aggressiveness. These factors are, of course, all affected by the environment, since all behaviour is to a greater or lesser extent determined by an interaction between innately determined and environmental influences. So far as the teacher is concerned, it is of value to note here the findings of a number of important studies which indicate the significance of influences apparently present from birth, since these findings will help her in her understanding of the children in her care.

Understanding a child's temperament

It is important for the teacher to understand the child's temperament and to realize that his behaviour is often a spontaneous expression of inner drives and needs and not something which the child can easily change. The studies of Thomas, Chess and Birch (1968) indicate that when the home or the school make demands which are in gross conflict with a child's temperamental characteristics then the child is put under heavy stress. What can reasonably be expected of one child is an unreasonable expectation when demanded of another. A young child with a high activity level should not be expected to sit still for long; a persistent child can be forgiven if he doesn't come quickly when called while he is engaged on a task; a child which finds all manner of approach-making difficult, whether to new people, objects or jobs, should not be chided for attempting to avoid such approaches. Similarly the highly extraverted child will need the stimulation which the presence of other people provides and to be left alone could be a particularly severe trial for him which might not trouble a more introverted child. The friendly, pleasant child who enters into everything with joy and who is obviously likeable is no more responsible for his sunny nature than the child who, from birth it seems, has found everything done to him, or which he has had to do, a trouble and a pain. It is obvious, too, that such naturally disadvantaged children often have had matters made worse for them by the way they are handled by non-understanding adults, who find them difficult to deal with and often quite unlovable. It is with such children particularly that the teacher can be of especial help, not only in her attitude to the child in class, but at times also in helping parents towards a better understanding of their child.

It is obvious that a child's temperamental characteristics not only affect his interaction with other people, but also influence his learning ability. A child with a basically good learning capacity may find learning difficult if he is easily distracted, and insufficient allowance is made for his having to learn in distracting surroundings. Again some children find it much more difficult than others to respond to external stimulation, while some others have a short attention span and cannot be expected to persist with an activity for as long as children who are not subject to this difficulty. Much emphasis has hitherto been laid on the relationship between a child's measurable IQ and how he should, therefore, be expected to perform in learning tasks, and too little attention has been given to temperamental factors which affect learning ability. Hamilton (1970) has shown that personality variables, as well as 'A' level results and IQ scores, differentiate the successful university student from the unsuccessful one. It is known, for instance (Eysenck, 1960), that highly extroverted adults find learning more difficult than introverted persons. Recent work (Eysenck and Cookson, 1970) with 4,000 eleven-year-olds seems to indicate that introverts are more frequently 'late developers' than extroverts. Generally one finds that the more stable child does better in school subjects than the anxious child, but results of a number of recent studies are somewhat contradictory, particularly as the sex factor—whether one is dealing with boys or girls—appears to enter into the relationship between extraversion, stability and scholastic achievement.

Understanding children's language use

Another factor worth bearing in mind when observing and listening to children is that when they speak they do not always mean what adults think they mean, nor are they always fully able to understand what adults say despite the fact that children use language so fluently from quite an early age. Reference is made in chapter 4 to language learning and to the difficulties experienced by young children in particular. Donaldson and Balfour

(1968) (page 117) have shown how children under four-and-a-half years of age could not differentiate between the meanings of the words 'less' and 'more'; 'less' meaning the same to them as 'more'. Again Cromer (1970) has shown how such phrases as 'John is easy to see' invariably means for the child under five-and-a-half years of age that John is *doing the seeing*! Even to children under six-and-a-half years of age the meaning is not always clear. The lessons to be learned from these studies is that when children appear to misunderstand adults they are not necessarily inattentive or dull, but that a particular turn of phrase, even when quite ordinary words are used, may not be within their range of comprehension.

The working-class child and school

When the child from a middle-class home enters school he enters an atmosphere which is only an extension or a variation of home, but the child from a lower-working-class home enters a community which from a social-class point of view is quite alien to him. Children go to school to learn, and the value which is placed on education is a middle-class value. Implicit in a belief in the value of education is a belief in the value of taking a long-term view of life; but such a view is alien to many people who, as Vernon (1969) has suggested, have little economic control over their future and who see little point in planning for it. In chapter 4 we see how profound is the influence of the different use of language by the two social classes on moral development, thought processes, and parent-child relationship. The child from a lower working-class home coming to a primary school enters a community where language is used as it is used in a middle-class home. When bright children from linguistically deprived and socially different homes go to a grammar school the pressures which they experience are great, despite their earlier partial familiarization into middle-class values through having attended primary school. The problems they encounter have been outlined by Jackson and Marsden (1962), and by Stevens (1970), who reports actual testimonies of pupils in her book. The strains under which such children have to work, and the conflicts and confused feelings which are engendered, are, apparently, no less when they are put into the top stream of a comprehensive school.

The fundamental cleavage which exists in our society cannot easily be overcome by equal educational opportunities from five years of age onward, though it might be reduced if more nursery-school facilities existed. Teachers will have to recognize that at present children from certain types of under-privileged homes will inevitably find it much harder to take advantage of what the school offers than children who are more fortunate.

The problem is not confined to difficulties with school work; in matters of behaviour children who are used to quick orders being given them, and who have as yet developed little internal control but rely on the physical strength and greater size of the teacher to exercise control over them, find the middle-class approach to discipline strange and possibly consider it a rather weak way for adults to behave. The idea that learning is a preparation for life and work, and that it is an example of taking a long-term view of living, is a difficult one for children whose training at home is so largely directed to the present.

Although teachers themselves now come from a variety of social classes and some may personally have experienced the difficulties which have been described, they have, through their training and by their association at work with persons from other classes, largely adopted middle-class speech forms and most middle-class values. It may, indeed, be more difficult for some teachers who have come from a linguistically-deprived background to show understanding for children from a similar background, for they may quite unconsciously tend to reject such children because they are a reminder to them of associations which they have discarded.

It has been suggested that probably these language differences and their associated problems are slowly declining in society, and we can presumably look forward to a society where the present divisions will not be so pronounced.

Understanding the child's view of the world

Practical use can be made of the many studies which have supported much of Piaget's work (chapters 2 and 4) which indicate how very egocentric and percept-centred the young child is. It is also important to remember that children do not interpret the behaviour of others nor understand motives for behaviour in the same way as adults do (chapter 5), and that their ideas of morality also change with age (chapter 5). By constantly reminding themselves of the inevitable difference between the young child's view of the world and the adult view, and also trying to see with the child's eyes, teachers may help themselves, to some extent at least, to understand the children they teach.

Knowing parents

Knowing the parents of children in her care is a help to the teacher in trying to understand the children's behaviour. This is often difficult, because for many parents schools and teachers reawaken unhappy childhood feelings and memories and this makes them reluctant to establish any but the most necessary contacts with their children's school. For working-class parents too the educated teacher is often seen as a middle-class authority figure. In addition many parents are simply not interested in their children's scholastic progress or emotional development. Unfortunately also it is the parents with whom contact is most desirable who are usually the least ready to come. However, most good schools can find some way of seeing parents occasionally. If a child does appear to have some kind of difficulty it is well worthwhile to try to see in what way, if at all, the home environment may be contributing to the child's problems. If the problem is severe it is, of course, vital for the parents to be seen. This need to obtain parental co-operation is further discussed when children who require special help are considered (pages 172f.).

Obviously parents vary greatly in their attitudes to such matters as discipline, work, progress at school and other factors affecting their children's behaviour. Evidence exists from a number of sources (chapter 8) to show that parents of disturbed children are more directive and restricting; they diminish their children's individuality, have little empathy and are lacking in imagination, when compared with parents of non-disturbed children (Adams, 1965). What was particularly noticed in the Adams study was such parents' *puzzlement* when the experimenters asked: 'How do you think the child sees that?', or, 'Do you, in addition to trying to discipline and teach your child, also try to stop occasionally and see things the way he sees them?' It is very difficult to influence such parental attitudes, but by knowing that a particular child has parents who are unable to understand their child the teacher can both allow for this in the child's behaviour and attempt to show understanding towards the child.

As well as a lack of parental understanding, there are other domestic circumstances which make the lives of children in certain families unhappy and affect their emotional development. Again ample evidence exists to show that children from intact homes are not often patients in out-patient psychiatric clinics. It seems that different types of disturbance at home —that is, whether the parents are divorced or separated, the mother unmarried and so on—can result in different types of disturbance in the child (Tuckman and Regan, 1966). One has to beware, though, of taking it for granted that, where such disturbances exist, they are due entirely to the family environment. The correlation which exists between the disturbed homes and disturbed children indicates a possible cause-and-effect relationship, but it is also possible that parents whose personalities prevent them from providing stable homes for their children have also handed on difficult personalities to the children. Indeed, such children may be doubly disadvantaged. One must also bear in mind that it by no means follows that a disturbed domestic situation inevitably produces behavioural problems.

Stress in normal childhood

It is difficult for most adults to reflect on the distress and anxieties they experienced in childhood, and beyond a certain age it is in any case not possible to recollect thoughts and emotions. Moore (1970) suggests that most adults and children experience three major forms of stress: one form is due to the ordinary strains of living. The second occurs whenever a child, or an adult, has to take a new step forward in life; in a child's life such steps occur at specific 'critical' periods when a new phase of development starts. The third cause for stress lies in special occurrences, such as separation from home and parents, loss of a parent, illness, the arrival of a new baby and so on. Moore says that one must assume that small children learn about human behaviour at least in part through the reactions of parents and siblings to stressful situations. However, we are only just beginning to understand rather inadequately what form this learning can take and what the effects of such experiences are on different kinds of children. We do not know what factors both in the environment and in the child himself can pinpoint either the damage that may be done by stress, or, alternatively, establish a resilience which may be helpful in later life. Yet, says Moore (1970), daily decisions are made about children, such as whether to send a child to nursery or boarding school, whether to provide him with a sibling this year or next, etc. Until we know much more about the way specific children react to particular factors in their environment we cannot make such decisions with any degree of certainty about their beneficial or damaging effects.

In an earlier paper Moore (1966) states that about 80 per cent of children experience difficulties in the infant school, of which surprisingly and unfortunately nearly half seem to be of moderate or marked severity. In a longitudinal study of 164 boys and girls aged from six to eleven years, Moore found that the greatest difficulty in adjusting to school occurred among only boys. The most common difficulty was a general reluctance to go to school; but children also seemed to have difficulties with teachers and with work, and they reported disliking school dinners and the lavatories! Less frequently reported were difficulties with other children. From this investigation it seems that many children in the infant school are daily afflicted with the anxiety of having to do something they do not wish to do, and of having to face conditions and experiences which potentially or actually trouble them. It is perhaps difficult for most adults to appreciate the many fears which small children experience in their first days and weeks at school, and the teacher of the reception class should be particularly sensitive to these fears.

Extremes of body-build and associated temperamental characteristics

Before discussing children who appear to suffer from more than the usual amount of stress and who can be termed 'emotionally disturbed', it is worth considering children whose body-build is extreme in one of three directions. There is a certain amount of evidence which indicates that children who are in build *predominantly* 'muscular', 'round' and 'linear' respectively vary in temperament from one another (chapter 3). (By 'linear' is meant a body-build of relatively greater height and lesser weight, and 'round' means 'roundness of physique and ability to grow fat'.) Vernon (1964) has said that work relating personality characteristics and temperament shows sufficiently high correlations to justify the assumption that persons with *marked* 'round,' 'linear' or 'muscular' physiques differ from one another in a number of important characteristics. In a sample of fifty boys and fifty girls of seven years of age who were classified in this way, Davidson, McInnes and Parnell (1957) found 'linear' children to be far the best readers of the three groups of children. A 'linear' child often seems to have a shy, protective shell and his inner world tends to be more important to him than what is happening outside. Although he is usually superior in academic performance to his peers, he is often less able to use his intelligence when confronted with non-academic situations. He is shy, not very responsive, has high standards and may lack confidence. He is also likely to be anxious and this anxiety often expresses itself in emotional unrest of various kinds —thumbsucking, nailbiting, temper tantrums, bedwetting, etc. However, it seems that more than a third of all supposedly healthy children indulge in one or other of these habits, so that only if such indulgence is very intense or persistent, or if three or more such habits are in evidence, would one consider such a child to suffer from emotional unrest.

The extremely muscular child has, as one might suspect, much more practical ability than children of the other two body-build types. In the study under consideration it was found that in school examinations at eleven such children did less well in reading than the other children and they obtained fewer grammar school places than children of the other types of body-build. The muscular child is not so prone to be anxious and he is least likely to be submissive. He is usually also a good communicator and is more likely to be aggressive.

The more than usually 'round' child is the great 'allrounder'. He is neither especially anxious nor aggressive. He comes out well on intelligence tests; he is emotionally responsive to his environment, so that he is more lively, socially well-adjusted and better able to cope with new situations than the other types of children. He has more confidence and his energies are often well-directed.

It would, of course, be unwise to categorize even those children who are extreme in body-build exclusively according to their physique. However, it would also be unwise to ignore such findings, since a child's bodily build is the most immediate, obviously noticeable feature about him. Knowing the strengths and weakness of children who are extreme in body-build can give teachers an indication of the kind of child with whom they are dealing; in particular, it can warn them what they should expect and what they should not expect from such children.

The emotionally disturbed child

In addition to using her knowledge of parents and parental circumstances to help her understand the normal child, the teacher has an important role in the detection of the emotionally handicapped child. If the teacher is aware of circumstances which might make life difficult for a child she can be watchful for possible effects on the child; but also by observing a child's unusual or excessive behaviour she can be ready to investigate possible causes for this.

Throughout this book emphasis has been laid on the importance of studying the individual child. Descriptions of how children develop will also have given the reader an insight into the difficulty of identifying possible causes of 'good' and 'bad' development. The reader will also be aware by now that to describe behaviour is not to explain it. Thus one may say that a child is 'for ever wanting my attention', as if one had thus explained something about this child when, in fact, one has done no more than to *describe* his behaviour. Perhaps it is apt, therefore, before beginning a section on children with various kinds of difficulties and maladjustments, to emphasize what Charlotte Bühler has written (Webb, 1967).

(1) 'Never assume that a problem can be explained by one specified cause.'

(2) 'Never believe that explanation can be given without study of the individual situation.'

(3) 'Do not accept descriptions of a child's behaviour as explanation.'

Webb (1967) has listed eleven different kinds of behaviour which worry teachers in infant schools in some way or another, and consideration will be given to the most important of these. The author has, indeed, incorporated many ideas expressed by Webb in the author's account of the aggressive, thieving, anxious and withdrawn child. Other aspects of infant and older children's behaviour, which new teachers in particular may find worrying or puzzling, are also considered.

When we consider children's maladaptive behaviour we have to remember that our society must present conflicting norms to the developing child: at times he is told to be gentle, at others that he must stand up for himself. He must not be aggressive, but he notices aggression daily displayed on television, and he can see that the more aggressive an actor is the more likely he is to defeat his adversary and win approval. He is expected 'not to be a baby' and to control his feelings, but he not infrequently sees adults both angry and upset. He may not take other people's possessions, but in the supermarket he will see his mother pick up goods which do not belong to her!

The aggressive child

Psychologists are not agreed whether aggression is initiated by an inner drive, which has to express itself in some form, or whether it is always a response to an external stimulus; this stimulus can be positive, such as threatening behaviour, or negative, in the form of frustration. Some psychologists say that, in the last analysis, all aggression is a response to frustration of some kind. One can, though, support the view that, whatever the ultimate origin of aggressive behaviour, the energies which might be used for such behaviour are normally channelled into activities of which society approves.

A certain amount of positive, forceful behaviour, or a naturally angry reaction to the annoying actions of another person, cannot be termed 'aggressive'. Teachers, however, vary in the amount of aggressive or assertive behaviour they can tolerate, and indeed in whether they call certain behaviour 'aggressive' or 'assertive'. It is salutary for the teacher to examine her own feelings when she is faced with forceful behaviour which she finds disturbing and to consider why she is so worried by it. We are here, however, chiefly concerned with the over-aggressive child, who is usually so obviously a nuisance or worse, that no subtleties are needed to interpret his activities.

Sometimes, though, aggression may be covert, presenting a trouble and a threat only to the child's peers; other children are normally good sources of information about such aggressive behaviour, and their tales can usually be relied upon if reports of such aggression come from more than one child (Williams, Meyersson, Eron and Semler, 1967).

Most small children are unable to tolerate frustration if it continues too long or comes their way too often. The younger the child the shorter the time he can bear to be frustrated or restricted, and obviously the less control he can be expected to employ. If, in addition, he comes from a home where his aggressive behaviour is met by inconsistent behaviour on the part of his parents, he will become confused and even less able to control the expression of his feelings. For instance, in some homes parents punish aggression when it is directed towards themselves, while at the same time positively encouraging their children to be aggressive outside the home. Parental behaviour of this type produces children who are either excessively aggressive or very anxious (Bandura, 1963). Over-indulgence by parents of children's aggressive acts also tends to increase such behaviour.

It seems that some aggressive children learn from their parents that aggression, at least outside the home, is not disapproved of; for other children aggressive behaviour is a form of attention-seeking which expresses a need to feel wanted or admired, and possibly also shows a lack of self-esteem. The need for admiration seems most obvious in children who lead aggressive gangs; such children at least relate to others, and express their need to be assertive in a social, even if not socially-approved, manner. By contrast the lonely aggressor is often the more disturbed child, possibly feeling rejected, and expressing his feelings and his surplus energy in destructive and hurtful activities. If such behaviour is very severe and the child appears to treat other children in his attacks as if they were mere objects he may be potentially psychopathic, and in such cases psychiatric help is urgent. It is obvious too that such a child can present a real danger to other children in the school and in the neighbourhood.

The method of dealing with children who display this kind of disturbance will depend on the exact nature of the aggression, the age of the child, and what is known of the parents. If the teacher discovers that the parents in fact encourage the child to 'stand up for himself' outside the home in a manner which he interprets as licence to attack, it may help to discuss the matter with the parents and explain the problem their child's attitude is creating in school. A child who is known to come from a home where he is likely to feel unwanted or rejected can be helped by being given work to do where he can organize and assist others, particularly if it involves working in a friendly relationship with a sympathetic adult. Being allowed to take mechanical objects or puzzles to pieces sometimes helps the child who is destructive of material things rather than aggressive towards people, though this by itself will not be much use without a personal interest in the child. One might postulate that it is the child with a great deal of surplus energy whose feelings of unhappiness, anxiety or rejection, will express themselves in aggressive behaviour rather than in some other kind of symptom; and it would seem important, therefore, to find him activities where he can expend his energy as well as enhance his self-esteem. It also helps such a child if he can learn through association with a helpful adult that he can often obtain by legitimate and socially acceptable means the things he needs so badly, such as attention, assurance and an enhanced view of himself, even if he does not consciously recognize his needs.

Sometimes older children, who were severely punished for aggression when they were young, express their aggressive feelings covertly and in time become adults who are strict law-enforcers, who desire severely to punish lawbreakers, and who tend to persecute minorities (Berkowitz, 1964). It would seem that for aggression, as for most other apparent misdemeanours, punishment for styles of behaviour, as opposed to isolated acts, serves only to drive the undesirable behaviour underground (chapter 8).

It is important when dealing with the over-aggressive child to handle him firmly and with consistency, and to let him see that all the adults in his world are acting together.

The attention-seeking child

Attention-seeking is nearly always a symptom of emotional disturbance, and some children constantly seek attention, either overtly and consciously, or covertly and possibly unconsciously. A particular example of the latter kind of attention-seeking is that of girls who have frequent accidents (Mannheimer and Mellinger, 1967). There are many other ways in which children of varying ages will seek to gain the teacher's attention: they make demands on the teacher, or they have always to be in the forefront; often they have to be the leader and cannot tolerate being a follower, and sometimes petty thieving and story-spreading are used as means. It is possible for this thieving to be seen as a symbolic form of 'stealing' love, though such pilfering can spring from a number of causes which will be considered later. Attention-seeking is a well-known symptom of the maternally deprived child (chapter 8), though the opposite symptom of withdrawal is also noted in such children. It is usually wise to find the cause of the trouble rather than to attack the symptom; it is possible that the origin may lie in a feeling of being rejected at home.

The terms 'maternally deprived' and 'rejected' indicate a culpability on the part of parents, particularly the mother, which they should not imply, for rejection of a child or children may be quite an inevitable act for some parents, and may often be unconsciously determined. Sometimes a bad birth experience for the mother, or a depression following the birth, will not enable her to feel as warmly towards a particular child in her family as she does towards the other children. Again some children are themselves unable to respond to affection, and persistent attempts by parents to evoke a response may end in their giving up the effort. However, this does not mean that the child itself is not in need of the affection it cannot demonstrably reciprocate. Sometimes mothers are unaware consciously that they feel rejection towards a child, yet they suffer a sense of guilt because they cannot respond as they feel they should respond, and this makes them over-anxious and over-protective. Evidence that such over-protection can cause emotional disturbance, which shows itself not infrequently in a child's difficulty in getting on with its peers, comes not only from clinical studies, but also from experimental work with animals (Harlow, 1962). The child who stands by himself in the playground may well have problems because of over-protection. This need not, of course, be due basically to rejection, but could indicate a severe anxiety on the part of his mother which it might help the teacher to know about.

The over-anxious child

Most children have what adults would term 'irrational' fears of some kind, but over-anxiety which is much more serious can show itself in a number of ways, not infrequently in the crying of the five-year-old when his mother leaves him at school. 'Anxiety is the expectation of something as yet unknown' (Rycroft, 1968), but it is also a fear which springs from unease. To be separated from his mother in a building probably never entered before, and to be left alone among strange adults and many children, can be a terrifying experience for the young child, particularly for the only child who has not previously mixed a great deal with other children. However, some five-year-old children's anxiety at separation continues for much longer than is usual. If the child appears too attached to his mother then the teacher should take suitable action with the head's approval. If by the end of the first term in the infant school a child will still not separate happily from his mother, then it would be wise to refer the child to the clinic. Apart from help which the child can be given, a social worker can also work with the mother. Action taken at this stage may prevent school refusal later.

It seems to be established that the aggressive as well as the withdrawn child, in fact all children who are emotionally disturbed, suffer from anxiety, but there are other types of anxious children who do not evidence the more severe symptoms of aggression and withdrawal. These children are ineffectual; they work below their capacity; they have restless habits. More is often expected of them than they can give, for parents and teachers may know them to be intelligent and accuse them of not trying. For these children school remains often a perpetual worry, for it seems to make demands which they cannot meet. All children at times suffer anxiety because they desire to please, but these over-anxious children particularly feel that they are constantly failing and have no excuse for doing so. This sense of failure becomes cumulative so that many such children fall further and further behind with school work the older they get. The teacher can do a great deal to help such children by giving them tasks well within their capabilities and by not making unnecessary demands. Jersild (as reported by Webb, 1967) has mentioned that 'the school dispenses failure on a colossal scale. . . !'

Parents too often make excessive and unrealistic demands in relation to their child's success at school, and some children are used by their parents in order to compensate for the parents' sense of failure or lack of opportunities. There is also little doubt that some adults use their power over a child to diminish the child's sense of self-esteem (chapter 8), which further increases the child's sense of failure. Sometimes a child may become acutely anxious due to the marital problems of his parents, but in such circumstances a teacher may be able to do little more than give him support.

The hyperactive child

This term is applied to children who are excessively restless. Such children obviously present a management difficulty for both parents and teachers; their quick movements can cause accidents and disturbances to others; they are more likely to break things and to get burnt or bruised themselves. When such over-activity is combined, as it sometimes is, with easy distractibility, then the child moves from task to task, whether in work or play, in quick succession, and his behaviour becomes unpredictable and hence anxiety-provoking in those around him. This variability in day-to-day behaviour and in school work has caused some mothers to describe their children as having 'Jekyll and Hyde' personalities (Stewart, Pitts, Craig and Dieruf, 1966). Over-activity is also at times combined with emotional intensity; if the child is pleased he may overwhelm another child with a hug which knocks him over; if he is upset or angry he will display his feelings with more vigour than the average child. For this reason the over-active child not infrequently angers both parents and teachers, who, finding that such a child apparently ignores their admonitions again and again, feel that he is deliberately disobedient, and their strictures may then in fact make him so.

These children need to be understood, and parents and teachers should attempt to deal patiently and cheerfully with their rapid and continual movements, and not too much must be expected of them, such as enforced sitting still for long periods and slower ways of moving. Although children who have a severe form of hyperactivity syndrome rate highly on anti-social symptoms, there is no reason to suppose that ordinarily such children are necessarily or even frequently anti-social in their behaviour. However, if the hyperactivity is severe they should be given expert help, for the vicious circle of over-activity leading to adult annoyance, which may in itself exaggerate the over-activity, should be broken early.

The rigid child

Teachers will occasionally have to deal with a child who appears to be living in a kind of psychological straitjacket. The first sign may be an extreme reluctance to get his hands or clothes messy with paint, clay or plasticine. Then the teacher may notice that the child has difficulty in thinking except in a very narrow way. Most children of eleven can classify objects in a number of ways (chapter 4) according to their function, colour, material, etc., but very rigid children cannot do this. Often they cannot even recognize a classification made by someone else, when this is not the way they think about the objects thus ordered. Leach (1964), who has interested herself in such children, has described how she grouped together a red apple, a red ball of knitting wool and a red tin. The very rigid children she tested said that these objects did not go together as, 'the knitting wool must go with mother's things. The apple is for eating.'

The moral judgements of such children too will be more limited than those of other children of the same age. We know that young children's moral judgements are dictated by effects and not by intentions (chapter 5), but the rigid child is even more restricted in his judgements than other children. Children of eleven years of age usually know it is a rule not to speak to strangers in the street. Leach showed both very rigid children and non-rigid children a picture of an old lady who had dropped her shopping in the street, and she asked them if it were all right to break the rule in order to help the lady. The non-rigid children said that in such circumstances the rule could be broken, but the rigid children tended to say that it would be wrong to stop as it was a rule that one should not speak to strangers.

It is possible that parents of very rigid children have, from the beginning of their children's lives, set standards of behaviour which are too high for their children to achieve. We have discussed anxiety in children (page 176) and how the fear of not pleasing is a potent source of worry for certain children. If a parent makes demands which a child cannot understand, he cannot meet these demands, and he becomes perplexed and highly anxious, for he cannot hope to please his parents however hard he tries. We will consider in chapter 8 the effects on children of authoritarian behaviour. Suffice it to say here that excessively high parental expectations can cause a child to adopt a rigid way of behaving in order to try to make sure that his behaviour will meet with approval.

Research seems to indicate (Leach, 1964) that, although the effects of such early upbringing can be very influential in forming rigidity in behaviour and thinking, a non-authoritarian liberal school atmosphere can modify such rigidity. Authoritarian parents usually lay great stress on scholastic success; even a liberal school will be seen by such parents as 'good'—as an organization representing authority and power, which they admire. If, therefore, a child can be persuaded to accept the norms of such a school his parents will usually support him if he does well, and the rigid bounds of his behaviour and thinking may be weakened.

It is important for the teacher to recognize a real emotional problem in the child who seems afraid of messing up his clothes and hands, and not to deal brusquely with such a child; often the fear of mess and untidiness is sufficiently strong to be labelled obsessional, and then the child will require additional help. Knowledge of the parents will usually shed light on the origins of the child's behaviour, and will give some clues about possible ways of overcoming the difficulty.

In older children and in adolescents the rebel may well be the boy or girl who has thrown away completely the rigidity of his upbringing. It is a pity that such behaviour, which often results in lawlessness, has to be met by society with the very forces of authority against which the young person is rebelling.

The withdrawn child

In several ways withdrawn children present the teacher with especially difficult problems; they do not readily come to the teacher's notice, yet they may need the teacher's attention more than the attention-seeking child. Unlike the hyperactive or aggressive child the withdrawn child gives few clues about his troubles because he does not express himself. One may, of course, notice the lonely child in the playground, or realize that a particular boy or girl appears never to make contact with other children or use apparatus or materials in the classroom; but there is a danger that, because he is neither noisy nor a nuisance, he will be thought of as 'shy' and consequently ignored. It is only when the teacher finds that she can remember nothing about the child, and has few records of his work, that she should begin to watch him more, and she may then notice how he keeps himself apart from human contact.

The kind of family problems which tend to produce withdrawal often seem to be problems which, if investigated, appear to infringe the parents' privacy; the possibly hyperanxious mother of the over-protected child may not readily wish to discuss her feelings with a teacher. In addition, since a child's withdrawal is not infrequently his response to severe mental illness in a parent, and this kind of illness is often, even today, considered a shame on the family, the remaining parent may not wish the teacher to ask questions and will probably refuse to come to the school.

Sometimes a child will withdraw from human contact after being bereaved, as a defence from having other potentially warm relationships broken; the fear of being hurt once more by making an emotional tie which may have to be severed is too great; so no contact is made in order to prevent the possibility of further hurt being experienced.

Such children are obviously in very great need of help, and if the situation is not too acute the teacher can do a great deal by keeping close to the child and showing him that she is interested in him. However, children who have been deprived of a warm and close personal relationship with a parent or a parent-substitute may suddenly form an intense attachment to a teacher, and the teacher should be most careful not to allow this attachment to develop too far, for undoubtedly such a relationship cannot continue indefinitely and the child might then experience a feeling of rejection. For this reason it is wiser usually to encourage other children to establish contacts with the withdrawn child, while at the same time displaying an interest in him without giving him too much special attention.

If a child is obviously acutely withdrawn psychiatric help must be sought.

Thieving in the classroom

Stealing in a classroom is often more upsetting to some teachers than any other form of misdemeanour. Because we live in a property-owning society our sense of security depends to an extent on the assurance that in most normal circumstances we can trust others not to take our possessions away. We often feel very angry with people who take our goods, not only because they threaten our security, but because our possessions become an extension of ourselves and we invest them with certain emotions. In a classroom there are additional complications; the teacher feels she must protect the other children from the pilferer, and yet the thief is often for a time unknown. Some teachers are driven in their anxiety to asking the culprit to own up, and acute tension can be created in the class which not infrequently ends in a sensitive child confessing to an act he did not commit. Often too such sensitive children, without actually confessing guilt, will blush and show every sign of guilt (page 137). When she discovers that pilfering is taking place it is as well for the teacher to remind herself that the intensity of the emotions possibly engendered in her is probably greater than is justified by the situation.

In an infant school there will be many children who have not learned fully to respect other people's possessions. Even in homes where it is made clear that one must not take other people's things it is difficult for the young child to differentiate between those things at home which belong to everyone, and those which are personal possessions; so at school he may not understand the difference between using materials in school and taking them home, or between what belongs to the classroom and what belongs to another child. We know well how very tenuous are children's concepts of morality (chapter 6) and in a society where mother picks up goods from a supermarket and is permitted to put them into one kind of basket (the shop basket) but not into another kind, it takes time to learn the rules.

In many homes too personal possessions are not valued, and the child comes to school with little idea that to take things which have not been specifically given to him is not approved.

Punishment for pilfering is mostly found to be ineffective, and long verbal explanations given to young children are usually worse than useless, for young children cannot cope with abstract concepts (chapter 4), and ideas about morality are abstract concepts. With many younger children free giving of the kind of goods, often small colourful objects, which they previously stole can be effective. Webb (1967) suggests that small children can be helped to learn about the private nature of personal possessions by the teacher making it her practice daily to empty her desk, tidy her pockets and generally make it clear that in tidying up she is returning various items both to the *people* to whom they belong, as well as to the *places* where they belong. It also helps to allow children to borrow things on the understanding that these are returned in due course to their owner. They must learn what can and what cannot be taken.

However, we know that children who are older and who have learned the importance in our society of personal possessions also sometimes begin to pilfer. It has already been suggested (page 175) that this is one form of drawing attention to themselves, and the teacher will either already know something about the child's background which will give her a clue about his behaviour, or she will be wise to try to find out. When children come from homes where there is disturbance of some kind the pilfering can be seen as a cry for help, or a compensation for feelings of rejection. It happens, though, that children from good and intact homes suddenly begin to show signs of disturbance, which may include thieving, and as domestic situations, particularly in young families, are seldom static, it is nearly always worth while trying to discover what changes may have taken place in the family set-up which may account for the child's behaviour.

Physical defects

The teacher in an infant or junior school is often the first person to detect a minor though important physical defect from which a young child may be suffering. Such children can be viewed as 'bridge' children between those with severe physical handicap, such as frequent illness or an obviously discernible disability, and those with emotional or educational problems and no *apparent* physical disabilities.

In many education authority areas there are now no longer any routine medical checks in school, except for tests carried out on entry at five years of age, and later the occasional 'sweep' test for hearing and sight. Poor sight is unusual in small children, and so the onset of myopia can easily be missed without regular eye tests. Teachers in both junior and secondary schools should be on the look-out for the child who screws up his eyes when trying to see the blackboard, or who complains of headaches.

Other children have been called 'brain damaged', and this term is used in at least three different ways (Furneaux, 1969):

(1) for the obviously severe disorders, such as cerebral palsy;
(2) to describe the possible origin of certain kinds of child *behaviour*, and
(3) to describe a number of disorders which have a common origin in damage to, or *dysfunction of, the brain.*

Wortis (1957) has said that there is no 'brain-injured' child, only a variety of brain-injured children, whose problems are quite varied, and whose condition calls for a more refined analysis than some of the current generalizations. However, Silver (1957) has specified three areas which brain damage influences:

(1) it causes *interruption of maturation*, and this means a retention of old behaviour patterns and difficulty in forming new ones;
(2) it makes it difficult for the child to *control impulsive actions*, and
(3) it makes it likely that such *children are anxious.*

A perceptive teacher will note the child who shows an unusual degree of anxiety, who has learning difficulties and who presents certain behavioural problems, such as either emotional lability*, sensitivity to frustration, a distorted body image and a controlling bossiness on the one hand, or a withdrawn, defensive and possibly compulsive kind of behaviour on the other hand. However, it by no means follows that children with some of these problems are brain-injured, but a combination of such difficulties should cause a teacher to observe the child more closely and to ask for specialized help for the child.

The loose use of the term 'brain-damaged' and the general lack of understanding of the many difficulties associated with this problem sometimes results in groups of children so designated being treated by similar methods, when they each need training tailored to their individual need.

Children who have marked spelling and reading problems may suffer from poor auditory or poor visual discrimination. Poor auditory discrimination is usually detected when the teacher notices that a child has difficulty in distinguishing between *d*s and *t*s, and between *p*s and *b*s. The Wepman Auditory Discrimination Test (1958), which can be used for children of eight and over, should indicate if a child can discriminate between certain sounds. In this test the child, its back to the teacher, is asked to say if the same word has been said twice, or if two different words have been spoken. The words will differ in either vowel or consonant; for example, 'shape—shake', or 'pat —pet'. A child who does poorly in this test, or who has obvious difficulties in discriminating between hard and soft consonants, should be sent for audiometric screening. It is, of course, possible that a poor speech model at home is responsible for the deficiency. On the other hand the child may be suffering from high-frequency deafness, or temporary deafness due to a head cold. If a child is subject to persistent or frequent head colds, progress in his reading and spelling can be adversely affected. Teachers in schools where reading is taught phonetically are more likely to detect a possible auditory problem, whereas in schools where reading is taught by emphasizing memory of whole words teachers are more likely to discover problems of visual discrimination.

Dyslexia

A discussion of subtle physical deficiences which may affect scholastic performance leads naturally to a consideration of reading problems, and what has been called 'dyslexia', or 'word blindness'. It has been suggested that this term has been used to cover so many different kinds of reading difficulty that it is of little value for the purposes of classification. There is no real agreement on diagnostic criteria, nor does one know how many children are at risk, nor whether there is one cause or several.

From a study undertaken between 1966 and 1969 and reported by Clark (1970) it seems clear that of a group of nineteen children in this study who were of *average* intelligence but who were two years or more behind in their reading all had difficulties other than not being able to decipher a printed word on a page. They had a wide diversity of disabilities and it did not seem possible to determine an underlying pattern of limitations. This group of nineteen children comprised only about 1 per cent of the population used in the investigation; fifteen were boys and only four girls. They were of average IQ but their verbal IQ was below ninety. It was common for children in this group to have speech defects and poor auditory discrimination as well as poor visuo-motor discrimination, while the parents were not particularly active in helping their children. A teacher will seldom meet children who are of average or superior intelligence and who have severe reading disabilities, and are also resistant to remedial help given in school. Such children need specialist guidance, but Clark (1970) points out that practically all other reading problems which teachers meet can be dealt with in the classroom, though it may be necessary to enlist the help of others in the school.

In the same study it was found that about 15 per cent of all the 1,900 children tested had no independent reading skill after having been at school for two years, but after three years only 6 per cent required assistance with basic reading skills. With these children reversal or inversion of letters, as well as reversal of letter order, was common: most of the children were of low average intelligence, and absence rate from school, and/or rate of change of schools, was high. Nearly a third had poor co-ordination. Vernon (1971) lists the four major psychological processes involved in reading, and states that a misfunctioning of any one of the four can cause difficulties in reading: visual perception, audio-linguistic perception, intellectual processes and motivational processes. She says that it is difficult to trace the relationship between various environmental deficiencies and backwardness in reading. Vernon considers that there may be a dyslexic syndrome in addition to the more usual causes of backwardness. The basic disability she describes appears to be a combination of failure to grasp 'the sequential spatial relationships of printed letters and the temporal sequential relationships of phonemes* in words', and an inability to relate these together to form meaningful words. So far no known cause of such a specific syndrome has been established.

It is most important for the teacher, particularly in the primary school, to be able to diagnose a child's reading difficulties and for her to be aware of the differences in skills between children in a group. Vernon also lays great stress on individual teaching. Research in the teaching of both reading and spelling to the backward child has shown how relevant is the role of the teacher in relation to the reading and spelling abilities of the primary children in her charge.

The gifted child

Relatively recently society has become interested in children whose only problem is that they are more gifted than the average child. The question has been asked whether we are educating such children to their best advantage, and, if special arrangements are to be made for them, whether it is wise to educate them with others of similar exceptional gifts separately from average children. The 'gifted' child has been defined as the child 'who shows consistently remarkable performance in any worthwhile line of endeavour' (*57th Year Book of the National Society for the Study of Education*, 1968). Such children are either of outstanding general intellectual ability or they show some specific ability, such as in arithmetic, or a particular artistic skill. A number of studies have shown that these children, contrary to common belief, are usually outstanding in personality characteristics, such as common sense, a sense of humour, conscientiousness, self-confidence, truthfulness and so on (Terman, 1926; Parkyn, 1949).

The gifted child usually has an extensive vocabulary for his age together with good powers of comprehension, observation, reasoning, memory and relational thinking (Shields, 1968). Although there appears to be some contradiction in the evidence from a number of studies regarding the relationship between intellectual gifts and creative gifts (Getzels and Jackson, 1962; Wallach and Kogan, 1965; Lovell and Shields, 1967), it does seem that most highly intelligent children obtain high ratings on creativity tests. Lovell and Shields (1967) consider that the scores gained in their study by highly intelligent children aged between eight-and-a-half and eleven-and-a-half years, with an IQ of 140 and over, on various tests of creativity, intelligence, logical thinking and mathematical ability, indicate the existence of creative thinking abilities. However, psychologists are as yet unsure exactly what they are measuring when they appear to measure 'creativity', and it may be that creativity is not a unitary factor at all; it may be that, as Burt suggests (1962), creative ability is highly specific and relates to a particular field of interest. It is possible also that creative ability is related more to personality factors, such as intellectual independence, less acceptance of authority and lack of emotional inhibition, than to extremely high intellectual gifts.

Regarding the education of the gifted child, one must differentiate between the child with high general intellectual gifts and the child with unusual artistic or other specific abilities. Burt (1967) has suggested the provision of special schools for the mathematically gifted, and other writers have put forward the idea that children of high intellectual abilities should be 'accelerated' by being placed in classes with children who are older, or by being given an enriched environment so that they can work at studies which their peers could not undertake. Children who are artistically gifted can attend special schools whose purpose it is to develop these gifts, but it is not usual for such attendance to start before the secondary-school stage. Arrangements which can be made for such children are described by Gold (1965), in *The Year Book of Education 1961*, and *The Year Book of Education 1962*. The Plowden Report commented on the needs of the specially gifted child and suggested that special schooling should be restricted to those children who are gifted in music, the arts or ballet.

It is important for the teacher to be as aware of the sensitivities and abilities of the gifted children in her class as it is for her to be aware of the difficulties which less fortunate children have. Because gifted children often have many abilities they should be given opportunities in the ordinary school of exercising these abilities as widely as possible; it is also important for these children, as indeed it is important for all children, to be provided with a curriculum which encourages flexibility and originality of thought. One must remember, though, that only the most exceptional child of junior age is capable of formal operational thinking (pages 110f.) and so such a child should be given a great deal of 'concrete' experience, though possibly of a more sophisticated kind from that of less able children (chapter 4).

The Plowden Report has also suggested that special arrangements might be made to give junior children 'interest' teaching, by obtaining help from local persons who have specialist knowledge or specialist abilities which reflect a child's interests. It is not unusual for a gifted child to have developed an expertise, or a range of knowledge, in a subject which surpasses that of many adults, and the interest of such children can be greatly fostered by their being able to discuss their subject with expert adults.

Groth and Holbert (1969) found that the emotional needs of gifted children showed more concern with self-actualization than those shown by normal children in their control group, and the ten to fourteen-year-olds in this study expressed a continuing desire for love and for belonging. It would seem then that there is a definite need for such children to express their high gifts. Wallach and Kogan (1965) seem to have found that the child who is highly creative but of *relatively* low intelligence finds life at home and at school more difficult than other creative children. They suggest that such children should have an environment which is as free from stress as possible.

Kellmer Pringle (1970) has identified what she calls the 'able misfit', the child with high ability who is unable to make full use of his ability. She stresses early identification of such a child, in the hope, not always realizable, that the provision of a helpful environment may enable such a child to develop his gifts. She suggests that when a child is performing badly in school but can still learn easily and quickly, has a good memory and a thirst for knowledge, then the teacher should investigate further.

The administration of tests

Reference has been made throughout this chapter to a number of methods by which a good teacher can evaluate and assess a child's capabilities and needs. We have not, however, so far considered the actual administering of formal tests. Most teachers give group intelligence tests to their class from time to time, and although there are some disadvantages attached to the giving of such tests, these are most probably counterbalanced by the teacher's personal knowledge of the children in her care. It is inevitable that when a test is administered to a number of children simultaneously, not all factors of influence and importance are under control, and there will inevitably be a margin of error which is not so great when an individual test is given. A low score in a group test is not very significant if the teacher knows the child to be capable, but a high score from a child who has not done well in school is significant. A test of this kind may first indicate to the teacher that she has an 'able misfit' (see above) in her class; indeed, the main function of the school group IQ test is to pick out the underfunctioning child; it is useful also to assist in the making of broad categorizations if these are required for a special purpose.

Teachers are sometimes concerned when an educational psychologist, whose help may be sought in special circumstances, appears to duplicate the teacher's work by administering an individual IQ test. This is done not because the psychologist doubts the teacher's findings, but because a great deal more information can be obtained from individually administered tests than from group tests. An individual test enables the psychologist to detect relevant factors other than cognitive functioning, such as the child's attitude to work and interest in work, whether he is capable of sustained effort, and whether he is emotionally disturbed. The trained and experienced educational psychologist can from this information get a fairly comprehensive picture of a child's emotional attitude to life, as well as being able to measure intellectual functioning with more important factors under control than when a group test is given. In addition, the educational psychologist can bring his clinical knowledge to bear on the interpretation of various additional projective tests which can also be administered by him.

If the psychologist's test result should differ somewhat from the teacher's findings then this need not mean that the teacher has administered her test badly; it is difficult to cross-compare IQ test results without knowing which particular areas of cognitive functioning are being tested, whether verbal or non-verbal reasoning abilities, spatial or number ability, etc.

Apart from administering and interpreting a variety of tests in accordance with his special training, the educational psychologist may at times be asked to give assistance when the school has difficulty in getting parents to co-operate. The educational psychologist has also been trained in an interview situation with adults to find the vital areas of trouble more quickly than a teacher can, and the fact that he is someone outside the school may result in some parents being less reluctant to discuss matters of difficulty with him than they would be with someone from within the school.

When a child exhibits deeply disturbed behaviour in one of the several ways we have considered, or when he is obviously grossly underfunctioning, then the educational psychologist's assessments may result in the child being referred to a clinic and in the assignment of a specially trained social worker to help him and his family.

The adolescent

A chapter on the understanding of children should not conclude without some mention of the particular problems adolescent children may present, though it should not be assumed that the period of adolescence need be especially difficult either for the adolescent or for the adults with whom he is in contact. A great deal has been written about these problems and most teachers who are in contact with this age group are only too well aware of them.

Margaret Mead (1958) and others have commented that the period of adolescence need not be turbulent, but that the climate of our culture makes it so. She found little evidence in primitive cultures of the disturbances we so often see. Many of life's problems, which the adolescent has to face more or less at the same time, such as taking on social responsibility, coming to terms with sex, deciding on his religious attitudes, are in primitive societies assigned to different ages, or are not met with at all. In addition, our society is an inconsistent society, in that we present conflicting standards, contrasting philosophies, a choice of religions and a choice of work; and during a prolonged period the adolescent is unplaced in society, whereas in most primitive societies even the abnormal have a place (Mead, 1958). So the adolescent is in a 'no-man's-land' of being neither biologically a child nor socially an adult. Our society provides a long educational period which, however beneficial, is seen by many adolescents as an enforced extended childhood, although nowadays many children are maturing physically earlier than they did at a time when education for the majority of the population finished at fourteen years of age. It is not surprising that this period should sometimes prove to be a difficult one alike for adult and adolescents in interaction with one another.

In an earlier chapter (page 145) we have seen how the young child's life and development centres largely around his family; we have also noted that the older junior child, and the child newly entering the secondary school, seeks to identify more and more with his peers. Through these attachments, first to the family and then to friends, the individual person emerges in adolescence, seeing himself as a unique being. However, his growing need for independence to develop himself is limited, at least for the adolescent still at school, by complete, or almost complete, financial dependence on his parents, and by the inevitable refusal of society to allow him to take on the adult responsibilities for which he is physically and intellectually ready. The adolescent needs help to develop his individuality and his independence, and opportunities should be provided to enable him to practise social behaviour until he finds the attitudes and behaviour patterns which both suit his personality and are also acceptable to others. The provision of such opportunities not only enables the young person to develop his personality and to exercise his growing abilities for taking responsibility and for acting maturely, but will make it unnecessary for him to assert his individuality in less acceptable ways.

Alice Laing (1966) has suggested that, in addition to formal teaching, teachers might at times attempt to teach informally in self-selected groups. The rationale behind this suggestion is that, since in adolescence the important relationships are no longer between the 'child' and the adult, but between the adolescents themselves, and since such adolescent groups tend to form themselves, teachers should utilize the energy which such groups exhibit for learning purposes. Some success has been achieved by teaching adolescent groups in this way.

In discussions on the advisability of sex education in school, thought is not usually given to the possibility that adolescents at least may find the problems of human relationships, whether or not these are of a sexual kind, more troubling than ignorance about sexual matters. Several investigators have found that children do not normally reflect on their own feelings until early adolescence, nor do they seem self-consciously to review their relationships with others until that time; but by about thirteen years of age or so adolescents are much more aware of their own feelings and how the behaviour of others impinges on them (Wood, 1968). However, there is often little opportunity for young people to discuss such feelings and relationships with helpful adults, and for this reason the increasing practice of making opportunities for adolescents to talk with teachers, or with the school counsellor, about their feelings and about possible problems which they are encountering in their relationships with other people, is likely to prove very helpful to them.

Adolescents often have high ideals, and from their standpoint criticize the frequently 'less idealistic' views of adults. It is hard for adults who have lived much longer and achieved much more than a young person to accept criticism and bitterness without indicating anger and resentment; it is equally difficult at times to listen to an expression of views about, say, world affairs, which may be high-handed and uninformed. There is little doubt, however, that the attitudes of adults towards the adolescent are of great importance in helping him to live through this period of his life. The enhancement of self-esteem is probably even more important for the adolescent than for the younger child. Because the teenager so often displays a kind of arrogance, which may well be a cover for feelings of uncertainty, adults, misunderstanding his behaviour, tend to diminish his self-esteem just when it most needs enhancing. If parents and teachers can see the idealism behind the criticism and the insecurity behind the assertiveness and if they can understand rather than condemn, then the difficulties experienced during the years from twelve to twenty can be lived through more easily than without this understanding.

FURTHER READING

WEBB, L.: *Children with Special Needs in the Infants' School* (Smythe, London, 1967).

THOMAS, A., S. CHESS, AND H. G. BIRCH: *Temperament and Behaviour Disorders in Children* (Viking Press, New York, 1968).

VERNON, M. D.: *Reading and Its Difficulties* (Cambridge University Press, 1971).

FURNEAUX, B.: *The Special Child* (Penguin Books, Harmondsworth, 1969).

SHIELDS, J. B.: *The Gifted Child* (National Foundation for Educational Research, 1968).

8

The adult as interactor with the child

Loevinger in an amusing article called 'Patterns of Parenthood as Theories of Learning' (1959) makes the point that child-rearing patterns only work if one can be sure that the child is aware what effect the parent (or teacher) intends to produce with the particular child-rearing pattern which has been adopted. It is unlikely, though, that the child will be aware of this intention, and, she says, since children generally seek the gratification of their own impulses they will in any case mostly find ways of circumventing the social learning methods which their parents have adopted. 'A shift in parentmanship is countered by a shift in childmanship.' Loevinger suggests that there are three different kinds of social learning theories available to parents:

Parent One will use a reinforcement theory, whereby a child is punished for wrongdoing, probably by physical means, and rewarded for rightdoing, though the latter is mostly overlooked and children are seldom rewarded as conspicuously as they are punished.

Parent Two believes in learning by insight. Parents (and teachers) explain why certain acts are wrong and persuade children to behave differently another time.

Parent Three is sure that children learn mostly by identification; that is, he believes that children model themselves on adult behaviour (chapter 2) and that the way children are controlled should never be by means which in themselves set a bad example.

However, whatever the intentions of adults, the children may see the matter quite differently; reinforcement theory, particularly when physical punishment is used, may be interpreted by a child as if he were being reared by identification theory; and children of parents *two* and *three* may not understand about insight and identification, and merely enjoy the lack of serious consequences following a particular misdemeanour!

This somewhat frivolous approach to a serious problem—which, as indicated in chapter 1, has troubled and is still troubling most conscientious people who want to act in the best way in relation to the children in their care—emphasizes the very real difficulty experienced by so-called experts when asked by parents and teachers how they should treat children. Loevinger herself suggests that the main value of a parental (and teacher) social-learning theory for behaviour (chapter 2) lies in demonstrating to a child the ability of adults to curb their own impulses simply because it is better for the future welfare of another person, the child, that they should do so. This is, of course, adopting basically a theory of identification. However, although consistency in behaviour is important, it may also be possible, by understanding the level of development which a particular child has reached, to use successively a number of learning theories, each appropriate both to the particular misdemeanour it is intended to correct and also to the child's developmental stage.

Methodological problems of investigating the relationship between rearing habits and personality development

It is very difficult to demonstrate a definite relationship between *specific* methods of child rearing and children's subsequent behaviour, because so many variables inevitably intervene between the rearing and the behaviour.

In addition, studying the relationships between parental rearing habits and child personality involves acute methodological problems. For example, reports from parents are frequently, though not always, retrospective; when parents and children are observed instead of questioned on their interaction there is the problem of·the effect of the observer on the interaction. There is usually too the assumption that parental behaviour is consistent, both in dealing with any one child and in dealing with all the children in a family, and yet one knows that the best parents are affected by circumstances which make it unlikely that they will be consistent in the handling of even one child. In a longitudinal study which included a study of consistency, Bayley and Schaefer (1960) found that mothers were usually stable in their *affectional* attitudes, but they were not consistent in their attitude to the child's need for freedom and in the degree of autonomy they allowed. Evidence is also available to show that different kinds of personalities of children in the same family call forth different responses from parents, and also that the socialization processes are by no means unidirectional (Bell, 1968). In addition there is the common assumption that the *mother's* rearing methods have the major influence on the children. Although there is some justification for this view, since the mother normally spends much more time with a child than the father does, and consequently her influence may be greater, there is evidence to show that where delinquency or other problem behaviour is exhibited in a child, the father's contribution to causing such behaviour appears to be by no means negligible (Burton and Whiting, 1961; Grygier, Chesley and Tuters, 1969).

An additional difficulty is that the methods parents adopt to rear their children are necessarily affected by their own personality structure, yet there are no means of knowing whether the characteristics which their children exhibit are due chiefly to the rearing methods used or to the inheritance of certain of the parents' personality features. Eysenck (1965, and elsewhere) suggests that the introverted child socializes more easily than the extraverted child. There is also some evidence that very active restless children are more difficult to socialize, perhaps because they are not able to pay sufficient attention to the relevant socializing cues. Again, there appear to be no studies which explicitly relate parental rearing methods individually to *all* the children in a family. It is known, for instance, that different methods of handling have different effects on boys and girls respectively; it has been found, for example, that a warm and giving mother produces boys who are leaders and who have a strong Superego but produces girls who are dependent and have a low conscience! As Burton (1968) states: 'It is difficult to accept . . . the idea that the same child-rearing practice by the same parent should produce opposite effects in a son and a daughter.' It may be equally difficult to accept, yet not impossible to find evidence, that the same child-rearing practice by the same parent can produce differential effects in each and *all* the children of one family, though it is doubtful, as has been suggested before, whether in fact parents do use the same rearing methods for all their children. The research area is also vastly complicated by the different ways in which parents and children perceive one another. Stott (1941) reports finding poor consistency between reports given by siblings of their home environment. Again, parents may report not how they *actually* behaved towards their children, but what they feel would have been the *appropriate* way to behave.

These research problems are mentioned in order to emphasize the very real difficulty which exists when attempts are made to define causes and effects in the upbringing of children, and they are also mentioned in the hope of inculcating a certain wariness in the reader, so that when he encounters dogmatic statements about how to treat children he will recollect that in this area many problems still remain to be solved. However, various studies carried out over a number of years with increasingly strict methodological control, employing a variety of methods and using children from different age groups, do seem to indicate a reasonable consensus of opinion about the kinds of rearing methods which appear to be *more likely* to produce children with certain characteristics and not others.

Possible relationship between personality characteristics and rearing

Several studies in the past have investigated the development of aggression; there seems little doubt that parental aggression, or what others may prefer to call excessive physical punishment, produces overt or covert aggression, depending on the severity of the punishment administered (chapter 7). Up to a certain level of punishment the child may *show* aggressive behaviour, but beyond this level the aggressive feelings, which could be engendered by the parents' punishment, express themselves mostly in fantasy or in punitive and restrictive ideas about other people's behaviour. Anthropological work which indirectly supports these findings shows that societies which worship aggressive gods also appear to use punitive child-rearing methods.

Both aggressiveness and dependency are viewed differently by our society according to whether they are displayed by boys or girls. Normally a degree of aggressiveness is permitted for boys but discouraged in girls, and conversely girls are encouraged to be dependent and boys to be independent. In chapter 7 reference is made to the finding that aggressive behaviour is stimulated when parents punish a child when he displays aggression towards themselves, particularly when at the same time they encourage him to be aggressive outside the home. However, it also seems that extreme permissiveness in the face of the child's aggression may encourage its further expression (chapter 7).

The whole question of whether to punish children, and if so, when and how, and the place of rewards and punishment in child-rearing methods, is a complex one. We discussed earlier the consistency which parents may or may not adopt in their behaviour. In relation to rewards and punishments, consistency can mean either the rewarding or punishing *techniques* adopted by parents and teachers, or always rewarding and punishing the *same specific acts*. A number of studies indicate that while it is important always to reward or punish particular acts (if one punishes at all), so that the child is informed what is approved, and what is not approved, behaviour, it is better not to make any kind of reward or punishment which will be administered predictably. It is important also to give the child verbal explanations of approved and disapproved behaviour, so that he can understand how he should act another time in a similar situation but in a different place (Burton, 1968). Because this kind of cognitive support for approved and disapproved behaviour is mostly lacking in a linguistically deprived home, a child from such a home is relatively handicapped in the internalization of authority, and also in the ability to generalize behaviour from one specific act to other similar acts (page 119).

It has been implied earlier (page 191) that social teaching by identification is probably the most suitable method for adults to adopt. There is a danger, however, that this could be confused with the giving of 'unconditional love' in all circumstances. Whiting and Child (1953) say that if the giving of 'unconditional love' were, in fact, consistently applied in principle, a child could not learn to discriminate, and that such a method would produce children whose behaviour would be 'directionless, asocial and completely unpredictable'. It seems necessary, therefore, to indicate to a child approval for some acts and disapproval for others, and somehow to reconcile this with adult behaviour with which the child can identify, ideally at all times.

It might appear that to rely on rewards for approved acts and punishments for disapproved acts is a fairly straightforward way of teaching social behaviour, particularly if one were not concerned with problems of identification. Indeed, early learning theorists were of the 'common-sense' opinion that responses which are rewarded are 'stamped in', and responses which are punished are 'stamped out' (Thorndike, 1911). However, Logan and Wagner (1965) pinpoint something sophisticated learning theorists have known for a considerable time, which is that the terms 'reward' and 'punishment' cover complex happenings in widely varying situations, so that behaviour arising from such situations depends on the timing, quantity and quality of reward or punishment, together with the probability of receiving or not receiving such appropriate treatment, and that all these factors, as well as extraneous situational cues, have to be controlled if the would-be modifier of a child's behaviour wishes to be successful in the kind of behaviour he seeks to inculcate. The problem of when, how, and how often to give rewards and punishments is a complex one when the experimental animal is a rat; how much more complex is such an endeavour when the animal is a human child! It is probably because the problems associated particularly with punishing children have been viewed in too simple a fashion that this method of controlling a child is still used so extensively, but also often so unsuccessfully.

Effects of punishment

Sears, Maccoby and Levin (1957) and others appear to have established that physical control, such as the giving of tangible rewards, administering physical punishment and removing privileges, are negatively associated with the development of a strong conscience. It has been found that punishment produces anxiety, and it is possible, though by no means inevitable, that the extremely anxious child is also a heavily punished child (chapter 7). Punishment also encourages the production of techniques for avoiding punishment rather than producing desirable behaviour; it also has other complex effects. It is possibly quite effective in momentarily stopping some disapproved act, but physical punishment may generate hostility; it may drive the act underground; also it may provide an example of punitiveness and possibly aggressiveness; the child may very likely identify with the punisher, seeing him as an aggressor. There is a good deal of experimental and observational evidence to show that punishment produces fear of being found out, rather than the establishment of an internal control. Sluckin (1970) has also suggested that the effects of punishment 'over-generalize' (to use learning-theory terminology)—that is, the effects spread to activities which are associated by the child, probably unconsciously, with the punished activity, but of which it is not the intention of the adult to disapprove. Punishment may, therefore, be more extensive in its effects than the punisher intended it should be. An example of this is illustrated when parents punish children for playing with their genitals, and this for the child generalizes to feelings of guilt later associated with all sexual activities.

Sears, Maccoby and Levin were interested in isolating the factors which, in a general way, make for the production of strong Superego formation, and they were not so interested in indicating how the development of particular kinds of behaviour could be fostered, nor in showing what other kinds of behaviour could be prevented, and by what specific means.

A good deal of work by other researchers had until recently supported their other finding that psychological punishment, or love withdrawal, was the more effective means of inculcating a sense of unease whenever disapproved behaviour was contemplated. Bernstein (chapter 4) has also commented on the fact that this kind of attitude—often adopted by middle-class parents towards their children as opposed to the more frequently administered physical punishment used by working-class parents towards their children—is one of the reasons why middle-class children normally develop a stronger Superego, whereas a child from a working-class background relies on physical strength either to control others or to be controlled by them. Freud also considered that conscience formation rested on fear of loss of love, though he also postulated that the need for the child to identify with the parent of the same sex while working through the Oedipal situation contributed to Superego growth (chapters 2 and 5).

However, Freud, Bernstein, and Sears *et al.* were essentially interested in the *total* parent-child relationship and in the use of punishment by the parents within that relationship. More recent work has differentiated between general punitiveness on the part of parents, which appears to have a deleterious effect, and punishment for specific acts which may have an 'informative effect' (Marshall, 1965). Similarly Walters and Parke (1967) consider that punishment is a more effective control technique than had been supposed, particularly when it is judiciously timed, and if the punisher is able both to elicit and simultaneously strengthen an alternative response to the response being punished. This would seem to be a method which could be used in the training of animals, and is, indeed, highly effective, but parents are mostly too involved emotionally in the misdemeanours of their children to be able to calculate the niceties of timing rewards and punishments!

Support for the findings that physical punishments are probably not effective as a normal means of inculcating desirable behaviour and eradicating undesirable behaviour, particularly with older children, comes from recent work reported by Minturn (1969). Minturn designed a cross-cultural study involving six hundred children from six countries aged ten to fourteen years of age, 50 per cent boys and 50 per cent girls, with half the children from lower-class homes and half from middle-class homes. All the children supported the hypothesis that it was more wrong for a child to hit an adult than for a child to hit another child, and that it was less wrong for an adult to hit a child. The children also confirmed the hypothesis that an aggressor using physical aggression will be judged as being more wrong than an aggressor using verbal aggression; but the children did not assume that a child who was being hit must necessarily have been naughtier than a child who was merely being told off. The children in this cross-cultural study were virtually unanimous that hitting was very wrong, and Minturn considers that this finding has important relevance for parents and teachers, in relation to the use of physical punishment.

It would seem, then, that the use of physical control is, by and large, not very effective, at least not in the way it is normally used by adults in their dealings with children. The work of Sears, Maccoby and Levin (1957) and others contrasted only two kinds of rearing methods—what have been termed the 'physical control' method, and the 'love withdrawal' method, whereby parents and teachers indicated their disapproval by coldness of manner and other non-physical ways of indicating anger. However, Hoffman and Saltzstein (1967) have described a study which investigated the use of three different kinds of control methods, the two methods mentioned above and what they call 'induction'—that is, a method whereby adults indicate to the child the consequences to others of his acts. The children in this study were thirteen- to fourteen-year-olds, and the experimenters were concerned to 'tap' different aspects of conscience, such as guilt-intensity feelings and the use of moral judgements about other people based on internal rather than external considerations. They were also interested in seeing how far the child confessed his misdeeds and accepted responsibility for them and what consideration he showed for other people. They found that the use of the induction method by *middle-class mothers* was consistently associated with advanced moral development, but the findings regarding the use of different methods of control by the *fathers* did not fit any apparent pattern, though there is substantial evidence that where children are maladapted the father's behaviour is usually a contributory factor. Curiously enough the 'love withdrawal' method was negatively associated with strong moral development. With the *lower-class* sample of children there appeared no particular relationship between the child's moral development and the mother's disciplining methods, and the writers conclude that for a child from a lower social class the mother's method of disciplining her child may be less crucial and singular a factor in such a child's developing moral standards than it is for the child from a middle-class home. They say that although more work needs doing to compare the effects of different disciplining methods used by parents from different social classes, one might conjecture that the bases for internalizing authority and values may be quite different for children from the two classes, and that different *kinds* of morality develop in consequence. It certainly seems important for teachers to bear this in mind when dealing with children from different social backgrounds (chapter 7).

Parents and teachers cannot, however, use explanations of consequences of behaviour when children's moral knowledge (page 135) or their knowledge of causality (chapter 4) is too limited to make such explanations comprehensible to them. Scott, Burton and Yarrow (1967) report work with nursery-school children which will appeal to tender-minded parents and teachers. They achieved success in changing the behaviour of small children from undesirable to desirable acts by ignoring in every way undesirable behaviour and responding immediately with affectionate attention to desirable behaviour.

If one looks at the literature which compares observational work on children's moral development with parental child-rearing practices one can make a few tentative generalizations, though it is too early to draw definite conclusions about the relationship between parental behaviour and child morality. It does seem that physical coercion is more conducive to establishing *fear* of detection and *fear* of external punishment as inhibitors, rather than contributing to the establishment of internal controls.⋅ A frequent expression of warmth and affection towards a child helps identification with the parent. Explanations about why a child should not behave in a certain way appear to help the formation of a strong conscience, though when children are very small, or the situation very complex, ignoring (where possible!) an undesirable act and quickly rewarding with affection a desirable act, helps to stamp out the former and encourage the latter. There is experimental evidence too that clearly labelling behaviour—that is, giving cognitive support—helps a child to discriminate between approved and disapproved behaviour, and to transfer this learning to other situations.

Parental personality traits and child personality development

It is of value to look at a number of studies which have compared parental (usually maternal) personality traits as they show themselves in the way parents behave towards their children. The findings of some of these studies appear at times to be contradictory, particularly in relation to the effects of either permissive or firm discipline, but it is of interest to understand what the apparent contradiction may mean. As part of the longitudinal Berkeley growth study which is still going on, Bayley and Schaefer (1960) found that generally children of hostile and controlling mothers had a greater tendency to be maladjusted, whereas children of loving and autonomy-granting mothers had a greater tendency to be well-adjusted; they also found, however, that this tendency was stronger for girls than it was for boys; but they also write (1967) that they cannot say 'whether the mother-child interactions are primarily determined by the behaviour tendencies of the mother or the child'. In most studies it appears that parents who are hostile to their children are also unusually controlling, and parents who are loving are autonomy-granting. Baumrind (1967), however, in her study of three-and four-year-old children found that those children who came from homes which were loving and understanding, but also firm and demanding, showed greater self-control, more affiliation and self-reliance, more exploratory drive and more self-assertion than children whose parents were either only moderately loving and lacking in control, or unaffectionate and punitively firm. Baumrind specifically makes the point that the spontaneity, warmth and zest of the children with loving, but firm, parents were not affected adversely by the high parental control exercised. However, an earlier study by Watson (1957), in which the personalities of children from good and loving, but *strictly disciplined*, homes were compared with those of children from good and loving, but *excessively permissive*, homes showed that the children from the permissive homes displayed significantly greater initiative and independence, better socialization and co-operation, greater affiliation, less hostility and more spontaneity than the children from the strictly disciplined homes. Still a third group of studies by Coopersmith (1967) on the development of high self-esteem have indicated that children with high self-esteem had parents who were non-punitive, but firm; who used rewards rather than physical punishments or threatened love-withdrawal, who showed an interest in the child's welfare, and who saw their child as a significant person who was worthy of their deep interest. These parents too set definite rules of behaviour, and fostered a well-structured, demanding environment, rather than a largely unlimited permissiveness and 'freedom to explore in an unfocused way'. Lindenauer (1968) also has stated that flexibility within a consistent framework of rules is an important complement for the development of a secure and responsible character. The importance of parental recognition of the individuality of each child is also stressed.

It would seem from these studies that some contradictory information is presented: on the one hand there is some evidence that where the home is good and loving, permissiveness develops to a greater degree the commendable qualities which, on the other hand, are produced by an equally loving and understanding home which is, however, firm and demanding. It is thus possible that whether parents are permissive or firm is not as important as the presence of other qualities in their relationship with their children—love, understanding, valuing the child as a person to be respected, being non-punitive and rewarding. Again it may be that some children work more happily in a structured atmosphere and others in greater freedom, providing always that the other positive qualities are present. Burton (1968) indeed has suggested that a number of what *he* calls 'positive' parental characteristics usually cluster together, such as using the disciplinary techniques of rewarding, praising and reasoning; providing a warm home environment; developing the children's talents and showing an interest in their happiness; and he suggests that such a 'cluster' seems to produce children who are high on such characteristics as: low aggression, feelings of responsibility, high level of conscience, low undesirable dependency and high sociability. Conversely parents who display the so-called 'negative' qualities of scolding, derogating, threatening and punishing by physical methods, who are unloving or only moderately loving and who show little interest in their children, appear to produce children who display in their behaviour traits which are the reverse of those children who have parents with 'positive' characteristics. There is no mention in Burton's list of either permissiveness or firmness; but reference is made to the disciplinary techniques of rewarding, praising and reasoning.

It would seem reasonable, then, to suppose that the display of what we have called 'positive' characteristics by parents and teachers, rather than punitive or permissive behaviour, will provide a home and school atmosphere which is more conducive to the growth of qualities which make for a happy and responsible relationship with other people and for effective functioning in life generally. One has, however, also to bear in mind that not only are parental attitudes towards their children influential in forming the child's personality, but that the way a child *interprets* parental behaviour, and also the way he sees himself in fantasy in relation to the other important people in his life, that is, in relation to his parents and siblings, that these factors too are influential in personality formation. The remark of Kelly quoted on page 147—that we are not so much the victims of our history as of our construction of that history—is important when one tries to assess the influences of adult behaviour on children. Unlike animals, when children are being 'trained' they are able to interpret the possible alternative meanings of the training, as Loevinger has pointed out (pages 190f.). They are also able to indulge in a fantasy life which may at times become mistaken for memory. In a review of the family characteristics of normal, neurotic and schizophrenic people, Frank (1965) concluded that a child's psychopathology may not be determined so much by his experiences of life as by his proclivity towards fantasy distortion of reality (page 159). From this one may assume that children who develop behavioural difficulties or unfortunate personality traits may be afflicted with fantasy perceptions which distort their view of the behaviour of others.

It is also worth remembering that the child's own characteristics affect parental behaviour. Bell (1968) (page 139), in a review in which he sought to look anew at correlations between child behaviour and parental behaviour, suggested that models which explain child and animal socialization in terms of the effects of the *parents on the child* are too limited. He has written that, obviously, a correlation between parental treatment and child characteristics shows a *relationship*, but it does not necessarily show a *direction* of effect, though the assumption is always made that the parental behaviour *causes* the child behaviour. He considers that the effect of children's behaviour on parents can no longer be dismissed as only a logical but implausible alternative for the usual explanation that only the parents' behaviour affects the child!

Some parents, and perhaps some teachers too, are unable to display the kind of behaviour which aids good personality growth in children when they are in the company of children, because they themselves have personality problems which often make their relationship with other people difficult, and which in some kinds of disturbed persons are particularly evoked when they deal with children. Thus it has been suggested that one of the reasons why some adults use physical methods of punishing is that for them punishing can be a satisfying activity; when such adults are frustrated and anger builds up which cannot be dissipated, the use of physical power over a child can be excused as being good for the child. In effect such a display of power will usually only be good for the adult who is releasing his pent-up emotion! Similarly it has been shown that people who are self-rejecting tend also to reject their children more than parents who have a reasonable degree of self-esteem (Medinnus and Curtis, 1963); and when one considers how important self-acceptance is in the development of a child's healthy personality, and how self-acceptance is related to acceptance of the self by important other people (Rogers, 1951), one can see how a parent with a low self-acceptance can influence the development of his child's personality in unhappy directions. Because, also, children are so powerless in relation to adults—indeed the only freedom they have is the freedom adults permit them to have—it is too great a temptation for some persons not to refrain from exercising their power over helpless children by making sarcastic comments and by belittling them. Teachers may indeed from time to time encounter a colleague who seems to be using one, or even several, of the children in her class as a scapegoat for her own inadequacies. Lindenauer (1968) has written of adults who use children to satisfy their own needs in this manner. It is a tragedy for all concerned when a teacher manages to pass through the various neecessary selection and training procedures but whose own personality difficulties make it hard for her to both treat children as individuals and to open up lines of communication with them.

Children's concepts of teachers as persons

What do children themselves think about teachers, and what is known about the most effective teachers? A number of studies have investigated children's views. Eleven-year-old children in a study by Taylor (1962) considered that the following are a teacher's most important qualities: ability to help, explain and encourage; knowledge of her subject; firmness in keeping order; fairness; good manners; patience and kindly understanding. Jersild (1940) found that children mentioned sympathy, cheerfulness and good temper as desirable qualities in a teacher, as well as having the ability to be a good disciplinarian. She must be fair, consistent, able to explain well, and permit an expression of opinion. Wood (1968) found that children within a wide age range often commented on helpfulness and ability to discipline as desirable qualities in a teacher. Bad-temper and roughness were disliked characteristics, and children of all ages disliked being shouted at. A sense of humour was also appreciated by children. Older children thought that the ability to produce a good atmosphere in class was important, and being able to get children to work was also referred to as an admirable trait! Indeed, Biber and Lewis (1949) say that the children they interviewed in their studies saw teachers as authority figures who were expected to exercise their authority even if the atmosphere in the school or the classroom is non-authoritarian; and it appears from more recent work that the views of children have not changed fundamentally in the last twenty years. It does seem that children see the teacher mainly as someone who should be helpful; who should enable them to learn; and who must be able to keep control. As Moore (1966) has put it: '[Teachers should display] teaching ability plus a combination of firmness and respect for the child as an individual.' In his study of the difficulties which the ordinary child has to face when adjusting to primary school, Moore comments that the lack of these qualities in a teacher can mar a child's happiness and progress at school. Although he is very sympathetic with the teacher who has to work with large numbers of children, he nevertheless comments that children cannot learn if they are frightened, angry, bewildered or bored; and he found that the sensitivities of small children to their own appearance, to the state of the school lavatories, to the enforced eating of food which may be strange and unpalatable to them—these sensitivities, if unappreciated by adults in the school, make it difficult for the child to use all his gifts.

A teacher's character and personality is thus of particular importance when young children are being taught, as Moore's findings emphasize. How a child is able to meet the inevitable anxieties of his first few weeks at school may powerfully affect his continuing attitude to school and to learning. The teacher's role, especially in the junior school, is in many respects not very different from that of a parent of a large family. In a classroom jealousies can arise, as they arise in families, and a class may react to the return after a temporary absence of a form teacher by 'trying her out' rather as children test a parent's love. The teacher who has empathy for children is likely to be a good teacher, largely because of her powers of understanding and her ability to be firm. Burt (1970B), quoting Ballard, an 'erstwhile and renowned' inspector of schools, says that it is the twin abilities of being able to keep order and being sympathetic which distinguish the good teacher from the bad; and seemingly children of all ages agree with Ballard's views.

FURTHER READING

MEDINNUS, G. R. (ed.): *Readings in the Psychology of Parent-Child Relations* (John Wiley and Sons, New York and London, 1967).

BURTON, R. V.: 'Socialization: Psychological Aspects' in the *Encyclopedia of the Social Sciences* (Collier-Macmillan, New York, 1968).

RETROSPECT

The reader who has perused the major part of this book will be aware by now that many traditional ideas about children, their development and their upbringing, have neither been supported by controlled observational or experimental work, nor have they invariably been derived from valid interpretations of clinical data. A number of such ideas have in themselves been contradictory, for example the idea that both punishment for misdeeds and a permissive type of rearing will produce moral and responsible adults. Again, the notion that children are miniature adults, who differ only from grown-up people because they know less and lack experience of life is an idea which was held almost universally until comparatively recent times, with the exception of psychoanalytic writers such as Susan Isaacs. Only since Piaget's work has become better known has it been realized that there is a *qualitative* difference not only between the mind of a child and that of an adult, but also that such differences exist between the various stages of development throughout childhood. The pedagogic implications of Piaget's work are profound.

The influence of the environment on child development, and the importance of a 'good' environment for healthy functioning, have been stressed in baby- and child-care books for decades. It is clear from material presented in this book that the definition of what is a 'good' environment is not as simple as it may have seemed at one time, and that such subtle factors as personality problems exhibited by a parent can in certain circumstances be more damaging than, for example, the prolonged absence of maternal care, which has been fully discussed by Bowlby and others. It is also now realized that important though good environmental conditions are, the mind of a child is not a *tabula rasa*, a blank sheet on which the experiences of life are written and thus form the personality, but that children may differ as much from one another in innate *psychological* characteristics, such as temperament and ability, as they do in such physical characteristics as height, facial and bodily features, and eye colour. We are far from understanding how great such innate differences are, or how far an enriched environment can compensate for a poor hereditary endowment, but it is certainly clearer now than it has been in the past that man's personality and abilities cannot be fashioned entirely by providing good environmental conditions. This is not to decry the importance of such conditions, but it does enable us better to understand the wide range of ability and of temperamental differences which exists naturally in a human population.

We have noted that children born into homes belonging to the lowest social classes are handicapped in many ways when compared with other children. It would seem that neither an egalitarian scholastic system, nor indeed the provision of nursery-school education, can in itself compensate for such handicaps. The disadvantages apparently suffered affect such children almost from the beginning of life, and it would seem that only by involving parents in the education of their children from an early age and by showing them how to maximize their children's abilities can society hope to help such children to overcome the handicaps from which they might otherwise suffer.

One of the major concerns of parents and of many teachers in bringing up children is that the children in their care should develop into moral and responsible adults, using the word 'moral' in its widest sense, and many parents suffer acute anxiety when quite young children display apparent immorality by telling lies or by seemingly behaving unkindly towards other children. From the results of careful observational and experimental work with young children it is clear that they do not have the same ideas about moral behaviour as mature adults have, and that the development of moral behaviour progresses through a variety of stages as the child grows up. Thus one cannot expect young children to understand adult concepts of morality, and in our handling of children their different ways of viewing so-called moral behaviour must at all times be borne in mind. It is also worth reminding ourselves that children cannot be *made* to do anything unless they are under compulsion, but that their willing co-operation can usually be enlisted. Fortunately most children do want to please other people most of the time!

We have seen that previous generations had clear ideas about the kind of human being they sought to produce through the adoption of specific child-rearing methods. Today it is realized that the universal application of a specific rearing method, regardless of the abilities and temperamental characteristics of the child with whom the adult is interacting, is of little value, and that in any case the indiscriminate application of such methods to all children denigrates the unique individuality of each child. Nevertheless, there are probably some common aims which all thoughtful adults in our society have when bringing up the children in their care. Two of these seem to be paramount: one is that to be able to live happily in the company of other people children must learn to get on well with them, respecting their rights and wishes; the other is that the adult-child relationship should be such that children can grow up able to use their natural abilities to the full. How far these aims can be fulfilled will depend to an extent on the child's own temperament and the ease with which he can respond to other people; on parental characteristics and the general environment in which parents and child find themselves; and on the extent to which the child's fundamental needs can be met. Kellmer Pringle (1972) has recently suggested that all children have four basic needs: a need for love and security, for praise and recognition, for responsibility, and for new experiences. She goes on to imply that the provision of these basic needs remains the ultimate responsibility not only of parents but of the whole of society through its health, housing, social and educational institutions.

GLOSSARY

NOTE: Words in italics are themselves to be found in the glossary.

ABREACTION: Employed by psychoanalysts for the process of releasing a repressed emotion by reliving in imagination the original experience (Drever, 1964).

ACCOMMODATION: In Piagetian developmental psychology, 'modification of behaviour as a result of experience' (Piaget, 1968).

ADAPTATION: In Piagetian developmental psychology, the combined effect of *assimilation* and *accommodation*.

AFFECT: Feeling or emotion.

ANAL STAGE: In psychoanalytic theory, the second of the *psychosexual* stages of development.

ASSIMILATION: In Piagetian developmental psychology, 'the incorporation of an object into the activity of the subject' (Piaget, 1968).

CONATION: Will or drive, striving.

CONSANGUINITY: Blood relationship (Concise Oxford Dictionary, 1964).

CONSCIENCE: An individual's system of accepted moral principles (Drever, 1969). In Freudian psychology, the restraining part of the *Superego*.

CRITICAL PERIOD: A stage in development during which the organism is optimally ready to learn certain response patterns. It is closely related to the concept of maturational readiness (Hilgard and Atkinson, 1967).

DEFENCE MECHANISM: In psychoanalytic theory, unconsciously adopted methods of behaviour which alleviate anxiety by distorting, denying or falsifying reality.

DENDRITE: Process of a *neuron* usually, though not always, short and branching, but defined scientifically as a process traversed by nerve impulses in the direction of the cell body (Drever, 1969).

DENDROGENESIS: The formation of a dendrite.

DISPLACEMENT: In psychoanalytic theory, the process by which energy is channelled from one *object* to another object (Hall, 1954).

EGO: In Freud's tripartite division of the personality, that part corresponding most nearly to the perceived self, the controlling self, which holds back the impulsiveness of the *Id* in the effort to delay gratification until it can be found in socially approved ways (Hilgard and Atkinson, 1967).

EGO-IDEAL: In psychoanalytic theory, that part of the *Superego* which sets a standard for behaviour.

ENACTIVE STAGE OF
COGNITIVE GROWTH: A mode of representing past events through appropriate motor responses (Bruner, 1964).

GENOTYPE: In genetics, the characteristics that an individual has inherited and will transmit to his descendants, whether or not he manifests these characteristics; (contrast with *phenotype*) (Hilgard and Atkinson, 1967).

HOMEOSTATIC: Term borrowed from physiology, employed by some psychologists for compensatory adjustments to meet any threat to the personality (Drever, 1969).

ID: In psychoanalytic theory, part of Freud's hypothesized tripartite personality system. The Id is present from birth, represents the biological aspects of the personality, is the repository of all psychic energy and operates on an unconscious level.

IDENTIFY: A process by which an individual, unconsciously or partially so, as a result of an emotional tie, behaves, or imagines himself behaving, as if he were the person with whom the tie exists (Drever, 1964).

INTROJECT:	Psychoanalytically, taking into oneself the characteristics of another person.
LABILE:	Unstable, liable to displacement or change (Concise Oxford Dictionary, 1964). In psychological contexts usually meaning emotionally unstable.
LATENCY PERIOD:	In psychoanalytic theory, that period of a child's life, approximately between five and puberty, when, according to Freudian theory, sexual drives are latent.
MECHANISMS OF DEFENCE:	See *defence mechanisms*.
MORPHOLOGY:	Study of the structure or form of organisms.
NEO-FREUDIANS:	Meaning 'new Freudians', those persons who have helped to develop Freudian psychoanalytic theories and ideas since Freud's death.
NEURON:	The body of a cell, together with its processes.
OBJECT:	In psychoanalytic theory, any thing or person on whom psychic energy is expended to satisfy an instinct.
OEDIPAL COMPLEX:	In psychoanalytic theory, the largely unconscious complex, developed in a son from attachment (sexual in character, according to analysts) to the mother and jealousy of the father, with the resulting feeling of guilt and emotional conflict on the part of the son, held to be normal in some form or other in any family circle (Drever, 1964).
OEDIPAL STAGE:	In psychoanalytic theory, the stage of development during the *phallic* period of *psychosexual development* when the Oedipal complex is resolved.
ONTOGENESIS:	The evolution and development of the individual; (contrast with *phylogenesis*) (Drever, 1969).
ORAL STAGE:	In psychoanalytic theory, the first of the *psychosexual* stages of development.
OREXIS:	The *conative* and *affective* aspects of experience—impulse, appetite, desire, emotion (Drever, 1969).

PHALLIC STAGE:
In psychoanalytic theory, the third period of *psychosexual* development.

PHENOTYPE:
In genetics, the characteristics that are displayed by the individual organism—e.g. eye colour, intelligence, as distinct from those traits which he may carry genetically but not display; (contrast with *genotype*) (Hilgard and Atkinson, 1967).

PHONEME:
A unit of significant sound in a given language (Concise Oxford Dictionary, 1964).

PHYLOGENESIS:
Origin and evolution of race or species; (contrast with *ontogenesis*) (Drever, 1969).

PLEASURE PRINCIPLE:
The tendency inherent in all natural impulses or 'wishes' to seek their own satisfaction independently of all other considerations; according to Freudian theory, the principle ruling the individual at the start, and remaining always as the guiding principle in the unconscious (Drever, 1969).

PRIMARY PROCESS:
In psychoanalytic theory, the process which produces a memory image of an object that is needed to reduce a tension (Hall 1954). The primary process serves the *pleasure principle;* (contrast *secondary process* and *reality principle*).

PROJECT:
In psychoanalytic theory, the attributing unconsciously to other people, usually as a defence against unpleasant feelings in ourselves —such as feelings of guilt, or inferiority feelings—of thoughts, feelings, and acts towards us, by means of which we justify ourselves in our own eyes (Drever, 1964).

PSYCHOPATH:
An unstable individual who has usually no marked mental disorders, but who has been defined as a 'moral imbecile'.

PSYCHOSEXUAL:
In psychoanalysis 'psychosexual' refers to the theory that development takes place through stages, *oral, anal, phallic,* each stage characterized by a zone of pleasurable stimulation . . . (Hilgard and Atkinson, 1967).

PSYCHE:
Variously defined, but often used as a substitute for mind or soul.

REALITY PRINCIPLE:
In psychoanalytic theory, the postponement of energy discharge until the object which will satisfy a need or reduce tension is found (contrast with *pleasure principle*).

REINFORCEMENT:
In learning theory, a process akin to, but not necessarily synonymous with, reward, which seeks to ensure the repetition of a response in a learning (conditioning) set-up.

SECONDARY PROCESS:
In psychoanalytic theory, the process which aims at discovering in reality (as opposed to fantasy) objects or actions which bring satisfaction of needs and/or reduce tension. The secondary process serves the *reality principle;* (contrast *primary process* and *pleasure principle*).

SENSORI-MOTOR:
Term employment with reference to structures, processes, or phenomena involving both the sensory and the motor aspects, or parts, of the human organism. In Piagetian theory, the first stage of child development before about twenty-one months of age.

SUPEREGO:
In psychoanalytic theory, part of Freud's hypothesized tripartite personality system. The Superego, made up of the *conscience* and *Ego-Ideal*, is the moral part of the personality which both restrains the *Ego* and strives to fulfil the demands of parents and society. It operates mostly at an unconscious level by producing conscious feelings of guilt and anxiety.

SYMBOLIC STAGE OF COGNITIVE GROWTH:
Bruner's final stage of cognitive development, when the child can 'translate his experience into symbol systems' (Osser, 1970).

TEMPERAMENT:
General nature of an individual, especially on the *orectic* side (Drever, 1969); that is, the *conative* (drive) and *affective* (emotional) aspects of the personality.

TRAUMA:
Any injury, wound or shock, most frequently physical or structural, but also mental, in the form of an emotional shock, producing a disturbance, more or less enduring, of mental functions (Drever, 1969). More usually now used to refer to some kind of psychological shock.

BIBLIOGRAPHY

ADAMS, P. L., J. J. SCHWAB AND J. F. APORTE: 'Authoritarian Parents and Disturbed Children' in *American Journal of Psychiatry 121* (1965).

ADORNO, T. W., E. FRANKEL-BRUNSWIK, D. J. LEVINSON AND R. N. SANFORD: *The Authoritarian Personality* (Harper, New York, 1950).

ALLPORT, G. W.: *Personality: a Psychological Interpretation* (Henry Holt, New York, 1937).

ALTMAN, J., G. D. DAS, AND W. J. ANDERSON: 'Effects of Infantile Handling on Morphological Development of the Rat Brain: an Exploratory Study' in *Developmental Psychobiology I* (1968).

ALTUS, W. D.: 'Birth Order and Its Sequelae' in *Science 151* (1966).

AMBROSE, A. (ed.): *Stimulation in Early Infancy* (Academic Press, New York and London, 1969).

ANASTASI, A.: 'Heredity, Environment and the Question "How?" ' in *Psychological Review 65* (1958).

ARONFREED, J.: *Conscience and Conduct* (Academic Press, New York and London, 1968).

BANDURA, A.: 'Social Learning and Imitation' in M. R. Jones (ed.), *Nebraska Symposium on Motivation* (University of Nebraska Press, 1962).

BANDURA, A.: 'The Influence of Rewarding and Punishing Consequences to the Model on the Acquisition and Performance of Imitative Responses' in Bandura and Walters, *Social Learning and Personality Development* (Holt, Rinehart and Winston, London, 1963).

BANDURA, A.: 'A Social Learning Theory of Identificatory Processes' in D. A. GOSLIN (ed.), *Handbook of Socialization Theory and Research* (Rand-McNally, Chicago, 1968).

BANDURA, A. AND R. H. WALTERS: (1963) 'Aggression' in *Child Psychology: The Sixty-second Yearbook of the National Society for the Study of Education, Part 1* (The National Society for the Study of Education, Chicago, 1963).

BARTLETT, SIR F. C.: *Remembering: A Study in Experimental and Social Psychology* (Cambridge University Press, 1932).

BAUMRIND, D.: 'Child Care Practices Anteceding Three Patterns of Pre-school Behaviour' in *Genetic Psychology Monographs 75* (1967).

BAYLEY, N. AND E. S. SCHAEFER: 'Relationships between Socio-economic Variables and the Behaviour of Mothers towards Young Children' in *Journal of Genetic Psychology 96* (1960).

BAYLEY, N. AND E. S. SCHAEFER: 'Maternal Behaviour and Personality Development: Data from the Berkeley Growth Study' in G. R. Medinnus, *Readings in* the *Psychology of Parent-Child Relations* (John Wiley and Sons, New York and London, 1967).

BEARD, R. M.: 'The Order of Concept Development: Studies in Two Fields' in *Educational Review 15* (1963).

BEARD, R. M.: 'An Investigation into Mathematical Concepts among Ghanaian Children' in *Teacher Education* (May 1968).

BEARD, R. M.: *An Outline of Piaget's Developmental Psychology* (Routledge and Kegan Paul, London, 1969).

BELL, R. Q.: 'A Reinterpretation of the Direction of Effects in Studies of Socialization' in *Psychological Review 2*, vol. *75* (1968).

BENEDICT, R.: 'Continuities and Discontinuities in Cultural Conditioning' in M. Mead and M. Wolfenstein, *Childhood in Contemporary Culture* (University of Chicago Press, 1955).

BERKO, J.: 'The Child's Learning of English Morphology' in *Word, 14* (1958).

BERKOWITZ, L.: *The Development of Motives and Values in the Child* (Basic Books, New York, 1964).

BERNSTEIN, B.: 'Some Sociological Determinants of Perception' in *British Journal of Sociology 9* (1958).

BERNSTEIN, B.: 'Language and Social Class' in *British Journal of Sociology 11* (1960).

BERNSTEIN, B.: 'Social Class and Linguistic Development' in A. H. Halsey, J. Floud and C. A. Anderson, *Education, Economy and Society* (The Free Press, New York, 1961).

BERNSTEIN, B. AND D. HENDERSON: 'An Approach to the Study of Language and Socialization' in L. Hudson (ed.), *The Ecology of Human Intelligence* (Penguin Books, Harmondsworth, 1969).

BETTELHEIM, B.: *The Children of the Dream: Communal Child-rearing and its Implications for Society* (Paladin, London, 1971).

BIBER, B. AND C. LEWIS: 'An Experimental Study of What Young Children Expect from Their Teachers' in *Genetic Psychology Monographs 40* (1949).

BLOOM, B. S.: *Stability and Change in Human Characteristics* (John Wiley and Sons, New York and London, 1964).

BOWLBY, J.: 'Forty-four Juvenile Thieves' in *International Journal of Psychoanalysis 25* (1944).

BOWLBY, J. AND J. ROBERTSON: 'Responses of Young Children to Separation from Their Mothers' in *Courrier de la Centre Internationale de l'Enfance 2* (1952).

BRIDGES, K. M.: 'Emotional Development in Early Infancy' in *Child Development 3* (1932).

BRITTON, J.: *Language and Learning* (Allen Lane, The Penguin Press, London, 1970).

BROWN, R. W.: *Social Psychology* (The Free Press, New York, 1965).

BROWN, R. W. AND U. BELLUGI: 'Three Processes in the Child's Acquisition of Syntax' in E. H. Lenneberg (ed.), *New Directions in the Study of Language* (M.I.T. Press, Cambridge, Mass., 1964).

BRUNER, J. S.: 'The Course of Cognitive Growth' in *American Psychology 19* (1964).

BRYANT, P. E.: 'A Young Child's Understanding of Quantity', paper delivered to the British Association, Swansea (1971).

BÜHLER, C.: 'Social Behaviour of the Child' in C. Murchison (ed.), *A Handbook of*

Child Psychology (Clark University Press, Worcester, Mass., 1933).

BÜHLER, C.: *From Birth to Maturity: An Outline of the Psychological Development of the Child* (Routledge and Kegan Paul, London, 1935).

BURGESS, E. W. AND H. J. LOCKE: *The Family* (American Books, New York, 1956).

BURKE, K.: *Language as Symbolic Action* (University of California Press, 1966).

BURT, C.: *The Factors of the Mind* (University of London Press, 1940).

BURT, C.: 'The Evidence for the Concept of Intelligence' in *British Journal of Educational Psychology 25* (1955).

BURT, C.: 'General Introduction: the Gifted Child' in G. F. Z. Bereday and J. A. Lauwerys (eds.), *The World Year Book of Education, 1962* (Evans Bros., London, 1962).

BURT, C.: 'Critical Notice' in *British Journal of Educational Psychology 37* (1967).

BURT, C.: 'The Concept of Intelligence: History of the Concept' in *Journal and News Letter of the Association of Educational Psychologists* (1970A).

BURT, C.: 'Urgent Issues in Educational Psychology', paper read to the British Psychological Society Annual General Conference (1970B).

BURT, C.: Letter in *Bulletin of the British Psychological Society 82* (1971).

BURTON, R. V.: 'Socialization: Psychological Aspects' in *International Encyclopedia of the Social Sciences* (Crowell, Collier and Macmillan, New York, 1968).

BURTON, R. V. AND J. W. M. WHITING: 'The Absent Father and Cross-sex Identity' in *Merrill-Palmer Quarterly Journal of Behaviour and Development 7* (1961).

BUTCHER, H. J.: *Human Intelligence: Its Nature and Assessment* (Methuen, London, 1968).

CANTER, S.: 'Personality Traits in Twins', unpublished paper read to the Annual Conference of the British Psychological Society (1969).

CATTELL, R. B.: *The Scientific Analysis of Personality* (Penguin Books, Harmondsworth, 1965).

CHOMSKY, N.: *Syntactic Structures* (Mouton, 's-Gravenhage, Netherlands, 1957).

CLARK, M.: 'Reading Difficulties in Schools' in *Penguin Papers in Education* (Penguin Books, Harmondsworth, 1970).

CONNOLLY, K.: 'The Evolution and Ontogeny of Behaviour' in *Bulletin of the British Psychological Society 83* (1971).

COOPERSMITH, S.: *Antecedents of Self-esteem* (W. H. Freeman, London, 1967).

CORTÉS, J. B. AND F. M. GATTI: 'Physique and Self Description of Temperament' in *Journal of Consulting Psychology 29* (1965).

CROMER, R. F.: ' "Children are Nice to Understand": Surface Clues for the Recovery of a Deep Structure' in *British Journal of Psychology 61* (1970).

CROW, J. F.: 'Genetic Theories and Influences: Comments on the Value of Diversity' in *Environment, Heredity and Intelligence* (Harvard Educational Review Reprint Series, 2, 1969).

DAVIDSON, M. A., R. G. MCINNES AND R. W. PARNELL: 'The Distribution of Personality Traits in Seven-year-old Children: a Combined Psychological, Psychiatric and Somatotype Study' in *British Journal of Educational Psychology 27* (1957).

DAVIS, E.: 'Tendency among Children to avoid Words with Unpleasant Connotations' in *American Journal of Psychology 49* (1937).

DE MONCHAUX, C.: (iii) 'The Contributions of Psychoanalysis to the Understanding of Child Development', 'Symposium on the Contribution of Current Theories to an Understanding of Child Development' in *British Journal of Medical Psychology 30* (1957).

DENENBERG, V. H.: 'An Attempt to Isolate the Critical Periods of Development in the Rat' in *Journal of Comparative and Physiological Psychology 55* (1962).

DENENBERG, V. H.: *Education of the Infant and Young Child* (Academic Press, New York and London, 1970).

DEUTSCHE, J. M.: *The Development of Children's Concepts of Causal Relations* (University of Minnesota Press, Minneapolis, 1937).

DONALDSON, M. AND G. BALFOUR: 'Less is More: a Study of Language Comprehension in Children' in *British Journal of Psychology 59* (1968).

DREVER, J.: *A Dictionary of Psychology* (Penguin Books, Harmondsworth, 1969).

ERIKSON, E. H.: *Childhood and Society* (Hogarth Press, London 1950; Penguin Books, Harmondsworth, 1969).

ERLENMEYER-KIMLING, L. AND L. F. JARVIK: 'Genetics and Intelligence: a Review' in *Science 142* (1963).

EYSENCK, H. J. AND D. PRELL: 'The Inheritance of Neuroticism; an Experimental Study' in *Journal of Mental Science 97* (1951).

EYSENCK, H. J.: *The Scientific Study of Personality* (Routledge and Kegan Paul, London, 1952).

EYSENCK, H. J.: *The Structure of Human Personality* (Methuen, London, 1959).

EYSENCK, H. J.: *The Structure of Human Personality* (2nd ed.) (Methuen, London, 1960).

EYSENCK, H. J.: *Fact and Fiction in Psychology* (Penguin Books, Harmondsworth, 1965).

EYSENCK, H. J. AND D. COOKSON: 'Personality in Primary School Children—Family Background' in *British Journal of Educational Psychology 40* (1970).

EYSENCK, H. J.: 'The Experimental Study of Freudian Concepts' in *Bulletin of the British Psychological Society 89* (1972).

FAIGIN, H.: 'Social Behaviour of Young Children in the Kibbutz' in *Journal of Abnormal Social Psychology 56* (1958).

FANTZ, R. L.: 'The Origin of Form Perception' in *Scientific American 204* (1961).

FARRELL, B. A.: 'The Scientific Testing of Psychoanalytic Findings and Theory' in *British Journal of Medical Psychology 24* (1951).

FLAVELL, J. H.: *The Developmental Psychology of Jean Piaget* (D. Van Nostrand, Princeton, 1963).

FLAVELL, J. H. AND J. P. HILL: 'Developmental Psychology' in *Annual Review of Psychology 20* (1969).

FRANK, G. H.: 'The Role of the Family in the Development of Psychopathology' in *Psychological Bulletin 64* (1965).

FREEDMAN, D. G., J. A. KING AND O. ELLIOT: 'Critical Period in the Social Development of Dogs' in *Science 133* (1961).

FREUD, A. AND D. BURLINGHAM: *Infants without Families* (International Universities Press, New York, 1944).

FREUD, A. AND S. DANN: 'An Experiment in Group Upbringing' in *Psychoanalytic Study of the Child*, Vol. 5 (1951).

FREUD, S.: *Two Short Accounts of Psycho-Analysis* (first published 1910; Penguin Books, Harmondsworth, 1962).

FREUD, S.: *Beyond the Pleasure Principle*, Vol. 18 of Standard Edition of the

Complete Psychological Works of Sigmund Freud (Hogarth Press and Institute of Psycho-Analysis, London, 1920).

FREUD, S.: *Civilization and Its Discontents* (Hogarth Press, London, 1930).

FRIJDA, N. H. AND E. PHILIPZORN: 'Dimensions of Recognition of Expression' in *Journal of Abnormal Social Psychology* 66 (1963).

FURNEAUX, B.: *The Special Child* (Penguin Books, Harmondsworth, 1969).

FURTH, H. G.: *Thinking without Language: Psychological Implications of Deafness* (The Free Press, New York, 1966).

GAGE, N. L., G. S. LEAVITT AND G. C. STONE: 'The Intermediary Key in the Analysis of Interpersonal Perception' in *Psychology Bulletin 53* (1956).

GALTON, SIR R.: *Hereditary Genius* (first published 1869; Watts and Co., London, 1950).

GESELL, A. AND F. ILG: *Child Development: The Child from Five to Ten* (Harper, New York, 1946).

GETZELS, J. W. AND P. W. JACKSON: *Creativity and Intelligence* (John Wiley and Sons, New York and London, 1962).

GLUECK, S. AND E. GLUECK: *Unraveling Juvenile Delinquency* (Commonwealth Fund, New York, 1950).

GOLD, M. J.: *Education of the Intellectually Gifted* (Charles E. Merrill Books, Columbus, Ohio, 1965).

GROTH, N. J. AND P. HOLBERT: 'Hierarchical Needs of Gifted Boys and Girls in the Affective Domain' in *Gifted Child Quarterly 13* (1969).

GRYGIER, R., J. CHESLEY AND E. W. TUTERS: 'Parental Deprivation: a Study of Delinquent Children' in *British Journal of Criminology 9* (1969).

HALL, CALVIN S.: *A Primer of Freudian Psychology* (Mentor Books, New York, 1954).

HAMILTON, V.: 'Non-cognitive Factors in University Students' Examination Performance' in *British Journal of Psychology 61* (1970).

HAMILTON, V.: 'The effect of maternal attitude on the development of logical operations' in *Symposium on Cognitive Development and Socialization*, paper read to British Psychological Society Conference (1971).

HARLOW, H. F.: 'The Formation of Learning Sets' in *Psychological Review 56* (1949).

HARLOW, H. F.: 'The Heterosexual Affectional System in Monkeys' in *American Journal of Psychology 16* (1962).

HARLOW, H. F.: 'Sexual Behaviour of the Rhesus Monkey' in F. A. Beach (ed.), *Sex and Behaviour* (John Wiley and Sons, New York and London, 1965).

HARRELL, R. R., E. WOODYARD AND A. I. GATES: 'The Effect of Mothers' Diets on the Intelligence of the Offspring' in *Columbia University Teachers' College Record* (New York, 1955).

HARRIS, L. AND I. ALLEN: 'The Effects of Stimulus Alignment on Children's Performance in a Conservation-of-length Task' in *Psychonomic Science 23* (1971).

HARSH, C. M. AND H. G. SCHRICKEL: *Personality Development and Assessment* (John Wiley and Sons, New York and London, 1950).

HARTSHORNE, H., M. A. MAY, J. B. MALLER AND F. K. SHUTTLEWORTH: *Studies in the Nature of Character* (3 vols.) (Macmillan, New York, 1928–1930).

HAWKES, G. R. AND D. PEASE: *Behaviour and Development from Five to Twelve* (Harper and Row, New York, 1962).

HAYHURST, H.: 'Some Errors of Young Children in Producing Passive Sentences' in *Journal of Verbal Learning and Verbal Behaviour 6* (1967).

HEBB, D. O.: *The Organization of Behaviour* (John Wiley and Sons, New York and London, 1949).

HEBB, D. O.: *A Textbook of Psychology* (Saunders, Philadelphia and London, 1958).

HECKHAUSEN, H.: *The Anatomy of Achievement Motivation* (Academic Press, New York, 1967).

HERRIOT, P.: *An Introduction to the Psychology of Language* (Methuen, London, 1970).

HIGARD, E. R. AND R. C. ATKINSON: *Introduction to Psychology* (Harcourt, Brace, Jovanovich, New York, 1967).

HINDE, R. A.: 'Some Aspects of the Imprinting Problem' in *Symposium of the Zoological Society of London 8* (1962).

HINDLEY, C. B.: 'Contributions of Associative Learning Theories to an Understanding of Child Development' in *British Journal of Medical Psychology 30* (1957).

HINDLEY, C. B.: 'Individual Differences in the Development of Intelligence related to Social Class and Family Background', paper read to the Annual Conference of the British Psychological Society (1971).

HOFFMAN, M. L. AND H. D. SALTZSTEIN: 'Parent Discipline and the Child's Moral Development' in *Journal of Personal and Social Psychology 5* (1967).

HONKAVAARA, S.: 'The Psychology of Expression' in *British Journal of Psychological Monographs 32* (1961).

HORNEY, K.: *Neurosis and Human Growth* (Norton, New York, 1950).

HUTT, C.: *Males and Females* (Penguin Books, Harmondsworth, 1972).

ISAACS, S.: *The Nursery Years* (Routledge and Kegan Paul, London, 1929).

ISAACS, S.: *Social Development in Young Children: a Study of Beginnings* (Routledge and Kegan Paul, London, 1933).

JACKSON, B. AND D. MARSDEN: *Education and the Working Class* (Routledge and Kegan Paul, London, 1962).

JACKSON, L.: *A Test of Family Attitudes* (Methuen, London, 1952).

JAHODA, G.: 'Social Class Differentials in Vocabulary Expansion' in *British Journal of Educational Psychology 34* (1964).

JENSEN, A. R.: 'Environment, Heredity and Intelligence' in *Harvard Educational Review 59* (1969).

JERSILD, A.: 'Characteristics of Teachers who are "liked best" and "disliked most" ' in *Journal of Experimental Education 9* (1940).

JERSILD, A.: *Child Psychology* (Staples Press, London, 1955).

JONES, H. E.: *Development in Adolescence: California Adolescent Growth Study* (Appleton-Century-Crofts, New York, 1943).

Jones, M. C.: 'A Laboratory Study of Fear: the Case of Peter' in *Journal of Genetic Psychology 31* (1924).

KAGAN, J.: 'The Child's Perception of the Parent' in *Journal of Abnormal Social Psychology 53* (1956).

KAGAN, J. AND H. A. MOSS: *Birth to Maturity: A Study in Psychological Development* (John Wiley and Sons, New York and London, 1962).

KAY, W.: *Moral Development: A Psychological Study of Moral Growth from Childhood to Adolescence* (Allen and Unwin, London, 1969).

KELLY, G. A.: *The Psychology of Personal Constructs* (Vol. 2) (Norton, New York, 1955).

KING, F. T.: *Feeding and Care of Baby* (Oxford University Press, 1937).

KLINE, P.: *Fact and Fantasy in Freudian Theory* (Methuen, London, 1972).

KLINE, P.: 'The Experimental Study of Freudian concepts: a reply to H. J. Eysenck', Bulletin of the British Psychological Society, Vol. 26, 1973.

KOHLBERG, L.: 'The Development of Children's Orientation toward a Moral Order' in *Vita Humana* 6 and 9 (1963).

KOPPITZ, E.: 'Relationship between some Background Factors and Children's Interpersonal Attitudes' in *Journal of Genetic Psychology 91* (1957).

KRETSCHMER, E.: *Physique and Character* (Harcourt Brace Jovanovich, New York, 1925).

LAING, A. F.: *The Psychology of Adolescence* (Faculty of Education, University College of Swansea, 1966).

LAURENDEAU, M. AND A. PINARD: *Causal Thinking in the Child* (International Universities Press, New York, 1962).

LEACH, P. J.: *Social and Perceptual Inflexibility in School Children in relation to Maternal Child-rearing Attitudes*, London University Ph.D. Thesis (unpublished, 1964).

LEWIS, M. M.: *Language, Thought and Personality in Infancy and Childhood* (Harrap, London, 1963).

LINDENAUER, H.: 'Importance of Flexibility in Parents' in *Journal of Emotional Education 8* (1968).

LINDZEY, G., H. D. WINSTON AND M. MANOSEVITZ: 'Early Experience, Genotype, and Temperament in *Mus Musculus*' in *Journal of Comparative Physiological Psychology 56* (1963).

LIU, C. H.: 'The Influence of the Cultural Background on the Moral Judgement of the Child,' unpublished doctoral dissertation at Columbia University (1950).

LIVESLEY, W. J. AND D. B. BROMLEY: 'Studies in the Developmental Psychology of Person Perception', Bulletin of the British Psychological Society, vol. 20, 1967.

LOEVINGER, J.: 'Patterns of Parenthood as Theories of Learning' in *Journal of Abnormal Social Psychology 59* (1959).

LOGAN, F. A. AND A. R. WAGNER: *Reward and Punishment* (Allyn and Bacon, Boston, 1965).

LORENZ, K.: 'Der Kumpan in der Umwelt des Vogels; Der Artgenosse als auslösendes Moment sozialer Verhaltungswisen' in *Journal of Ornithology 83* (1935).

LOVELL, K. AND J. B. SHIELDS: 'Some Aspects of a Study of the Gifted Child' in *British Journal of Educational Psychology 37* (1967).

LURIA, A. R.: *The Role of Speech in the Regulation of Normal and Abnormal Behaviour* (Liveright, New York, 1961).

LURIA, A. R. AND F. I. YUDOVICH: *Speech and Development of Mental Processes in the Child* (Staples Press, London, 1959).

MANNHEIMER, D. I. AND G. D. MELLINGER: 'Personality Characteristics of the Child Accident Repeater' in *Child Development 38* (1967).

MARSHALL, H. H.: 'The Effect of Punishment on Children: a Review of the Literature and a Suggested Hypothesis' in *Journal of Genetic Psychology 106* (1965).

McCARTHY, D.: 'Language Development in Children' in L. Carmichael (ed.), *Manual of Child Psychology* (2nd ed.) (John Wiley and Sons, New York and London, 1954).

McCLELLAND, D. C.: *Studies in Motivation* (Appleton-Century-Crofts, New York, 1955).

McCLELLAND, D. C.: 'The Use of Measures of Human Motivation in the Study of Society' in J. W. Atkinson (ed.), *Motives in Fantasy, Action and Society* (Van Nostrand, Princeton, 1958).

McCLELLAND, D. C.: *The Achieving Society* (Van Nostrand, Princeton, 1961).

McCLELLAND, D. C., J. W. ATKINSON *et al.: The Achievement Motive* (Appleton-Century-Crofts, New York, 1953).

McNEILL, D.: 'Developmental Psycholinguistics' in F. Smith and G. A. Miller (eds.), *The Genesis of Language* (M.I.T. Press, Cambridge, Mass., 1966).

MEAD, G. H.: *Mind, Self and Society* (University of Chicago Press, 1934).

MEAD, M.: 'An Investigation of the Thought of Primitive Children with Special Reference to Animism' in *Journal of the Royal Anthropological Institute of Great Britain and Ireland 62* (1932).

MEAD, M.: *Sex and Temperament in Three Primitive Societies* (Mentor Books, New York, 1935).

MEAD, M.: *Coming of Age in Samoa* (William Morrow, New York, 1938).

MEAD, M.: 'Theoretical Setting—1954' in M. Mead and M. Wolfenstein (eds.), *Childhood in Contemporary Cultures* (University of Chicago Press, 1955).

MEAD, M.: 'Adolescence in Primitive and Modern Society' in E. E. Maccoby, T. M. Newcomb and E. L. Hartley (eds.), *Readings in Social Psychology* (Henry Holt, New York, 1958).

MEDINNUS, G. R. AND F. J. CURTIS: 'The Relation between Maternal Self-acceptance and Child Acceptance' in *Journal of Consultative Psychology 27* (1963).

MILLAR, S.: *The Psychology of Play* (Penguin Books, Harmondsworth, 1968).

MINTURN, L. AND R. D. HESS: 'Authority, Rules and Aggression: a Cross-national Study of the Socialization of Children into Compliance Systems' in *International Journal of Psychology 4* (1969).

MITTLER, P.: *A Study of Twins* (Penguin Books, Harmondsworth, 1971).

MOORE, T.: 'Difficulties of the Ordinary Child in Adjusting to Primary School' in *Journal of Child Psychology and Psychiatry 7* (1966).

MOORE, T.: 'Stress in Normal Childhood' in *Human Relations 22* (1970).

MOTTRAM, V. H.: *The Physical Basis of Personality* (Penguin Books, Harmondsworth, 1944).

MOWRER, O. H.: *Learning Theory and Behaviour* (John Wiley and Sons, New York and London, 1960).

MURPHY, L. B.: *Social Behaviour and Child Personality* (Columbia University Press, New York, 1937).

NASH, J.: *Developmental Psychology: a Psychobiological Approach* (Prentice-Hall, Englewood Cliffs, New Jersey, 1970).

NEWSON, J. AND E. NEWSON: *Infant Care in an Urban Community* (Allen and Unwin, London, 1963).

NEWSON, J. AND E. NEWSON: 'The Pattern of the Family in Modern Society' in *Public Health (London) 81* (1967).

OSSER, H.: 'Conceptual Development' in T. D. Spencer and N. Kass (eds.), *Perspectives in Child Psychology* (McGraw-Hill, New York, 1970).

PARKYN, G. W.: *Children of High Intelligence* (New Zealand Council for Educational Research and Oxford University Press, London, 1949).

PAIGET, J.: 'Les Traits Principaux de la Logique de l'Enfant' in *Journal de Psychologie Normale et Pathologique, 21* (1924).

PAIGET, J.: *The Language and Thought of the Child* (Harcourt Brace Jovanovich, New York, 1926).

PIAGET, J.: *Judgement and Reasoning in the Child* (Harcourt Brace Jovanovich, New York, 1928).

PIAGET, J.: *The Child's Conception of the World* (Harcourt Brace Jovanovich, New York, 1929).

PIAGET, J.: *The Moral Judgement of the Child* (Routledge and Kegan Paul, London, 1932).

PIAGET, J.: *Play, Dreams and Imitation in Childhood* (Norton, New York, 1951).

PIAGET, J.: 'A Theory of Development' in *International Encyclopedia of the Social Sciences* (Crowell, Collier, Macmillan, New York, 1968).

PIAGET, J.: *Six Psychological Studies* (University of London Press, 1968B).

PRINGLE, M. L. KELLMER: *Able Misfits* (Longman Group, in association with the National Bureau for Co-operation in Child Care, London, 1970).

PRINGLE, M. L. KELLMER: *Address to Chief Police Officers* (County Councils' Association, London, 1972).

RABIN, A. I.: 'Culture Components as a Significant Factor in Child Development' in *American Journal of Orthopsychiatry 31* (1961).

RHEINGOLD, H. L. AND N. BAYLEY: 'The Later Effects of an Experimental Modification of Mothering' in *Child Development 30* (1959).

RICHARDSON, S. A., S. M. DORNBUSCH AND A. H. HASTOF: 'Children's Categories of Interpersonal Perception' (National Institute of Mental Health, 1960).

RITCHIE, R. R.: 'Brain Development: First Two Years' in E. H. Lenneberg, *Biological Foundations of Language* (John Wiley and Sons, New York and London, 1967).

ROBERTS, E. AND S. MATTHYSSE: 'Neurochemistry: at the Crossroads of Neurobiology' in *Annual Review of Biochemistry 39* (1970).

ROGERS, C. R.: *Client-centred Therapy* (Houghton Mifflin, Boston, Mass., 1951).

ROSEN, B. C.: 'The Achievement Syndrome: a Psychocultural Dimension of Social Stratification' in *American Sociological Review 21* (1956).

ROSEN, I.: 'A Brief Summary of the Psychoanalytic Views on Aggression', paper read to the International Congress of Psychology (1969).

RUTTER, M.: *Maternal Deprivation Reassessed* (Penguin Books, Harmondsworth, 1972).

RYCROFT, C.: *Anxiety and Neurosis* (Allen Lane, The Penguin Press, London, 1968).

SCARR, S.: 'The Inheritance of Sociability', paper read to the American Psychological Association, Chicago (1965).

SCHNEIRLA, T. G. AND J. S. ROSENBLATT: 'Critical Periods in the Development of Behaviour' in *Science 139* (1966).

SCOTT, J. P.: 'Critical Periods in Behavioural Development' in *Science 138* (1962).

SCOTT, P. M., R. V. BURTON AND M. R. YARROW: 'Social Reinforcement under Natural Conditions' in *Child Development 38* (1967).

SEARLE, L. V.: 'The Organization of Hereditary Maze-brightness and Maze-dullness' in *Genetic Psychology Monographs 39* (1949).

SEARS, P. S. AND E. R. HILGARD: 'The Teacher's Role in the Motivation of the Learner' in *Theories of Learning and Instruction, 63rd Yearbook of the National Society for the Study of Education, Part 1* (National Society for Study of Education, Chicago, 1964).

SEARS, R. R.: 'Experimental Analysis of Psychoanalytic Phenomena' in J. McVicar Hunt (ed.), *Personality and the Behaviour Disorders* (Ronald Press, New York, 1944).

SEARS, R. R.: 'Identification as a Form of Behavioural Development' in D. B. Harris (ed.), *The Concept of Development* (University of Minnesota Press, Minneapolis, 1957).

SEARS, R. R., E. E. MACCOBY AND H. LEVIN: *Patterns of Child Rearing* (Row and Peterson, Evanston, 1957).

SHELDON, W. H. AND W. B. TUCKER: *The Varieties of Human Physique* (Harper, New York, 1940).

SHIELDS, J.: *Monozygotic Twins Brought Up Apart and Brought Up Together* (Oxford University Press, 1962).

SHIELDS, J.: 'Summary of the Genetic Evidence' in *Journal of Psychiatric Research 6* (1968).

SILVER, A.: 'Behaviour Syndrome associated with Brain Damage in Children' in *Journal of Insurance Medicine 6* (1957).

SKINNER, B. F.: *The Behaviour of Organisms* (Appleton-Century-Crofts, New York, 1938).

SKINNER, B. F.: *Verbal Behaviour* (Appleton-Century-Crofts, New York, 1957).

SLATER, E.: 'Types, Levels and Irregularities of Response to a Nursery School Situation of Forty Children observed with Special Reference to the Home Environment' in *Monographs of the Society for Research in Child Development 4* (1939).

SLOBIN, D. I.: 'Comments on "Developmental Psycholinguistics" in F. Smith and G. A. Miller (eds.), *The Genesis of Language* (M.I.T. Press, Cambridge, Mass., 1966).

SLOBIN, D. I.: 'Imitation and Grammatical Development in Children' in M. S. Endler, L. R. Boulter and H. Osser (eds.), *Contemporary Issues in Developmental Psychology* (Holt, Rinehart and Winston, New York, 1968).

SLUCKIN, W.: *Early Learning in Man and Animal* (Allen and Unwin, London, 1970).

SMITH, M. E.: 'An Investigation of the Sentence, and the Extent of Vocabulary in Young Children' in *Studies in Child Welfare 3* (University of Iowa, 1926).

SOWERS, A.: 'Parent-Child Relationship from the Child's Point of View' in *Journal of Experimental Education 6* (1937).

SPEARMAN, C.: *The Nature of 'Intelligence' and the Principles of Cognition* (Macmillan, London, 1923).

SPIKER, C. D., I. R. GERJEROY AND W. O. SHEPHARD: 'Children's Concept of Middlesizedness and Performance on the Intermediate Size Problem' in *Journal of Comparative Physiology and Psychology 49* (1956).

SPOCK, B.: *Baby and Child Care* (The Bodley Head, London, 1957).

STERN, W.: *The Psychology of Early Childhood* (Allen and Unwin, London, 1924).

STEVENS, F.: *The New Inheritors* (Hutchinson Educational, London, 1970).

STEWART, M. A., F. N. PITTS, A. G. GRAIG AND W. DIERUF: 'The Hyperactive Syndrome' in *American Journal of Orthopsychiatry 36* (1966).

STOTT, I. H.: 'Parent-adolescent Adjustment: Its Measurement and Significance' in *Character and Personality 10* (1941).

SULLIVAN, H. S.: *Conceptions of Modern Psychiatry* (William Alanson White Psychiatric Foundation, Washington D.C., 1947).

SUNLEY, R.: 'Early Nineteenth-century Literature on Child Rearing' in M. Mead and M. Wolfenstein (eds.), *Childhood in Contemporary Cultures* (University of Chicago Press, 1955).

TAYLOR, P. H.: 'Children's Evaluations of Characteristics of a Good Teacher' in *British Journal of Educational Psychology 32* (1962).

TERMAN, L. M.: 'Mental and Physical Traits of a Thousand Gifted Children' in *Genetic Studies of Genius* (vol. 1, 2nd ed.) (Stanford University Press, 1926).

THOMAS, A., S. CHESS AND H. G. BIRCH: *Temperament and Behaviour Disorders in Children* (Viking Press, New York, 1968).

THOMPSON, P.: 'Memory and History: Report on Preliminary Interviews' in *Social Science Research Council 6* (1969).

THORNDIKE, F. C.: *Animal Intelligence* (Macmillan, New York, 1911).

TRASLER, G. B.: 'The Shaping of Social Behaviour', an inaugural lecture delivered at the University of Southampton in 1966 (University of Southampton, 1967).

TUCKMAN, J. AND R. A. REGAN: 'Intactness of the Home and Behavioural Problems in Children' in *Journal of Child Psychology and Psychiatry 7* (1966).

TUDDENHAM, R. D.: 'The Constancy of Personality Ratings over Two Decades' in *Genetic Psychology Monographs 60* (1959).

VERNON, M. D.: *Human Motivation* (Cambridge University Press, 1969).

VERNON, M. D.: *Reading and Its Difficulties: A Psychological Study* (Cambridge University Press, 1971).

VERNON, P. E.: *The Structure of Human Abilities* (2nd ed.) (Methuen, London, 1950).

VERNON, P. E.: 'The Assessment of Children' in *Studies in Education* (vol. 7) (University of London Institute of Education and Evans, 1955).

VERNON, P. E.: *Personality Assessment* (Methuen, London, 1964).

VERNON, P. E.: *Intelligence and Cultural Environment* (Methuen, London, 1969).

VYGOTSKY, L. S.: *Thought and Language* (John Wiley and Sons, New York and London, 1962).

WALLACH, M. A AND N. KOGAN: *Modes of Thinking in Young Children* (Holt, Rinehart and Winston, London, 1965).

WALTERS, R. H. AND R. D. PARKE: 'The Influence of Punishment and Related

Disciplinary Techniques on the Social Behaviour of Children: Theory and Empirical Findings' in B. A. Maher (ed.), *Progress in Experimental Personality Research* (Academic Press, New York, 1967).

WATSON, G.: 'Some Personality Differences in Children Related to Strict or Permissive Parental Discipline' in *Journal of Psychology 44* (1957).

WATSON, J. B.: *Behaviourism* (Norton, New York, 1925).

WATSON, J. B.: *Psychological Care of Infant and Child* (Norton, New York, 1928).

WEBB, L.: *Children with Special Needs in the Infants' School* (Smythe, London, 1967).

WHITE, R. W.: 'Motivation Reconsidered: the Concept of Competence' in *Psychological Review 66* (1959).

WHITE, R. W.: 'Competence and the Psychosexual Stages of Development' in M. R. Jones (ed.), *Nebraska Symposium on Motivation* (University of Nebraska Press, 1960).

WHITEMAN, M.: 'Children's Conception of Psychological Causality' in *Child Development 38* (1965).

WHITING, J. W. M. AND I. L. CHILD: *Child Training and Personality* (Yale University Press, New Haven, 1953).

WILLIAMS, J., L. J. MEYERSON, L. D. ERON AND I. J. SEMLER: 'Peer-rated Aggression and Aggressive Responses Elicited in an Experimental Situation' in *Child Development 38* (1967).

WILLIAMS, N.: in J. Wilson, N. Williams and B. Sugarman, *Introduction to Moral Education* (Penguin Books, Harmondsworth, 1967).

WILLIAMS, R. J.: 'The Biological Approach to the Study of Personality' in F. McKinney (ed.), *Psychology in Action* (Collier-Macmillan, London, 1960).

WILSON, J., N. WILLIAMS AND B. SUGARMAN: *Introduction to Moral Education* (Penguin Books, Harmondsworth, 1967).

WITKIN, H. A., R. B. DYKE, H. F. PATERSON, D. R. GOODENOUGH AND S. A. KARP: *Psychological Differentiation Studies in Development* (John Wiley and Sons, New York and London, 1962).

WOLFENSTEIN, M.: 'Fun Morality: an Analysis of American Literature on Child Training' in M. Mead and M. Wolfenstein (eds.), *Childhood in Contemporary Cultures* (University of Chicago Press, 1955).

WOOD, M. E.: 'A Study of Children's growing Social and Motivational Awareness', unpublished Ph.D. thesis, London University (1968).

WORTIS, J.: 'A Note on the Concept of the "Brain-injured" Child' in *American Journal of Mental Deficiency 61* (1957).

YARROW, L. L. AND M. S. GOODWIN: 'Effects of Change in Mother-figure during Infancy' in N. S. Endler, L. R. Boulter and H. Osser (eds.), *Contemporary Issues in Developmental Psychology* (Holt, Rinehart and Winston, New York, 1960).

INDEX